FALLACIES
AND
FANTASIES

of Air Transport History

FALLACIES AND FANTASIES

of Air Transport History

R.E.G. Davies

Paladwr Press

I dedicate this book to
Richard M. Clarkson, member
of the superbly intuitive
de Havilland design team,
and one of the great aerodynamicists
of all time. Under his tutelage,
I acquired a healthy respect for the
beauty and depth of the English language
and also learned never to take things
at their face value.

Published 1994 by Paladwr Press,
1906 Wilson Lane, Apt. 101, McLean, Virginia
22102-1957

Manufactured in Hong Kong

Maps by R.E.G. Davies

Edited by R.E.G. Davies and John Wegg

Typesetting/Layout by Spot Color

Pre-press Production by The Drawing Board

ISBN 0-9626483-5-3

First Edition

Contents

Exhibits

Foreword

by Patrick V. Murphy
Acting Assistant Secretary for
Aviation and International Affairs
U.S. Department of Transportation

Once again R.E.G. Davies has given us an outstanding work on aviation history. In *Fallacies and Fantasies of Air Transport History* Ron brings to the reader some of the key lessons involving the development of the airline industry. The chapters present the reader with a wide range of topics varying from flying boats to monorails, from aircraft that flew at less than 100 miles per hour to Mach 5 designs, and from World War I and the Russian Revolution to the very latest events involving aerospace engineering.

These history lessons are important to understand because the air transportation system has become essential to the economies of the world. Aviation and the aerospace industry are key sectors of the U.S. economy which will lead the nation into the 21st century. After all, the U.S. airline and aerospace industries directly employ about 1.5 million people in high-skilled, high-waged jobs. In the U.S., the aerospace manufacturing industry is the nation's largest exporter, while worldwide travel and tourism is a $3 trillion per year business.

In spite of these impressive measures, the airline and aerospace industry has been suffering over the last several years. In the past four years U.S. airlines have lost over $11 billion, and airlines worldwide have suffered their own extremely large losses. It was because of these difficult times that President Clinton and the U.S. Congress appointed the "National Commission to Ensure A Strong Competitive Airline Industry" in May of 1993. Not long after, the European Commission appointed the "Comité des Sages for Air Transport." Both these bodies were charged with analyzing the financial problems in their industries and reporting on what steps could be taken to improve performance. Looking at the recommendations of these two commissions, it is apparent that many of the lessons from this book have been learned, while others have not. The reader would do well to understand the lessons of history from *Fallacies and Fantasies* and compare them to the views of these distinguished commissions. For myself, I found that the author's chapter on airline deregulation gave me the most difficulty as I believe that airline deregulation in the United States has led to lower fares, more competition and many benefits to the American consumer. My friend Ron Davies disagrees, but I encourage you to read his chapter and understand his perspective.

For those who believe that the golden days of aviation set out in *Fallacies and Fantasies* have passed and no exciting decisions remain, I would point out that aviation officials continue to grapple with issues such as the development of global airline alliances, high speed civil transport technology, the development of 700–800 seat aircraft, the completion of more efficient surface links to airports and many more topics. In 1994 the U.S. will see the opening of a new Denver airport which is twice the size of the island of Manhattan. The F.A.A. has just authorized airlines to start using satellite signals for navigation and is studying the shift of air traffic control services to a government corporation. Airlines are trying unique methods of lowering costs, including more employee ownership and possible employee control of one of the world's largest airlines, United Airlines.

As aviation leaders deal with these and many other issues, Ron Davies provides guidance from the past, from his own analyses, which certainly make very enjoyable reading. We at the U.S. Department of Transportation will try not to provide him with additional chapters on fallacies and fantasies.

Author's Preface

During the course of air transport history, many aircraft, or families of aircraft, or episodes in airline development, have been awarded a prominence and implied importance far beyond their true worth, measured in terms of their contributions to the main stream of technical or operational progress. Often the result of creative and innovative minds diligently seeking the solution to an apparently insuperable problem, certain aircraft—the Lawson Airliner and the Dorner DoX are examples—were honorable failures, in that the ultimate target was correctly perceived, but the means of achieving the goal was not, partly because the innovative minds were ahead of the necessary supportive technology.

The first nine chapters of this book deal with some of the fallacious ideas of the pre-World War II years, those that are sometimes called The Golden Age of Aviation. These chapters are a reminder that all that glittered was not necessarily gold, and that there were a number of white elephants among the successful types. Strangely, some of the myths have been perpetuated and there are still people today who will claim that large flying boats or giant dirigibles should still be operated.

Not all of the essays of this period are specific criticisms of what was attempted. They are reviews of what may be termed brave tries and such adverse comment that is included is aimed at the prolonged promotion given to ideas that were proved to be fallacious, or to expose claims that were fallaciously made. In the very first chapter, the fallacy is inverted, as my objective is to summarize recent research by others that has shown the traditional historians to have been in error, not the aircraft designer.

I am more concerned with the lessons to be learned in the post-World War II years. The fallacies and fantasies, even bare-faced falsehoods, are perpetuated in unabated exercises in fanaticism. Again, the first of the postwar essays begins with a recognition of the immense technological breakthrough made by the de Havilland company in England in designing the world's first jet airliner, but whose supreme accomplishment was overshadowed by the tragedy that was the result, partially if not wholly, of crossing the threshold of existing knowledge, breaking new ground, and clearing the way for others. But this is an exception. There have been postwar parallels to Lawson and Mayo, although the responsibility for gigantic mistakes bears a collective rather than an individual responsibility. Over-riding all other ventures into the unorthodox, the supersonic mania—and it is no less than that—needs to be thoroughly recognized for what it is: a self-serving program designed to maintain a hypothetical standard of technological prowess, to be paid for by the taxpayer but with no worthwhile product to show for it. Into this category go the Concorde, the U.S. SST, and the so-called Orient Air Express. The development costs alone for these much-publicized and -promoted schemes are counted in billions of dollars, but, as I show by my Supersonic Market Law, the market for such aircraft can be counted on the fingers of a couple of hands or so.

Supersonic and hypersonic airliner protagonists assert that everyone must have faith, observing, correctly, that many experts and aeronautical specialists said that commercial jet airliners would not work. This is not an argument, at least not one of logic. Some of the experts, of course, mainly at Hatfield, England, said that the jet airliner would work. And they were right. Many aeronautical experts in the late 1920s, at a time when the majority opinion favoured airships for long-range air transport, claimed that these ungainly machines would not work. And they were right. Equally there were many who suspected that the trans-ocean flying boat that conquered the Atlantic and the Pacific in the 1930s was also doomed to ultimate retirement. And they were right too. Every age has its innovators and every age has its complement of crazy schemes, and air transport has progressed because there have been enough level-headed designers and engineers who have managed to steer a compromise course between the innovative and the idiotic, stick firmly to the mainstream of technical progress, and maintain their balance.

One reason too commonly quoted as the key to success for jet airliners and the beginning of the jet age is that the spectacular increase in speed—the first Comet almost halved the journey time from London to South Africa—attracted the travelling public. Thus, so the argument goes, an even more spectacular increase in speed, such as that offered by the Concorde and other projected supersonic airliners, will also attract more travellers. This is one of the greatest of all the fallacies, and unfortunately one that continues to be repeated by the over-enthusiastic promoters of Mach 2, 3, 5, and 25 airliners.

The truth is that speed was only one of the elements that attracted the public and brought almost instantaneous success to the jet airliners and their operators. Most important, it was only one of several contributing factors that created the far superior economics of the jet airliner. Fuel costs were found to be far lower than anticipated, because the fuel consumption itself was lower and the kerosene was cheaper than gasoline. Maintenance costs plummeted because of the smooth running of turbine engines. And one aircraft could, because of the speed, earn far more revenue every year. In short the jet airliner was a better money-maker and could offer cheaper fares than its predecessors.

This is not the case with the supersonic airliner. The Concorde, while demonstrably a technical miracle, has been an economic disaster, costing $2 billion of the taxpayers' money (sterling and francs) in development costs alone and bringing solace to only a fraction of the travelling public—those that can afford the extortionate fares. Furthermore, the technical miracle was achieved largely at the expense of the British industry's hopes to expand the marketing base on a wide front. All the British eggs were crammed into one basket, or nest, and the Concorde cuckoo threw the rest out. Sadly, the lessons have not been learned, and the supersonic and hypersonic fanaticism still brings in the converts.

Lest the reader might think that this book is inviolate and that the author is acting only as an armchair quarterback after the game is over, the last chapter will give all the defenders of SSTs, HSTs, STOLs, VTOLs, airships, flying boats, and even the Lawson Airline, a chance to get their own back. After a career spent pursuing the high-risk occupation of airline market research and air traffic forecasting, and having been sorely frustrated at being over-ridden by engineers and accountants and the good old gut feel, I am still a devotee of Clement M. Keys, that airline promoter and conglomerate assembler of the embryo years of U.S. air transport. He once said that 90 percent of aviation is on the ground. After sixty years, the airlines have not yet come to terms with this basic truth. Roughly half of the world's air travellers spend as much time going to and from the airport and waiting at it as they do actually flying in the airplanes. If about one cent in every dollar spent on feasibility studies for hypersonic airliners was spent on improving ways to travel to and from the airport, total journey times for half of the world's air travellers would be reduced. The solution to the ground access problem may not be as spectacular or as sensational, but it will be more effective and, I guarantee, much cheaper. And so I invite the reader to sample my own pet fallacy and to challenge the assumptions and recommendations on which it stands.

R.E.G. Davies

Acknowledgements

Most books of reference are only as good as their sources, and this is no exception. I have tried to recognize the innumerable books, magazines, pamphlets, and other written material that I have consulted, in an extensive bibliography, a method which I believe to be infinitely preferable to a surfeit of footnotes which grace—I hesitate to say disgrace—many learned works. A well-organized book list is preferable to a thousand ibids.

In addition, I would like to acknowledge certain historians and writers whom I have consulted on specific chapters. They have advised and encouraged me in ways that supplement their own publications and by doing so have added veracity to my own views. Carl Bobrow and Dr. Von Hardesty, for example,were most generous in sharing with me their extensive knowledge, drawn from their own researches, on the Il'ya Muromets aircraft. Equally, Peter Brooks, who has guided me in so many ways during the past half-century, helped me to make what I believe to be a fair judgement of the role of airships in the whole scheme of aviation progress. My many friends in Pan American Airways, whose full contribution to airline development has yet to be fully acknowleged, augmented my thoughts on several subjects, especially the review of flying boats. Mike Ramsden, veteran of the de Havilland Tech School, and editor of *Flight International* for so many years, gave a masterly synopsis of the achievements of the first Comet, on the occasion of the 50th Anniversary of the Hatfield branch of the Royal Aeronautical Society; and I have dipped freely into the written version of that memorable lecture. I must acknowledge too the Archives Department of the National Air and Space Museum, a source of knowledge which, if properly pursued and systematically excavated, reveals a cornucopia of wonderful material which is a joy to the researchers' heart.

To preserve a sense of balance, however, I must also mention the other side of the coin, and note that, in some cases, acknowledgement of assistance has to be offset by an acceptance of just the opposite. During my life in the aviation industry, I have never encountered so many examples of "don't confuse me with the facts, my mind is made up" as in the fanatical determination of countless legions of supersonic airliner supporters. And this applies to the public relations artists who claim that the Concorde makes a profit, to those who believe that the United States should have built its competitor, and above all, to those who cling to the fantasy that a hypersonic airliner flying in three hours from New York to Tokyo is an achievable commercial proposition. Difficult questions about basic elements such as the true operating costs of an SST are met with a combination of obfuscation and a wall of silence.

In making these acknowlegdements, I must stress that all the views expressed in this book, in subjects ranging from the early successes and failures of the age of aviation infancy to the current challenges of the modern age, are my own. I do not wish to pass the buck on to my many colleagues who may happen to agree with much of what I say, but not necessarily all of it. And for those who may feel that my iconoclastic approach has been perhaps a little too harsh, I offer my head on a platter in the last chapter, and leave the reader to make his or her own judgement.

The Il'ya Muromets
(1913–1922)

One of the longest prevailing myths in the chronicle of transport aircraft development is that the large multi-engined biplanes designed by Igor Sikorsky in Russia before and during the Great War of 1914–1918 were either few in number, or failures, or both. Many even believe that only a couple of prototypes were ever built. Others think that they were something of a joke, too ungainly to perform adequately, and that their reputation drifted into oblivion because they never did anything worth recording. And in discussion concerning the first bomber airplanes, credit is normally given to the German Gotha or R 'planes as being the first.

The complete reverse is true. The Il'ya Muromets and its prototype, the *Grand* (also called the *Russkiy vityaz*, or *Russian Knight*), were the first four-engined airplanes ever built, pre-dating all other bombers, German, French, or British, by four years. It was demonstrating engine-out performance, even with both engines stopped on one side, within days of its first flight. It set many records, although these were not always recognized, or even known, by the international authorities. There were no documented instances of the aircraft ever breaking down completely. On one occasion, with all four engines immobilized by enemy gunfire, an Il'ya Muromets was able to glide to a safe landing. Contrary to the common understanding that only a few were built, reliable estimates put the total production of all variants to more than eighty individual aircraft.

When Igor Sikorsky first proposed the idea to Mikhail Shidlovskiy, chairman of the Russo-Baltic Wagon Company at St. Petersburg early in 1912, he had convinced himself that an aircraft should not rely upon a single engine for its (and its pilot's) survival. Engines at that time were notoriously unreliable and he asserted that to have one or more engines in reserve was better than to convert a single-engined machine instantly into an overweight glider. And so, on 30 August 1912, construction began on the first Sikorsky giant, the first multi-engined aircraft in the world. Shidlovskiy's influence was

1

The Sikorsky Il'ya Muromets made its first flight in St. Petersburg in 1913. Seen here in a dramatic demonstration, this giant biplane was the world's first multi-engined heavier-than-air machine and was several years ahead of its nearest rivals in western Europe. (United Technologies)

was far-reaching and he played an important role in molding Sikorsky's thinking as well as in his practical patronage.

There was only one of the first type, at first referred to as the Grand, and this may have led to some of the misunderstanding about the whole series. It was modified successively, as were most of Sikorsky's designs, and three different versions were produced. The first had only two German Argus 100 horsepower engines, the second had four of these in tandem pairs, and on the third variant, the *Russkiy vityaz*, the four engines were mounted in line on the leading edge of the wing.

When the *Grand* made its debut at Korpusnoi airfield at St. Petersburg on 26 May 1913, it must have been an awesome sight. It was not only large, but by the standards of aircraft aesthetics of the day, it was handsome. Compared with the flimsy single-engined monoplanes, biplanes, and triplanes that were proliferating in the leading industrial nations at the time, it was a solid workmanlike job. Built of wood and fabric by a team of skilled Russian carpenters, it weighed 3 1/2 tons and could carry a 1,600 lb load at 50 mph. To quote K.N. Finne (whose book, written in 1930 while in exile in Jugoslavia, has been so ably rejuvenated by Carl Bobrow and Dr. Von Hardesty for the Smithsonian Press in 1987) "This successful flight of the *Grand* belongs to the annals of historic flights as a triumph of human ingenuity over nature."

Igor Sikorsky was born in Kiev in 1889, the son of Ivan Sikorsky, a professor at the Imperial University of St. Vladimir. With an innovative and imaginative mind—as a youth he was an ardent fan of Jules Verne—Igor studied at the Kiev Polytechnic Institute and also in Paris. Passionately interested in aeronautics, he was still studying, at the age of 22, at the St. Petersburg Polytechnic when the idea of a multi-engined transport airplane first occurred to him.

During the summer of 1913, the Emperor Nicholas II inspected the *Grand*, which had a forward balcony, a design feature soon abandoned. But these were years of experiment. All over the world, aircraft designers, most of

This picture of one of the many different variants of the Il'ya Muromets shows a typical layout of engine mounting, gravity-feed fuel tanks, twin-wheeled landing gear, and spacious cabin with excellent visibility for crew and passengers. (United Technologies)

The true measure of the Il'ya Muromets's achievement is epitomised in this picture of the passenger cabin. Even in 1913, when all other aircraft had open cockpits, Sikorsky's transport aircraft offered a standard of comfort that was unmatched until after the end of the 1914–18 Great War. (United Technologies)

them ignorant of the principles of flight or aerodynamics, were promoting ideas and designs far more bizarre.

The *Grand* had some shortcomings. It could not climb to a high altitude and its 50 mph speed was unimpressive. Even the third variant could not ascend beyond 2,000 feet. Accordingly, Sikorsky set the Russo-Baltic Works craftsmen to work on a better machine, eliminating the balcony, and with improved aerodynamics. They started on the first Il'ya Muromets—named after a hero from Russian folk legend—in the fall of 1913. After some test flying, Igor made another historic flight, taking off on a bright day in February 1914 with 16 passengers and Korpusnoi airfield's mascot, the dog Shkalika. The total load was almost 1 1/2 tons. The passengers sat in wicker chairs, the cabin was heated—a wise precaution in northern Russia in February—and it was lit by electricity. Such was Sikorsky's confidence in the principle of engine-out safety that he flew low over St. Petersburg, whence large crowds marveled at the astonishing sight.

The altitude and speed problems of the Grand were partially solved. The Il'ya Muromets was about 10 mph faster and could ascend to about 4,500 feet. A second aircraft, with more powerful engines, increased this to more than 6,000 feet. Most of the pictures taken at the time, and since reproduced in innumerable publications, show the aircraft flying low over St. Petersburg, giving rise to the mistaken idea that it could not fly higher, and therefore something of a freak, loaded up for a very short flight, at the expense of range and altitude. The reason why no photographs were taken of high-flying Sikorskys, at least until after their participation in the Great War, is that no photographer could get near one.

Sikorsky took practical steps to dispel any possible uncertainty concerning the truly remarkable performance of his aircraft. On 30 June 1914, with a crew of three besides himself, he took off from Korpusnoi at 1.00 a.m. and headed south. With 1 1/4 tons of fuel on board, the Il'ya Muromets cruised at 1,500 feet and landed at Orsha, 370 miles from St. Petersburg, at 9 a.m. to refuel. Soon after takeoff, a fire in one of the fuel lines forced him to land, delaying the resumption of flight until 4 a.m. the next morning. Nevertheless, even after losing the way because of turbulence and bad visibility, the aircraft arrived triumphantly at Kiev in the early afternoon of the next day, after a 9-hour flight.

The return from Kiev to St. Petersburg on 12 July was even more noteworthy. Stopping only briefly at Novo-Sokolniki to refuel, the 660-mile journey was accomplished on the same day in only 13 hours, from 4 a.m. to 5 p.m., a magnificent performance, and one that should, like the notorious Ten Days, have Shaken the World, at least the world of aviation (see map). If nothing else, it opened up vast new horizons for the Russians whose problems in overcoming the huge distances from eastern Europe to the Far East, embracing no less than eleven time zones, were immense.

But oddly it did not. Although Sikorsky had received royal acknowledgment from the Tsar, and no doubt the Il'ya Muromets's flights over St. Petersburg were the Talk of the Town, the aviation community was not impressed, obsessed as it was to admire all things foreign and to disparage indigenous products. This was a reflection of a national characteristic that stemmed perhaps from the Imperial family's own yearning after the products of western Europe. As the Russians entered into the 1914 conflict, and as the hostilities increased in intensity, Sikorsky faced much opposition from the advocates of the use of smaller and more maneuverable aircraft.

Arguably, the Russians paid heavily for this conceit. When, in 1913, Igor launched the idea of a large load-carrying airplane, his objective was to carry passengers and goods, perhaps mail, across the wide spaces and endless

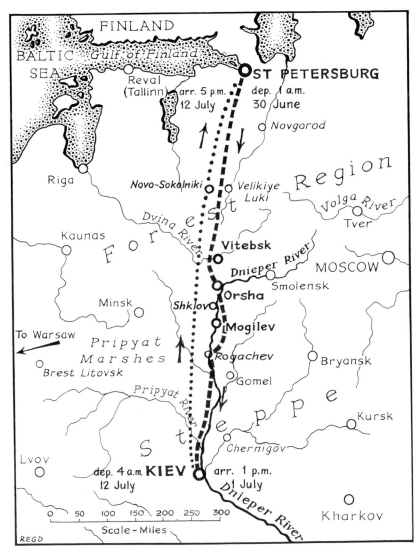

The Epic Flight of the Il'ya Muromets, 30 June and 12 July 1914. *During the summer of 1914—just a month before the outbreak of World War II—Igor Sikorsky and a crew of three flew the 660 miles from St. Petersburg to Kiev in 17 hours, with one stop; and made the return flight two weeks later. The four-engined biplane was clearly several years ahead of its time.*

distances of the Tsarist empire. The thought of war of European proportions was at the time only a distant possibility. The Sarajevo plot was still several months away, and the use of the Il'ya Muromets as a bomber or any kind of military machine was not on the priority list, if it was thought of at all.

Yet, with the onset of the Great War in August 1914, civil development had to be curtailed and the first use of Sikorsky's magnificent machine was for military purposes. When war broke out, only two Murometsy were available, but the Ministry of War ordered them into production. How they would be put to use was not clear, as the only previous wartime experience with aircraft had been in relatively limited operations in North Africa between the Italians and the Turks in 1911 and in the Balkan Wars of 1912 and 1913. Combat skills included aerobatics and there was one case of ramming another aircraft (a technique used more widely by the Soviet Air Force in World War II). Aircrew were sometimes equipped with personal armour. One ingenious proposal was for a 3-inch gun that would have fired two projectiles simultaneously in opposite directions with a single cartridge. No thought was given to a preferred operating altitude, as anti-aircraft firing potential was unknown.

With no experience or example to follow, the Russians used the great biplanes well, even intelligently, for both bombing and reconnaissance, but not nearly as much as their demonstrated capability should have demanded. For want of perseverance and confidence in an outstanding piece of equipment, the Russians may have neglected an advantage that would have made a vital difference to the conduct of the war on the Eastern Front.

The lukewarm support from the authorities meant that the Murometsy started their military career with many disadvantages, not least from the aircrew themselves. The pilots saw themselves as daredevil heroes destined to demonstrate flying skills in aerial duels rather than to routinely seek a target or to take photographs. They were all convinced that French or British machines were the best, even though the Sikorsky giants were demonstrably safer, able to crash-land even, without loss of life and seldom of limb. Even after scores of successful combat missions, the bias against the big airplanes persisted.

Not only that, but poor organization and inadequate preparation led to slow and inefficient delivery of the first aircraft to the front at Bielostok. But such was the quality of the Il'ya Muromets that it had its strong supporters too, for the achievement in flying long ranges with heavy loads, as demonstrated on the St. Petersburg-Kiev round trip, could not be ignored. The Russo-Baltic Works chairman, Shidlovskiy himself, pleaded the case to the Stavka, the Supreme High Command, with the result that in December 1914 he was instructed to create the Escadra vozduzhnykh korablei (E.V.K.) or

Squadron of Flying Ships, equip it with a fleet of Il'ya Murometsy, and take command.

This decision to put a civilian in charge was unpopular with the military establishment. When the E.V.K. party arrived at Jablonna, near Warsaw, the reception was lukewarm. This attitude continued even when Igor Sikorsky made a test flight on 24 January 1915, climbing to 8,000 feet in 49 minutes with twelve passengers on board; and with the cabin stripped for military use, climbing to 11,000 feet. In compensation, some momentum was building up at the Russo-Baltic Works where the carpenters were turning out excellent airframes that needed only to have the engines attached to the wings. This permitted a choice of engines, including French Renaults, British Sunbeams, even the occasional American Hall-Scott or the Italian Fiat, as well as the original German Argus or the home-built R-BVZ, which was one of the best.

The first official combat flight by an Il'ya Muromets was conducted on 27 February 1915 and the next day it saw action by bombing trenches in enemy territory. Steady activity during the ensuing months, with successful bombing raids on railway junctions and in reconnaissance on the deployment of enemy troops, led to a change of attitude by the Russian forces on the East Prussian front. Compared with the frightening losses of the flimsy single-engined aircraft that comprised the majority of the air fleets of the belligerent forces on both sides, the grand total of only three Murometsy lost by enemy action throughout the entire course of the war on the Eastern Front was to be an astonishing statistic, and such resilience and reliability should have been put to better use earlier in the campaign. The German adversaries certainly regarded the Murometsy with considerable respect.

In one incredible incident on 18 July 1915, Ship No. 143, the Il'ya Muromets *Kievskiy,* in a four-hour bombing mission, had traded some of its own armament for extra bombs and was consequently more vulnerable to enemy fire. Hit by 60 rounds and with both engines on one side immobilized, it lost the other two just before reaching base because the gasoline tanks had been pierced also. Yet it was able to glide in to land, in a muddy field, and was ready for service the next day after minor repairs.

Had the Murometsy been more energetically deployed on the East Prussian front in the summer of 1915, German troop movements might have been observed and the catastrophic tactics that led to the splitting of the Russian forces might not have occurred. The Battle of Tannenburg, 26–30 August 1915, might not have resulted in the near-annihilation of the Russian Army, which could perhaps have held the line. but the German intelligence as to the deployment of Russian troops, benefiting from aerial reconnaissance, was the critical factor. Unhappily, the E.V.K. squadron of Murometsy had already been re-deployed on 2 August to Lida, 200 miles to the north, and on 27 August 440 miles further north to Pskov (in which later move the six Murometsy made the journey nonstop) One of the newer ships, fitted with a Kireyev-designed R-BVZ engine, had attained an altitude of 11,000 feet with a load of almost a ton.

The fleet was operational as soon as it arrived at Pskov. In one raid, on 4 September, four aircraft destroyed the German seaplane station at Lake Angern, near the Bay of Riga, dropping 73 bombs weighing 1,700 lb altogether. In another raid, on 18 October, three attacked an important railroad junction near Riga, dropping 48 35-lb bombs and one 500 lb bomb. Such operations on the Western Front at that time would have been regarded as science fiction; yet still a certain amount of local disparagement of the E.V.K. continued.

This was in spite of a growing interest by the Allies. Great Britain, France, and Japan sent missions of inspection in July 1915, October 1915, and May 1916, respectively. Even with the evacuation of Riga, home of the Russo-Baltic Wagon Works, to Petrograd (St. Petersburg had been renamed), production continued—an act of defiant determination that was to be repeated in the heroic tank production during the siege of Leningrad during the Second World War.

Twenty aircraft were estimated to have been delivered in 1916. They were deployed on all parts of the Eastern Front and carried out countless missions. Performance continued to improve with design refinements in later models and the Russian-built engines proved to be of high quality. Even as the tide of war was turning badly against the Russians, the E.V.K. performed sterling service. In Galicia, in October 1916, Murometsy were attacking Austrian positions twice a day, and still maintaining an effort in the north, where one landed safely after receiving 293 bullet holes. (**See map** for East Prussian and Galician locations)

On 6 September 1916, the Type Yeh (E) had been tested, with a nose section that permitted almost 360° visibility both laterally and vertically. It could reach an altitude of 10,000 feet with 2 1/2 tons of payload. Sikorsky's giants had been developed into a formidable weapon that could have provided the Russian forces with a tactical trump card. But the line was collapsing. Lenin's return to Petrograd was only six months away and the regime was crumbling.

The E.V.K. had been moved from Pskov to Vinnitsa, that is, from the northern to the southwestern sector of the Eastern Front, to back up the offensive planned on the Rumanian front in the spring of 1917. But the dissention in the Russian forces was going from bad to worse and discipline was deteriorating, even without revolutionary encouragement. This did not apply,

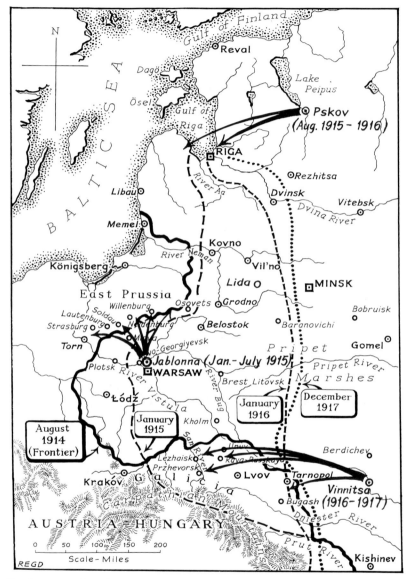

Deployment of the Escadra vozduzhnykh korablei (E.V.K.) on the Eastern Front, 1914–1917. *During World War I, the specially created squadrons of the E.V.R. performed well on the Eastern Front, in East Prussia and in Galicia. They were used for reconnaissance and sometimes for bombing and were well able to defend themselves.*

however, to the E.V.K. Possibly because of the pride inspired by their fine equipment, good morale and discipline were maintained by officers and enlisted men alike, and sustained even after the fires of revolution were ignited across the nation.

Even in May 1917, as the heart was going out of Russian troop morale, Ship No. 15 was engaged in a heavy aerial battle and destroyed two of three attacking Fokker aircraft while absorbing the enemy fire and returning safely. This was becoming a familiar story, typical of dozens of which records have been lost, and which pay tribute to the remarkable ruggedness of the aircraft design, and put Igor Sikorsky and his brilliant talent (not to mention those of his carpenters) on an aviation pedestal of that era. For only then were the German Gotha bombers making their appearance, and Frederick Handley Page's 'bloody paralysers' were to be ready only in the closing weeks of the great War, in November 1918, and never did fulfil their mission.

The E.V.K. surrendered to the revolutionary Cossack troops at Vinnitsa on 9 November 1917, at the close of the short-lived Kerensky regime. Amid much confusion, in which Bolsheviks gave way temporarily to Ukrainians early in 1918, the E.V.K. evacuated the remaining Il'ya Murometsy in what would justly be described as an orderly retreat. One is known to have flown to Bobruisk, another to Borisov. The former was a Type E Il'ya Muromets, *Kievskiy III*, under the command of Colonel I.S. Bashko, who then flew on towards Moscow, crashing when two engines failed and he misjudged his altitude. After trying to protect the remaining ships from being drafted into the Red Air Fleet, Bashko escaped and joined the Lithuanian army.

But the Il'ya Murometsy lived on under the Bolsheviks. The remnants of the fleet were assembled and the residual production at the Russo-Baltic Works at Petrograd was taken up and mobilized into a unit, the Division of Murometsy. Records from that time onward have not yet been sifted, if they exist at all, and the research into the full circumstances of the fate of this fine aircraft present a challenge to aviation researchers the world over. The prejudice against Sikorsky and his works, of course, took a different form, as Igor Sikorsky himself defected to the United States, where his genius quickly found new outlets.

Some of the Il'ya Murometsy were used by the Civil Air Fleet of the newly-formed Communist administration and for a while provided a quasi-airline service, in May 1921, from Moscow to Kharkov, thus reverting to the purpose for which they had originally been designed, as passenger-carrying aircraft. The last surviving model was scrapped in 1924.

Until recently, Soviet aviation historians had been reluctant to give much credit (at least publicly) to Igor Sikorsky, who had given the Russian

SIKORSKY MULTI-ENGINED AIRCRAFT, 1913-17
Summary of Production by Type

Aircraft Variant		Date of First Flight	Engines			Remarks	Number Built
Type	Name (if any)		No.	Type	H.P. each		
—	Grand: Bolshoi Baltiskiy (Great Baltic)	March 1913	2	Argus	100	Original prototype, 2 engines	
		April 1913	4	Argus	100	Same aircraft, with 4 engines paired in tandem	1
	Grand: Russkiy vityaz (Russian knight)	July 1913	4	Argus	100	Same aircraft, with 4 engines on leading edge. Set a world record by carrying 7 passengers for 1 hour, 54 minutes	
—	Il'ya Muromets	October 1913	4	Argus	100	Also flown as floatplane, with 2× 115 hp Argus + 2×200 hp Salmson engines	1
A	Kievsky (prototype military conversion)	Spring 1914	2	Argus	100	Made the epic long distance flight, St Petersburg-Kiev (750 miles), and back, with Igor Sikorsky and crew of three, 30 June, 12 July, 1914	1
			2	Argus	125		
Б (Beh)	(Series production of military conversion)		4	Argus or	140	Five aircraft adapted for military use. Some, used only for training, had only two engines	5
			4	Salmson	140		
B (Veh)	Kievsky II (military version)	1914	2	Argus	140	Military version, with special modifications and aerodynamic improvements. "Kievsky II" was squadron name	1
			2	Argus	125		
B (Veh)		1914	4	Sunbeam	150	Production version of Type B(Veh)	36
D 1	DIM (IM = Il'ya Muromets)	1915	4	Sunbeam	150	Smaller and lighter model, with detachable wings, for ease of rail transport 3 rudders. First 2 had engines in tandem	13
D 2		1916	4	Sunbeam	150	Improved version of D1. Center rudder removed to instal tail gun	
B (Veh)	Modified as prototype for the G series	1915	4	Sunbeam	150	Advanced military version, with larger wing. Crew of six.	1
G 1		1915	2	Renault	220	Production version of G series	24
			2	R-BVZ	150		
G 2	Familiarly known as "Russobalts" or "Renobalts", according to the engine type used (R-BVZ or Renault, respectively)	1916	(see footnote)			Strengthened wing, tailgun with trolley access. One G 2, with Beardmore engines, attained a height of 17,000 ft.	
G3		1917				Bigger load, more defensive power	
G4		1917	4	Renault	220	Used in 1921 for first commercial air route in Soviet Union, Moscow-Nijni Novgorod (now Gorkiy)	
E (Ye-1)		1916-1918	4	Renault	220	Largest and most advanced of all the Il'ya Muromets types, with incresed bomb load and as many as 8 machine guns. Crew of eight.	8
E (Ye-2)							
TOTAL, all multi-engined types							91

Notes: The Il'ya Muromets — especially the G Series — had many different engine combinations. As suggested by their unofficial names, the Russo-Baltic Wagon Company's R-BVZ 150 hp engines were normally fitted in the G 2s, and Renault 220 hp engines in the G 3s. But several others, such as the Hall-Scott 150 hp, or the Argus 140 hp, were often used.

The numbers built include all airframes constructed. Some of these never flew, because engines were unavailable. A few sub-assemblies were never put together.

All information in this summarized tabulation is based on original research and detailed data compiled by Carl J. Bobrow and Harry Woodman

Note: Since this table was prepared, further recent research by Bobrow and Woodman reveals that 37 (not 24) Type Gs and only 2 (not 8) Type Es were built. The modified Type B (Veh) should not have been listed as an additional aircraft. The adjusted total is thus 97.

armed forces in the first World War a weapon whose potential in that era might be compared with that of the German V-1 or V-2 'secret weapons' of a different era of technological warfare. But times are changing and recognition of Sikorsky's genius is now generously and even proudly acknowledged in the Soviet Union. A replica of the Il'ya Muromets can be inspected at the Monino Air Force Museum near Moscow. It is a full-size replica and to stand alongside it is to recognize immediately that, far from popular opinion, the Il'ya Muromets was no fantasy. It was one of the most important, yet one of the most neglected aircraft in air transport history. Its introduction marked an historic advance in the progress of aircraft construction technology. Further research into its record of performance, drawn from expanded access to Soviet aviation archives, may force a reassessment of the nature and magnitude of Igor Sikorsky's great achievement, rivaling even that of the Wright brothers themselves.

The Lawson Air Line (1919)

Contrary to many assumptions made by some aviation writers and commentators, there never was a Lawson Air Line. This fallacy stems almost entirely from the thousands of photographs generously distributed by Alfred Lawson's admirers. The Lawson airplane made a remarkable 2,000-mile flight in 1919 and the words LAWSON AIR LINE were painted conspicuously in large letters on both sides of the fuselage. But there was only one successful flying Lawson airliner; and it made only one flight.

An airline is presumed to offer service to the public, customarily on a fixed schedule, between a number of city pairs; or at least to provide an air service of some kind, scheduled or otherwise. On his single flight, Lawson carried on impressive load of passengers—with comparative ease, let it be noted—but he never carried anything else ever again. The Lawson Air Line was a dream, one of many that its dreamer was to have. But Alfred Lawson possessed neither the judgment nor the financial backing to bring his dreams to reality.

Lawson was undoubtedly a visionary. Born in 1869, he was the son of Robert Henry Lawson, an Oxford graduate engineer. His mother was an economics student, so that his background was attuned to his later interest in flying for commercial purposes. In 1908 he founded the aeronautical magazine *Fly,* followed in 1909 by *Aircraft,* of which he was editor until 1914. He helped to organize the Belmont Air Meet in 1910 and the one at Chicago in 1911. He learned to fly in 1913, bought his own flying boat, a Thomas, and became the world's first air commuter on 10 October of that year, flying 35 miles from his home in New Jersey to New York's 75th Street where it reached the Hudson River.

In 1912 he was elected vice president of the Aeronautical Manufacturers Association of America and in the following year he was motivated to send an 'Aeronautical Message' to Congress, pointing out—correctly—that the United States was lagging behind the rest of the world, especially Germany, in aviation, and proposed that the U.S. Army should be granted an appropriation of $10,000,000 to purchase airplanes and to train pilots to fly them. Lawson never did things by halves. The recommended sum would be equivalent to about a quarter of a billion dollars today. Yet his action was prophetic.

In 1917 Lawson decided to stop talking and writing and to show the courage of his convictions by putting his ideas into practice. He set up a factory, with some local support, in Green Bay, Wisconsin, and completed his first airplane, a trainer, the M.T.1 (Military Tractor One) on 10 September. He followed this with a better machine, the M.T.2, on 1 May 1918, but the Great War ended before he was able to fulfil a contract for 100 of these. His backers withdrew, but at the suggestion of consultant designer Vince Burnelli, he moved to Milwaukee and on Armistice Day he laid his plans before the remnants of his Green Bay team.

Curiously, in Berlin, on the very same day, Professor Hugo Junkers was putting his team to work on the diminutive F 13, the world's first metal-built airliner, and one that was to provide reliable service for two decades.

Lawson sketched out an aircraft that was, at least in the United States, a giant. It was also revolutionary because it was built from the start to carry passengers in reasonable comfort and could at least lay claim to be an airliner, in the sense that we understand the term today. The public were taken a little by surprise. For in the United States after the end of the first World War, there seemed to be no future for commercial aviation, except perhaps to carry the mails or to take Prohibition-restricted revellers from Florida to nearby Cuba or the Bahamas.

Returning wartime pilots found that they could make a living by 'barnstorming'—flying time-expired pursuit or training airplanes around the land, making acrobatic demonstrations of stunt flying, wing-walking, and other dramatic and dangerous acts, literally creating flying circuses. Danger was emphasized. It had to be to market the product. So the public could not be blamed if it regarded flying as dangerous, even foolhardy.

The Lawson Airliner was cast in a different mould, and was revolutionary in its approach to flying, compared with the barnstorming machines that seemed designed at times to fall apart, which they frequently did. Lawson built an 18-seat biplane, mainly with plywood, and weighing six tons, fully loaded, with a fabric-covered 95-foot wing and 50-foot fuselage whose interior, unimpeded by cross-bracing wires, was high enough for a tall man to stand up in, and wide enough to allow for two lines of chairs. Each passenger had a window, of transparent celluloid, smoked for protection against sunglare. It was well-powered, a rare phenomenon in those days, with two 400 h.p. Liberty engines, giving it a cruising speed in excess of 100 mph. The gas tanks could provide a range of 600 miles.

The "Lawson Air Line" of 1919 was never an airline, but the name appeared on a large passenger-carrying biplane that gave rise to the misapprehension. The aircraft undoubtedly had great potential but it never fulfilled its early promise. (National Air and Space Museum)

Remarkably, this unique aircraft could carry more people than the 14-seat Ford Tri-Motor of 1926, the metal-built airliner that was to launch the T.A.T. transcontinental passenger service in 1929. And furthermore, it was even marginally faster.

But it was not, as some claim, the first such airplane. As early as 1913, Igor Sikorsky had built his Il'ya Muromets four-engined giant which could carry heavy loads and could be used either for passengers or bombs (see Chapter 1). but a combination of political prejudice and the absence of good records has obscured the Russian ship's claim to fame. After the 1918 Armistice, the Farman company in France produced the Goliath, which entered scheduled service in the spring of 1919; and although Handley Page's 'bloody paralyser' was not in time to bomb Berlin before hostilities ceased, it was plying the London-Paris air route by the summer of 1919. The Germans would certainly have been to the fore, had not the harsh—and understandable—terms of the Treaty of Versailles prevented progress. Not only were the Gotha bombers all destroyed, but so also were the Staakens, innovative heavy machines designed by Adolf Rohrbach, whose box-spar wing was years ahead of its time. The Farmans and Handley Pages, albeit slower than Lawson's single aircraft, were in regular service on the commercial air routes in Europe while Lawson was demonstrating with his one and only round trip from Milwaukee.

Lawson's ideas of flight deck conduct were unusual. He told his co-pilot Charles Cox: "I will be the captain, you will be the steersman. I will control the engines and you will take off, steer the plane and land it under my personal direction." Delegation of authority was not Lawson's strong point, but the system seemed to work. They made a test flight on 22 August 1919, the day it arrived at the vacant field at Lisbon Road in New Butler, the site of what was to become Milwaukee's municipal airport, and is now James Currie Park. Some idea of the size and weight of the enormous machine can be gleaned from the knowledge that the truck hired to tow it from the factory could not move the assembled aircraft up the narrow road to the field; and a team of brewery horses was engaged to help out.

On the second flight, on 27 August, a crew of five took the Lawson Airliner to Chicago, landing at Ashburn Field, 85 miles as the crow flies, only 58 minutes later. One feature of the flight was that neither Lawson nor his crew were adorned with the typical flying gear of the day, the statutory cap, goggles, heavy leather suit, and white scarf. They were all in their shirtsleeves.

Four days later, they set off on an historic journey, historic because no other flight even closely approaching it in distance-with-load had ever been made in the United States before; and historic because none would be made again until the Lindbergh-inspired T.A.T. proving flights with the Ford Tri-Motors carved a transcontinental network in 1929 along broadly the same route that Lawson had planned a decade earlier.

On this single flight, the Lawson Airliner flew from Milwaukee and Chicago to the East Coast, and back by a different route. The itinerary is shown on the accompanying map and little more needs to be said beyond noting that it was hailed across the nation by the newspapers as a great achievement, as indeed it was.

On each of the route segments, at least nine people were on board. Fourteen flew from New York to Washington, and on one of the special sight-seeing flights at the latter city, no less than fourteen distinguished guests, as well as the crew of three, enjoyed the comfort of a closed cabin in a tour of the District of Columbia and the neighborhood. This flight, had it ended in

This picture of Alfred Lawson's 1919 airliner shows the impressive dimensions of the passenger cabin, the size and comfort of which were not emulated in the United States until well into the 1930s. (National Air and Space Museum)

disaster, could have changed the course of history, for it took place just before the crucial vote on President Wilson's proposal to join the League of Nations, and Lawson had enough opposing Senators on board to have made the difference.

While the flight was an impressive demonstration that aviation did not consist only of dogfights on the Western Front or looping the loop at an aerial circus, there had been snags. The aircraft had received adverse publicity when it landed at Syracuse in a cabbage patch and ended up with its nose in a ditch at a 48° angle. This could have happened today to any airliner landing in a cabbage patch, and just as today, the reporters were on the spot immediately, with cameramen who delighted in recording the scene before the Lawson Airliner could be returned to a more dignified position. Repairing it took a week, as the material and tools were back in Milwaukee.

On his return trip, Lawson met stiff headwinds at 17,000 feet over the Alleghenies, and could not reach Dayton, and so had to land in a cornfield reported as Collinsville by Lawson himself—but he probably meant either Circleville or Cedarville, Ohio, to the east of Dayton. The airliner was dismantled and sent on flat cars by rail to Dayton, where it was re-assembled at the Wright Airplane Factory. Then at Indianapolis, where the famous Speed-

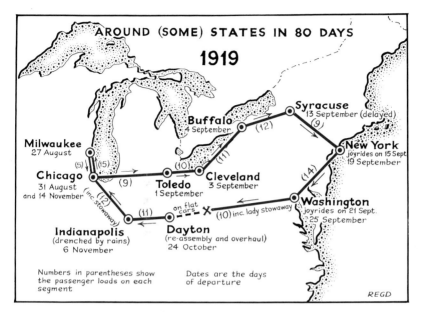

Around (Some) States in 80 Days. *The flight of the Lawson airliner in 1919, from Milwaukee to the East Coast and back, was an impressive feat; but it was the only flight of any consequence.*

burst-punctuated rain, a soaking that added considerably to the weight of the fabric and plywood.

The whole round trip from Milwaukee took 80 days. including a week at Syracuse, several days of local demonstrations in New York and Washington, a month at Dayton, and ten days of rain at Indianapolis. Such delays were not serious. The wonder was that, without en route repair shops, the journey had been completed with such speed at such an early date. But Lawson was dissatisfied. He felt that the Liberty engines might not be sufficiently reliable and decided to construct a new and larger airliner, with three engines to provide an extra margin of safety. He cherished the ambition to open transcontinental air routes and was encouraged by the award of Post Office mail contracts for routes from New York to Atlanta, Pittsburgh to St. Louis, and New York to Chicago. The new Lawson behemoth was built to carry 34 passengers, with berths and a showerbath, and three tons of mail. Both mail and passengers, it was claimed, would be transferred to a smaller airplane during flight through a chute in the floor.

THE LAWSON AIRLINER IN PERSPECTIVE

LARGE COMMERCIAL BIPLANES, 1914-1930

Date of First Service	1914	1919	1919	(1919)	1928	1930
Aircraft Type	Il'ya Muromets Type Б(Veh)	Farman Goliath	Handley Page 0/400 series	The Lawson Airliner	Handley Page HP 42/45	Curtiss Condor
Span (feet)	98	85	100	95	130	92
Length (feet)	56	48	63	50	90	58
Gross Weight (lb)	9,680	11,900	12,800	12,000	29,500	17,700
Max. Seating Capacity	10	12	11	18	38	18
Normal Cruising Speed (mph)	80	90	70	110	100	118
Normal Range (miles)	400	250	250	400	300	500
No. of Engines x horsepower	4 × 220	2×550	2 × 360	2×400	4×550	2×600
Number Built	70-80	50-60	33	1	8	6

The Lawson aircraft was similar in many respects, and may have drawn inspiration from, several contemporary machines flying in Europe immediately after World War I. Interestingly, the Curtiss Condor's performance, a full decade later, was remarkably similar.

This intriguing technique was never put to the test. One day in May, Lawson and four other crew members took off in defiance of the dictates of common sense. The prepared cinder and crushed rock strip was soft and the tires sunk into it, slowing up the takeoff run. The engines were not tuned well. The aircraft crashed on its first attempt to take off. With $55,000 owing to creditors and investors, this $10,000 instantaneous loss was irrevocable.

And so ended the biggest of all Lawson dreams. He had the imagination and foresight to visualize the shape of commercial aviation as it was to develop, and in fact was developing in Europe. The aircraft that he flew along two different routes between Chicago and New York, the most important route in the U.S.A. at the time, was almost clairvoyant in its choice of itinerary; and delays apart, put up a better performance than did the first airlines during the late 1920s, by which time the ground installations were in place. But why Lawson did not persevere with the twin-engined formula will remain as a question and a reflection on his good judgment that will never be explained.

Alfred Lawson went 'back to the drawing board' when he could have gone into production with a vehicle that seemed ready for further testing and refinement. But he turned, as so many dedicated and compulsive inventors do, to other things. He had already promoted a transoceanic floating platform system in 1918, an idea taken up by Edward Armstrong in the late 1920s. Lawson designed a two-tier railroad car for the Long Island Railroad in 1925, as well as a 104-seat two-tier aircraft, weighing 50 tons. His inventiveness, unfortunately, was never translated into practical application.

But there was a Lawson legacy. He founded the School of Lawsonomy, whose slogan was: "If it isn't Truth, it isn't Lawsonomy," and with the explanation of the word's derivation. "LAW stands for the procedure of God's Eternal acts; SON stands for the continuity of the procedure of God's Eternal acts; OMY stands for the process of the continuity of the procedure of God's Eternal acts." He claimed to have discovered the Cause of Sex and the Zig-Zag-and-Swirl Movement, among other surprising revelations, and his name lives on through the promotion by the Humanity Publishing Company of Detroit.

There was a Lawson Airliner. It made only one notable flight, in eleven stages. Only one was ever built. There was no Lawson Air Line.

The Armstrong Seadrome (1923–1943)

As a small boy, in about 1930, I remember seeing a silent movie, starring Conrad Veidt, the arch-villain of the screen at that time, and a good exciting yarn it was too. Entitled *F.P.1*—Floating Platform One—it was the story of dirty doings on the high seas, involving an enormous aircraft-carrier-like structure anchored halfway across the North Atlantic Ocean. It captured my youthful imagination; and at the time it was still capturing adult attention too as a serious engineering project that could be the answer to the problems of trans-oceanic aircraft flight.

The idea was first proposed by Edward R. Armstrong as early as 1913, and in 1915 an early design showed a combination of depot ship and artificial harbor for flying boats. These were to form a chain of stations across the ocean and the idea was modified by 1919 into the first floating platform scheme, for landplane or amphibian use. Rather like the airfields of the immediate post-World War I era, it was the wrong shape, unnecessarily wide and too short in length for safety, and a 1922 refinement rectified this shortcoming. By 1926 further modifications added extra width amidships, to provide space for buildings, and with only minor changes, this was the design that was promoted vigorously during the latter 1920s.

Edward Armstrong was a Canadian, born in 1878 in Mount Forest, Ontario. A delicate child at first, he studied physical culture to such good effect that by the age of 19 he was known as the Strong Boy of Canada. He gave exhibitions of strength and became a professional wrestler before taking up railroad surveying and civil engineering. Applying the same determination to study as he had done to exercise, he took up a serious career in mechanical engineering. Moving first to Cleveland, then to West Virginia and the Texas oilfields, he settled down permanently at the outbreak of the first World War with the E.I. du Pont de Nemours Company at Wilmington, Delaware.

By 1923 he was heading the engineering department of DuPont and was marshaling his ideas into a coherent plan for his seadrome project, backing it with much careful analysis, capital cost estimates and operating expenses, and traffic projections for a trans-Atlantic air route. Armstrong was both a competent engineer and a visionary, a formidable combination. As a senior executive of a manufacturing company with a reputation for innovative research, he was a man to be listened to. With his experience in mathematics and engineering combining with his belief in the enormous potential of air transport, he had an attentive audience from the technical community, an interested public, and a fascinated press.

Much of his case was well-founded and incontrovertible. He emphasized that attention should be concentrated on the North Atlantic. "On what other route do 2,500,000 passengers annually make a 3,500 mile voyage?" he asked. This succinct question alone was a sound reason to examine seriously the possibility of seeking a share of a vast travel market. But if this was to be done by air, a way had to be found to eliminate the contemporary range limitation of heavier-than-air aircraft. Airplanes could either carry large loads over short distances of about 400 miles, or small loads over long distances; but they could not do both.

The solution, Armstrong claimed, was to create "the engineering equivalent of nature's islands," spaced at economical and practical flight distances across the Atlantic. This was calculated at about 400 miles, based on the maximum 500-mile range capability of the best aircraft available. The solution demanded the combined talents of marine engineers and naval architects to contrive adequate areas for aircraft to use, and built so that pitching and rolling would be eliminated.

Edward Armstrong was thorough. His analysis of the preferred route, completed as early as 1921, was a masterpiece. Prevailing winds, storm frequency and distribution, the extent of freezing temperatures, ocean currents, and above all, the prevalence and distribution of fog, the greatest enemy of safe navigation by sea and even more by air: all these aspects were analyzed and researched in great detail. The resultant map and his traffic projections were widely accepted. No-one challenged his assumption that "10 percent of (1,600,000) passengers would travel by air if rates are at all comparable to first class steamship fares."

The seadrome derived inspiration from the large aircraft carriers, *Saratoga* and *Lexington*. Each seadrome would weigh 15,000 tons and would be 1,200 feet long, 200 feet wide, and 400 wide at the center section to allow for the deck structures. These latter were to include hangars, living quarters for the permanent staff, and a 40-room hotel. For passengers who felt like staying a night or two, or who may have been delayed by weather or by mechanical trouble, there was a radio in every room—sheer luxury in those times—and, comfortably beyond the three-mile limit of sovereignty—a bar

(Above) This artist's impression of the Armstrong Seadrome provides some idea of the breathtaking magnitude of the ambitious project that captured the public's imagination in the late 1920s. (National Air and Space Museum)
(Below) Another drawing of the Armstrong Seadrome, revealing the massive structure necessary to provide buoyancy and stability. The drawing does not, however, reveal the extent of the lines necessary for anchorage. These were calculated to require, in some parts of the Atlantic Ocean, cables that would have been three or four miles long. (National Air and Space Collection)

and even gambling for deprived Americans plagued by the Prohibition laws. If there was any problem with the U.S. authorities, Armstrong asserted, the seadromes would simply fly the British flag.

Each of these monsters would be supported, 70 feet above sea level, on 32 huge stilt-like columns, 270 feet tall, and incorporating large buoyancy chambers and ballast tanks. To ensure stability and freedom from pitching and rolling, 95% of the structure weight would be below the level of maximum wave disturbance.

The big problem was how to anchor these leviathans to the ocean bottom. The carefully chosen route was, for much of its course, over that part of the Atlantic that was three miles deep, so that five of the eight seadromes necessary to maintain the 400-mile separation had to be anchored by a system of cables and anchors whose design presented a formidable challenge. The platforms would always have to trail in line with the wind; but in compensation, the vast open sea provided unobstructed approaches from any direction, in contrast with many a land airfield, where buildings, poles, even trees, could threaten normal operations.

Consultation with the Baldt Anchor Company, of Chester, Pennsylvania, revealed some staggering requirements. Initial studies suggested cables of 2 1/4-inch diameter galvanized steel that had to be five miles long to allow for the catenary curve. These were to be attached to the seadromes via station buoys, each weighing 125 tons, acting as intermediate connecting points. At the sea bottom, these cables were to be secured by specially-designed anchors weighing six tons. The cable length was later reduced to 3 1/2 miles and anchor weight increased to fifteen tons.

Aircraft scheduling was relatively easy, just a series of 400-mile hops from seadrome to seadrome. Aircraft cruising at 115 mph were estimated to maintain trans-Atlantic schedules of just under 40 hours, leaving New York, for example, at 6 a.m. and arriving at Plymouth, England, after eight half-hour stops, at 4:30 p.m. the next day. Later modifications in 1929 suggested a limited-stop 150-mph service, with airplanes overflying every second seadrome. Armstrong may have had certain qualms about such an extension of the aircraft's range; but he did not pursue the theme. With normal extrapolation, the need for seadromes could quickly disappear.

Financial estimates were carefully presented, showing that, with an initial investment of $40,000,000, $18,000,000 would be for the eight seadromes. Annual operating costs would total $26,000,000 against revenues of $68,500,000, leaving an annual net income of $42,000,000, or 106% return on investment.

By 1927 Edward Armstrong's persuasive campaigning had made an impression, notably on his employers, who gave him a two-year leave of absence to pursue his ambitious project. He founded the Armstrong Seadrome Development Company at Wilmington, and proceeded to intensify his advocacy for the seadromes, using the 1926 design as the cornerstone of his plans. In a handsome promotional brochure, he invoked the spirit of Lindbergh, Chamberlain (sic), Byrd, and Brock; and pointed out that national progress and prosperity ran parallel with the utilization of transport, quoting Egypt, Rome, Carthage, and the British Empire as precedents.

Providing extensive detail to support the total North Atlantic traffic projections, estimated—reasonably—at 2,500,000 annually, he drew upon much special pleading to assume—unreasonably—that 1,000,000 of these would choose to fly by the seadrome route and would pay collective toll charges of $36,000,000. The matter of how much they would pay to make the trip itself was conveniently omitted from the study.

Support for the 400-mile separation was credited to no less an authority than Edward P. Warner, Assistant Secretary of the Navy, and a technical analyst in his own right, although curiously the chart to illustrate the theory fell far short of conviction.

Interestingly, the Sikorsky S-38 amphibian was featured as the best aircraft available to inaugurate the service, and Armstrong strongly implied that Igor Sikorsky himself was designing a new ship especially for the Seadrome project, a larger 18-seat amphibian. In spite of all his protests to the contrary ("It may be accepted ... as axiomatic...;" "It can be accepted without danger of contradiction.." and so on) the larger Sikorsky aircraft were to tear apart all Armstrong's beloved theories on the limitations on aircraft range. Nevertheless, test flights were made at Roosevelt Field on Long Island, using an area that was an exact replica of the proposed seadrome.

Early in 1928, Armstrong announced that construction of a test seadrome would start in August, that it would be stationed 350 miles from New York, and that the trans-Atlantic Airway would start in 1930. What actually happened, in October 1929, was the construction of a 1/32-scale seadrome model, complete with its S-38, at the Choptank River estuary in Chesapeake Bay, near Cambridge, southern Maryland. The model was 35 feet long, weighed a little more than a ton, and cost $10,000.

Work was to start on the real Seadrome, now increased in estimated weight to 29,000 tons, in December 1929, at the Sun Shipbuilding Company at Chester and the Belmont Iron Works at Eddystone, Pennsylvania. Naval architects were H.J. Gielow & Company, route studies and architecture were by Black and Bigelow, and the important cable contract was assigned to John

H. Roebling & Sons, of Trenton, New Jersey. Revised calculations had reduced the required cable length to about three miles, with a breaking stress requirement of 300 tons. Other contractors were the Baldt Anchor Company, General Electric, R.C.A., Sperry, and the Bureau of Standards; and the U.S. Navy, as well as Sikorsky, were also involved. The project was stated to be financed to the extent of $2,000,000—a rather modest sum compared to the far greater sums required—by a group of individuals from General Motors and DuPont, but those corporations themselves remained aloof, hedging their bets.

The complete seadrome was to be assembled at the mouth of the Delaware River, off Cape May, and then towed to a point halfway between New York and Bermuda. Cost estimates kept changing, but the price of one seadrome seemed to remain fairly constant at about $1,500,000, and the calculations still showed a net income of about $50,000,000. Opening day was postponed to May 1932. But the theories and special pleading were beginning to give way to some incontrovertible facts.

The results of the model tests were not completely supportive of the theories. A directional rudder was incorporated into the design, to prevent yawing in a moderate wind. Powerful winches would have to be installed to take up the slack of the cables in periods of calm, as the seadrome tended to drift towards the buoys. The route map was changed to include the Azores islands in place of one of the seadromes, with European termini such as Lisbon, Vigo, and Brest, none of which was exactly the preferred destination of most travellers. **(See Map)**

Problems of operational and financial management seem to have presented themselves, as there was now a Seadrome Corporation as a parent company, with North Atlantic Airways as a subsidiary. There were politico-legal problems concerning the sovereignty of a seadrome. At a Congress on Aviation Law in Budapest in October 1930, this was assigned to the builders; while a U.S. opinion decided that a seadrome was simply a piece of real estate, neither ship nor island.

Igor Sikorsky, significantly, had other customers, including one that enjoyed considerable favor in Washington. Pan American Airways, whose chairman, Juan Trippe, already had his own ambitions for conquering the world's oceans, was close to launching the S-40 40-seat flying boat, the first of the Clippers, on a 500-mile segment across the Caribbean from Kingston, Jamaica, to Barranquilla, Colombia. And this was only the beginning of flying boat development. While Armstrong was producing charts that included the obsolescent Commodore and the British Short Calcutta, Trippe was soon to commission the Sikorsky S-42, with 750 miles of range with full payload of 32 passengers. Consciously or unconsciously, Armstrong was making the classic

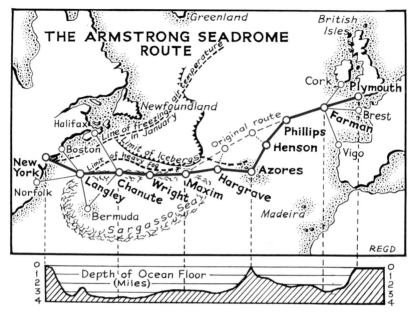

This was the modified plan of the early 1930s. Each floating platform was named after a famous aviation pioneer. The problem of anchoring them, sometimes to an ocean bottom three miles deep, would offer a severe technological challenge, even today.

mistake of comparing his own future product, still speculative, with obsolescent rivals that would themselves be superseded by inevitable developments.

Time was running out. And funds were running low. The Wall Street Crash of October 1929 threw cold water on investment opportunities that were in any way based on speculation. Bankruptcies and unemployment increased. Credit became almost inaccessible, especially for the volume of investment sought by Armstrong for his colossal project. Some slight consolation was derived from the discovery in the model tests that the diagonal and horizontal cross-bracing between the 32 huge supporting columns would not be necessary, thus saving some weight and cost. but these were insignificant compared to other problems that were emerging.

There was deep concern about the anchoring system. Illustrations of a new three-pronged type of anchor revealed a device almost as high as a two-storey house, with unspecified weight. Then, in a paper presented to the Society of Automotive Engineers at Detroit in January 1931 he revealed a new anchor design. If nothing else, this should have sent a warning signal to the minds of potential supporters or investors. He stated: "The anchorage system finally

worked out terminates in a large reinforced-concrete anchor of a spherical seg-
mental shape, 100 feet in diameter and weighing approximately 1,500 tons." He
then went on to describe the two parallel anchor chains and to explain why
chains had to be used as well as cables. There had clearly been serious problems
in ensuring that the seadromes could be safely anchored to the ocean bottom.

By 1931 the weights and costs of the seadromes were escalating. From
the 15,000 tons of 1922 and the 29,000 tons of 1929, the weight of each was
now 47,000 tons. The cost had almost trebled in three years from $1,500,000
to $4,000,000 each. Initial investment requirements had gone up from
$40,000,000 to $93,000,000. Annual operating costs rose from $26,00,000 to
$54,000,000. The cost side of the economic equation was getting out of hand.

Edward Armstrong appears to have faced these unpalatable facts by al-
tering the revenue assumptions, so as to maintain a figure of $71,000,000,
only slightly more than the earlier $68,000,000. This was estimated on the ba-
sis of ten daily flights in each direction with Sikorsky S-40s fitted with 30
seats each, after allowing for mail. The investment total had included 160
Sikorsky amphibians and 250 spare Pratt & Whitney Hornet engines.

The passenger estimate was 170,000, who were expected to pay $350
each, for an annual revenue, without mail, of almost $60,000,000. In 1931,
$350 was the equivalent, in terms of purchasing power, to about $4,000 today,
or about the price of a one-way Concorde ticket. During the Depression, the
prospects of persuading that many people to spend their hard-earned savings
(if they still had any) was remote. Such flights of fancy failed to make an impression on potential investors who, unlike journalists and their readers, were
inclined to read the small print and to ask penetrating questions. They were
not so gullible then as were their counterparts in Europe forty years later, who
swallowed the same kind of twisted economics, based on completely unsupportable assumptions, to justify the construction of the Concorde.

Armstrong still cherished the obsession that long range with adequate
payload was impossible. He insisted that "...it is not technically possible to
operate the Bermuda-Azores hop, exceeding 2,000 miles, with any payload at
all; so all such proposals must await the development of the superplanes
which apparently will be possible only by some revolutionary discovery that
cannot now be forecast." He further compounded the deception—to give him
the benefit of the doubt, self-deception—by using the Dornier Do X giant flying boat as an example of range limitation. But the Dornier was a white
elephant. The Sikorsky S-42, ordered by Pan American on 1 October 1932,
was not. Its 750-mile range was a foretaste of even better flying boats only a
few years of development time ahead. By 1936, Pan Am would be carrying
passengers across the Pacific.

The Austrian Credit-Anstalt Bank collapsed in May 1931, sending re-
verberations throughout the world's business communities. Several German
banks discontinued payments soon afterwards, Great Britain went off the gold
standard, as did the U.S.A. in April 1933. The investment climate went from
lukewarm to frigid. President Roosevelt launched the New Deal to improve
the welfare of the nation as a whole, not to benefit the privileged few who could
afford to spend a small fortune to cross the Atlantic. The Armstrong Seadrome
venture faded into oblivion, buried under the weight of escalating costs, false
assumptions, and declining prospects of even theoretical financial viability.

Not quite. In a bizarre sequel, the whole scheme was revived in 1943 by
none other than C. Bedell Monro, chairman of Pennsylvania-Central Airlines,
a U.S. domestic airline known to be a bit of a maverick. By this time the
weight of the seadrome was estimated at 64,000 tons and its cost at $10,000,000.
In compensation, the separation between seadromes had been increased to 800
miles and their number reduced to three, with the claim that the American
Bureau of Shipping had rated them A-1—whatever that may have meant.

A picture of a 1943 seadrome, slightly modified from the 1929 design,
but with more supporting columns and still with bracing wires, shows an airliner that appears suspiciously like the first four-engined Douglas DC-4E prototype, which had gone into service in June 1939. The Boeing 307 landplane
was already flying across the Atlantic, as were the Pan American 314 flying
boats, able to carry 40 trans-Atlantic passengers each, and which opened
scheduled Atlantic service in the summer of 1939, both by the mid-Atlantic
route via the Azores, and by the northern route via Newfoundland and Ireland.

While Monro was no doubt misguided, if not actually misled, he should
have known better. But Armstrong was a trained engineer and had become a
victim of his own ambition, which had become an obsession, leading to a
fanaticism that dismissed all arguments that inconveniently obstructed the
objective—again the analogy of the Concorde, the U.S. SST, and now the
HST, spring to mind.

For at least a decade, with faulty assumptions and a great deal of special
pleading, even wishful thinking, Edward Armstrong had captured the imagination of millions. Juan Trippe had claimed many airlines and their owners as
victims of his ruthless drive to expand the Pan American empire. Armstrong
could be considered, indirectly, to have joined the ranks of those unfortunates.
But he was more the victim of his own refusal to recognize the relentless
momentum of the technical development of the modern airliner, a progression
that Trippe understood, stimulated, and exploited. At all events, Armstrong
was never heard of again.

The Dornier Do X
(1929-1933)

Although it never went into commercial airline service, nor did it perform any operation to earn its keep, no single transport airplane has ever made a greater impact, upon technical and lay minds alike, than the Dornier Do X. Several successful airliners have been conspicuously successful because of their size, especially if this was combined with speed. The Boeing 707 started a new era because it was big and fast, as were, in their time, the Douglas DC-3 and the Lockheed Constellation, compared to all that went before them. The Boeing 747 succeeded because it was very big and derived great efficiency because of its size alone. But none of these pacesetters captured the imagination, stirred the emotions, or attracted such worldwide attention as the experimental aircraft built by the Dornier Works on Lake Constance in 1929.

Much of the Dornier Do X's impact, especially on the world's press, was because it was built in secret, and burst without warning on an unsuspecting aviation world. It was manufactured in Switzerland, just across the Bodensee (Lake Constance) from Dornier's base at Friedrichshafen, at the small community of Altenrhein. This situation was a residual hangover from the effects of the Peace Treaties and the harsh restrictions imposed on German aircraft builders after World War I. Although conditions had changed, Dornier continued production at Altenrhein as a matter of convenience.

Dr. Claudius Dornier himself was born in 1884, of Swiss-French parents, at Kempten, Bavaria, not far from the Bodensee. Possibly because of his parentage, he pronounced his name in the French manner, as though it were Dorné; and it is said that he preferred to be called Claude, rather than Claudius; but he was certainly German. He studied at the Technische Hochschule in Munich, became an engineer, and in 1911 was hired by the Zeppelin company at Friedrichshafen. He worked on the great airships until 1914, when he began to concentrate on metal skin techniques, a revolutionary idea in those days when fabric covering was normal and even thin wood cladding was considered an innovation.

During the early 1920s, Dornier production had been split fairly evenly between landplane and seaplane production, with factories in foreign countries, including Switzerland and Italy. The Komet/Merkur series of single-engined passenger landplanes were used not only in Germany but in the Ukraine, Japan, and in South America. Even more successful was the series of elegant flying boats, particularly the Wal (Whale), one of the greatest commercial flying boats in air transport history. Used by many airlines and for many historic flights, Wal production, at 320, totaled almost exactly the same as the famous Junkers-F 13's 322.

While the Wal proved to be an excellent example of aeronautical workmanship, and was doing splendid service in the Baltic, Mediterranean, and the Caribbean, its thoroughly deserved good reputation was, in one day, dramatically eclipsed by an usurper that drew its inspiration from the Wal's basic design, development, and operational record. The drama was not only the manner of its emergence, produced like a conjuror's rabbit, but the sheer size of the machine. It was not just big. It was enormous. Nothing even approaching it had ever been contemplated, much less seen before. With a wing span of 157 feet and a length of 131 feet, its all-up weight was almost 60 tons, six times as heavy as the largest German transport operating at the time, the Junkers-G 31. It was the Talk of Germany, of Europe, and of the World, taking over newspaper headlines as no other vehicle had ever done before.

Unlike many behemoths of the air, the Dornier Do X was also attractive to behold. It was twice as heavy but, in general appearance, not unlike the Boeing 314 which Pan American used to such good effect in the late 1930s— a decade and several generations of engine development later—and which is acknowledged as the most successful flying boat ever to enter peacetime commercial service. Strictly a sesquiplane, it had a high wing and sponsons at water level, like the Boeing. But in contrast with the famous Clipper's four engines, the Dornier Do X had twelve, mounted in tandem pairs on pylons above the large wing.

The plans for this enormous aircraft had first taken shape at Mansell, near Friedrichshafen, in September, 1924, for a smaller aircraft. Revised in June 1926, construction work on the final design began at Altenrhein on 19 December 1927. Piloted by Dornier's chief pilot, Richard Wagner, the Do X made its first flight on 12 July 1929. It had been built in nineteen months with about 240,000 man-hours of work.

The awesome dimensions were matched by its impressive load-carrying performance, at least for short distances. It demonstrated a take-off run of 33 seconds to carry 60 passengers and a ten-man crew. Considering the expected

The Dornier DoX of 1929 was magnificent and awe-inspiring by its sheer size. It was more than twice as big as the largest airplane of its era, and even this latter (the Junkers-G 38) was twice as big as any other. The DoX's size was not surpassed until midway through World War II, by the Martin Mars. (Lufthansa)

din from the twelve engines, the noise level was surprisingly low, the result of gearing the four-bladed wooden propellers to half the engine speed. Any doubts as to whether the Dornier Do X would ever really work were dispelled when, on 21 October 1929, 150 invited guests were carried aloft, and a later count revealed that nine stowaways brought the total to 169, a record that was probably broken only by some anonymous feats of airlifting during World War II, and commercially not until the age of the Big Jets in 1958.

Less publicized but well noted by the aviation fraternity was the absence of any servo-motors to assist the crew's control of the 60-ton aircraft. This alone provided evidence of a great design. The size permitted three decks with elaborate installations that included a radio room, navigation room, and a central engine control room. All these were on the upper deck and closely accessible to the cockpit, whose instruments included an elaborate warning light system. The seven passenger cabins in the middle deck included a smoking room and an executive suite, with kitchen, toilets, and a bar. It was the nearest thing to ocean liner luxury ever seen in the air, even exceeding the comfort of the *Graf Zeppelin.*

Only one shortcoming marred the technical success of the Dornier Do X. The twelve engines were 525-horsepower Bristol Jupiter air-cooled radials, built under license by the Siemens engine company. These were not powerful enough to lift the weight except at full power, and the rear line of the tandem-mounted engines overheated. The service ceiling of about 1,300 feet was unacceptable. During the summer of 1930, therefore, the entire engine installation was replaced by water-cooled 640-horsepower Curtiss Conquerors. This substantial modification brought an improvement but only enough to permit short flights with a full complement of 66 passengers.

Equipped with the Conqueror engines, the Dornier team made prepara-tions to give meaning to their name by crossing the Atlantic Ocean. Possibly they had visions of a future Atlantic air route. Wisely, they chose to take the shortest crossing and the one with the mildest weather, from North Africa to Brazil.

The entire odyssey as it eventually developed started from Altenrhein on 5 November 1930 and finished with a great welcome when it arrived back to Germany, at the Muggelsee, Berlin, on 24 May 1932. But the arrival could hardly be described as triumphant. It was not the convincing demonstration of air transport achievement that was intended. To describe the 535-day itin-erary **(see Map, page 36)** as leisurely would be an overstatement. Some of the delays were the result of ill-luck; some through technical problems that are typically encountered during the development stages of any airplane; but cumulatively the delays threw doubt on the Dornier Do X's credentials as a potential airliner, able to maintain the regularity and punctuality that are essential for scheduled air service.

The first section of the Atlantic flight was made up of six segments, ter-minating at Lisbon, and was intended as much for demonstration and public-ity purposes as to break any speed or endurance records. The stops included Amsterdam, Netherlands; Calshot, on Southampton Water, England; and Bordeaux, France. These were important centers of aviation development for those three countries which were among the world's leaders in aviation tech-nology at the time. The choice of route may have served to impress the na-tives. But more practically, it had to follow the River Rhine and stay over water as a sensible precaution against a possible emergency landing.

Certainly the huge craft attracted tremendous attention wherever it went, and at Calshot it welcomed on board the Prince of Wales. Barely more than a decade had passed since the Armistice. The British and Germans were barely on speaking terms. Penalized by reparations payments and obligations,

(Above) The Dornier DoX's take-off seemed to epitomise power; but in fact the aircraft was so under-powered that it could fly only at low altitudes.
(Below) The Giant Dornier flying boat at least excelled in one respect. Its comfort standards were not surpassed until the Hindenburg airship's in 1936.

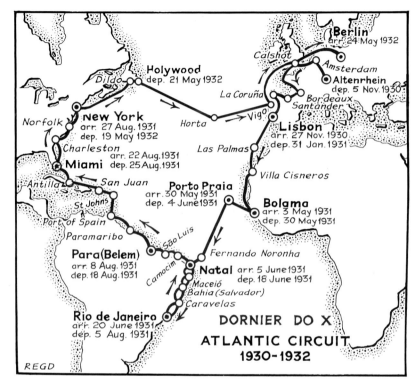

The map of the giant flying boat's circumnavigation of the Atlantic Ocean looks very impressive. But the journey took a year and a half to complete and was punctuated by many delays, including a long stay in New York, where new engines were fitted.

wounded by a financial crisis of unprecedented proportions, its great industries crippled, Germany needed a symbol to inspire confidence in itself. The Dornier Do X did more than any other single object or event, even the *Graf Zeppelin,* to give notice to the world that German industry, technology, and manufacturing prowess had revived and was ready to meet the world on equal terms again, as it had done in pre-war years.

The months that followed the arrival at Lisbon on 27 November 1930 were punctuated by frustrating delays, each for a different reason. On 29 November 1930, a serious fire in the wings, from an unknown cause, put the program back for two months and the Do X did not leave Lisbon until 31 January 1931. After flying the 830 miles to Las Palmas, in the Canary Islands, the hull was damaged and had to be repaired in an improvised dry dock dug out of the shoreline. On 1 May, the voyage was continued, with a stop at Villa Cisneros, to Bolama, Portuguese Guinea. Here a local revolution was in progress which did nothing to speed the ground servicing. The air was hot and humid and when the Do X departed, on 30 May, to Porto Praia, Cape Verde Islands, it had to cut the fuel load to a bare minimum.

Then came the real test. Even the shortest possible South Atlantic segment, from Porto Praia to the Brazilian island of Fernando de Noronha, was a distance of 1,440 miles. The Do X was loaded with 22 tons of gasoline, carried in the tanks in the lowest deck, with one of the 14 crew members on permanent watch. The all-up weight was 57 tons and, to meet the critical demands that would be made on the engine power, every superfluous piece of furnishing and equipment was stripped, and the crew left their toothbrushes and razors behind.

On 4 June, Captain Rudolf Cramer von Clausbruch, one of the great airline pilots in the annals of air transport history, attempted the take off. The Dornier Do X plowed through the water for three miles, unable to get up off the step of the keel, an essential procedure for flying boats to escape the drag of the water. Eventually, by an inspired piece of combined air- and seamanship, by rocking the aircraft from side to side so as to skim the waves and to escape the ocean swell, von Clausbruch coaxed the mighty machine into the air. For several hours, he was able to fly only about 30 feet above the water, taking advantage of the 'ground effect' on the enormous wing area. Only toward the latter part of the flight, at lighter weight because of the fuel burn-off, was he able to reduce power, fly at a more comfortable cruising height, and alight off the shores of the Brazilian island on 5 June 1931.

The trip down the Brazilian coast, from Natal to Rio de Janeiro, was uneventful, except that ceremonial receptions and celebrations, many no doubt in the uninhibited Brazilian style, added to the demands on the crew's stamina. Commander Friedrich Christiansen became so impatient that he protested to Dornier that his diplomatic and public relations duties were interfering with his work as a pilot and that the sojourn in Rio was unnecessarily long. He was over-ruled. Such were the international implications, in which Germany desperately wished to strengthen diplomatic and commercial overseas associations, that the Dornier Do X's presence had to be exploited to the fullest extent.

No man understood this better than ex-World War I pilot, Fritz Hammer, now the driving force behind the Condor Syndikat, the German aviation trading organization that had sponsored several airlines in South America. Christiansen returned to Germany 'for consultations' and Hammer took command of the Dornier Do X for the next part of the itinerary, up the coast of Brazil, departing from Rio on 5 August 1931, after 47 days in the Brazilian capital.

This picture of the Dornier DoX shows the positioning of the twelve tandem-mounted Siemens-Jupiter radial engines, and the huge wing area, which enabled the giant aircraft to use the additional lift created by "ground-effect" when cruising over the ocean at very low altitude, (Dornier)

At Belém, an engine had to be replaced, causing a ten-day delay, as the spare one had to be brought from Rio. The Do X left Belém on 18 August and arrived at Miami only four days later. With stage distances of 800 miles, the aircraft was more comfortable, and New York was reached on 27 August. On the last segment, from Norfolk, Virginia, 69 people were on board, the largest number carried by any aircraft in the United States until then. There were drinks and dancing, both novelties for air travellers at that time, and Captain Clarence Schuldhauer piloted the Do X in great style to alight at New York's Battery, having paid his respects to the Statue of Liberty. Thousands of people stood in line to visit the giant airplane when it was transferred to North Beach, the Curtiss airfield on Long Island.

Here the aircraft was completely inspected and overhauled, with the Conqueror engines receiving the first detailed attention since they were installed 300 flying hours previously. The Do X spent the whole winter in New York, in preparation for its greatest challenge, a return to Germany by the Central Atlantic route. After some test and demonstration flying around New York, once carrying 104 guests, it set off towards Newfoundland, alighting first at the island of Dildo, in Trinity Bay, then at Holyrood, in Conception

Bay. Here, to face the 1,360 miles to Horta, in the Azores island group, it took on 6,250 gallons of gasoline, for an all-up weight of 55 tons. All calculations had to made with absolute precision, and safety margins had to be bigger on this segment, even though it was shorter than the Cape Verde Islands-Fernando de Noronha stretch, because the North Atlantic weather was notoriously less reliable than that of the South. For five hours, the Dornier Do X flew at its long-range cruising altitude of about 30 feet before reaching landfall at Vigo, Spain, on 22 May 1932. With only one stop, at Calshot, it arrived back in Germany, at the Muggelsee, Berlin, two days later, almost two years after leaving the Bodensee. **(See Map)**

During the month in Berlin, no less than 200,000 visitors paid homage to the great machine before it departed on the last voyage. It had become a museum piece even before it stopped flying. Then, on 23 June, it headed northwest to Stettin and Königsberg, before turning back eastwards, calling at all the main German Baltic Sea ports and at North Sea points before reaching Hamburg on 12 August. Three weeks later, on 5 September, it flew via the North Sea and the Dutch Zuider Zee (to avoid unnecessary flying over land) to tour the Rhineland, with side trips to Frankfurt and Zurich, to come back home to Altenrhein on 14 November 1932.

In 1933, it flew to Passau, on the Danube, on 9 May, and this appears to have been its last flight. It ended its days in retirement in the Berlin Aeronautical Museum in 1934, and was totally destroyed by United States Air Force bombs in 1943.

The Dornier Do X never went into full production, although two more were ordered by the Italian Government, with 12 Fiat A-22 600-horsepower engines. the *Umberto Maddalena* was delivered from Altenrhein to Spezia, flying across the Alps at a respectable 12,000 feet, on 28 August 1931. The *Alessandro Guidoni* followed on 13 May 932. The former made a circuit of Italy, visiting all the main coastal cities and Lake Como in September and October, 1931. The two Italian Do Xs were intended for regular air service as far as Tripoli but this never materialized and they were allocated to the Italian Navy.

The giant Dornier flying boat's life was a short four years, of which far too much was spent on, rather than above the water, and even in the latter condition it was usually precariously low. But when it did fly, it did so with style and grace, in spite of its gargantuan size. After Germany's disastrous post-war decade, it sent a signal to the world proclaiming that German aviation technology was back on its feet. It was a brave try.

The Dornier engineers and designers crossed new thresholds of technical excellence, failing only to appreciate that the level of engine power and efficiency of the time could never permit acceptable operational standards or

THE DORNIER DoX IN PERSPECTIVE

Basis of Comparison	Biggest Aircraft until WWII	Largest Contemporary Landplane	Subsequent increase in flying boat size						
Year of First Service (Flight)	1929	1929	1931	1934	1935	1935	(1942)	(1947)	(1952)
Aircraft Type	Dornier DoX	Junkers-G 38	Sikorsky S-40	Sikorsky S-42	Martin M-130	Boeing 314	Martin Mars	Hughes H-4	Saunders Roe Princess
Span (feet)	162	147	114	114	130	152	200	320	219
Length (feet)	131	75	77	69	91	106	120	219	148
Gross Weight (lb)	123,000	52,800	34,000	38,000	52,250	82,500	145,000	400,000	330,000
Max. Seating Capacity	66	34	38	32	41	74	106	250	105
Normal Cruising Speed (mph)	115	112	115	150	130	180	170	200	300
Normal Range (miles)	500	800	900	1,200	2,500	2,500	3,000	3,000	4,000
No. of Crew	14	10	6	6	7	5	8	(8)	6
No. of Engines x horsepower	12×500	4 × 650	4×575	4×700	4×830	4×1,500	4×2,300	8×3,000	10×3,780
Number Built	3	2	3	10	3	12	7	1	3

For all its shortcomings, the sheer size of the German flying boat of 1929 was impressive. It was more than twice as big as any of its contemporaries, and not until the construction of the Martin Mars during World War II did a larger craft exceed it in gross weight.

commercial applications. There were no air routes that could produce the traffic to match its size, and no infrastructure to cope with the stringent servicing demands.

But it was no fantasy, as anyone who ever stood near it and gazed in awestruck wonder at its dimensions and its beautiful lines will testify. The Dornier Do X raised aviation's sights to a hitherto undreamed-of level, and gave German engineers priceless experience in studying the problems of building and operating large aircraft. Rather in the same way that the ill-fated post-World War II giant Bristol Brabazon airliner paved the way for the Britannia and helped to stimulate Britain's post-war aviation recovery, the Dornier Do X reaped untold dividends, measured in attitudes rather than aluminum, in the years to come.

Legalized Murder
(1934)

There are lies, damned lies, and statistics. The reality of this frequently-quoted axiom is all too common. Statistics are manipulated by selective citation or by the error of omission to prove almost anything, especially when percentages are involved, with the small print of the footnote obscuring rather than clarifying the exact definition of the parameters. During the hectic period of the early months of 1934, statistics concerning air safety were thrown around irresponsibly to exploit the emotional effect of a time-dishonored device, the statistically misleading ploy of generalizing by the particular.

In this instance the particular was a series of sensationally publicized accidents by pilots and airplanes of the U.S. Army Air Corps which, ill-prepared, ill-equipped, and at very short notice, were called upon by the President to take over the carriage of the air mail, hitherto conducted under the subsidized umbrella of 28 surviving Post Office mail contracts that were held, with only two or three exceptions, by the three giant conglomerates that, by 1933, had maneuvered themselves into a protected air transport oligopoly. It was rather as if the airlines of today were to abandon the air mail and the U.S. Air Force was asked to take over with its B-52 bombers.

There had been a scandal with enormous financial undercurrents. The airlines had been investigated by a special Senate committee, chaired by Senator Hugo Black, to inquire into allegations that the Postmaster General had used the privileges of his office to circumvent the intent, if not the precise letter of the law—and there was much doubt about the latter too. The investigation substantially confirmed a previous finding by the Crane Committee of February 1933, to the effect that "interlocking financial interests have in the past prevented the full, free, and independent development of aviation. They have resulted in the waste of public funds and run counter and do violence to the very purposes for which the subsidy has been provided."

Post Office Department estimates for the three years after the passage of the 1930 McNary-Watres Act, whose real architect was Postmaster General Walter Brown himself, revealed a massive public expenditure of $46,000,000, of which $8,000,000 had gone to the Post Office in handling costs, $18,000,000 to buy stamps, and no less than $38,000,000 in subsidy to the airlines. This was a lot of money, possibly three times the costs, and had been shared almost entirely by three corporations: General Motors, which controlled T.W.A., Western Air Express, and Eastern Air Transport; the Aviation Corporation of America, which controlled American Airways; and the United Aircraft & Transport Corporation (Boeing Aircraft and Pratt & Whitney Engines), which owned United Air Lines.

Brown's intentions were sensible and ultimately were demonstrated to be sound, but the means be which he achieved his ends were highly suspicious, especially as the contracts seemed to have been allocated by a Machiavellian interpretation of the law—Brown's own. Disbursements were concentrated into the bank balances of the Big Three, with two small independents, National Parks and the Pittsburgh Aviation Corporation, picking up the crumbs, with not a morsel left for new aspirants to a share of the air mail subsidy.

The evidence was convincing, overwhelming, and damning. The Attorney General gave his opinion: "...the arrangements, understandings and agreements out of which the route certificates subsequently grew (before 1934, and following the 'Spoils Conferences') were highly irregular and interfered with the freedom of competition contemplated by the statutes." The public seemed to be in no mood to learn about the dispersal of its tax money to the directors of General Motors, AVCO, Boeing, and Pratt and Whitney. The ideal scapegoat was Frederick B. Rentschler, head of Pratt & Whitney, whose $253 investment in United Aircraft became $29,675,000 in the boom of 1929. He had drawn $800,000 in salary between 1929 and 1930, had taken a profit of $9,000,000 out of his investment, and with bonuses, cleared $10,500,000—which would be worth about $120,000,000 today.

President Roosevelt took swift action, cancelling the Air Mail contracts at 4 p.m. on 9 February 1934. There was much weeping and gnashing of teeth from the boardrooms of the deprived air mail contractors. Newspaper headlines described a grave injustice in vivid phraseology. *Fortune* summed it up as well as it could: "The President of the U.S. put United Aircraft out of the air-mail business, at least temporarily. He also put Errett Lobban Cord (American Airways) out of it; and General Motors ... and a half dozen small operators. He threw 800 men and women out of work and made 6,000 others fear for their jobs. He kicked askew the underpinnings of a $250,000,000 investment shared by 200,000 stockholders." *Fortune*'s "half a dozen" was actually only two, but the article voiced the conventional protests of big business. The best-mannered comment from an authoritative aviation source—but from one

Aircraft such as these: the Douglas O-38B observation aircraft (top); the Douglas O-38E (middle); and the Douglas B-7 bomber (bottom) were never intended to carry the mail on a regular schedule, as they were called upon to do during the Air Mail Crisis of 1934 (Western Air Lines)

who was drawing a generous income from consultation work with T.W.A. and Pan American—was from Charles Lindbergh: "...action does not discriminate between innocence and guilt and places no premium on honest business."

Nevertheless, Roosevelt turned his back on the contractors and asked the Army to carry the mail, asking General D. Foulois, Chief of the Army Air Corps, if he could take over. Foulois was damned if he did and damned if he didn't. He knew that his men and machines were not ready, and had campaigned for years for improvements; yet he could not refuse the President's request, thereby admitting incompetence.

And so the Army carried the mail, from 19 February to 10 March 1934; and then, after a pause to lick its wounds and reorganize, from 19 March to 1 June, by which time the commercial airlines were progressively resuming air mail service under renegotiated contracts. The Air Corps' record was widely condemned as an utter failure. The worst accusation was that many human lives had been needlessly sacrificed, because of a plethora of accidents. The emotion generated in some directions reached a peak, amounting almost to hysteria, in a syndicated cartoon portraying the new Postmaster General Farley—and by implication Roosevelt—as harbingers of what was freely described as "legalized murder." The basis of this outpouring was a total of 66 accidents causing 12 pilot deaths during the short initial period of Army Air Corps operations between mid-February and the end of March.

Closer examination reveals that the Army Air Corps' record was not as disreputable as it had been portrayed, and that the statistics were selectively quoted. Though reference was made in subsequent reports and commentaries to the abominable weather—the worst in half a century, the inexperience of the pilots, and the inadequacy of the aircraft, these factors were brushed aside or ignored. They were not held as sufficient explanation, much less excuse, for the alleged carnage that Roosevelt had enacted. The President concluded that his decision had been ill-judged, although to have allowed the commercial contractors to carry on misusing the taxpayers' money would not have been wise either. But he followed the Dale Carnegie wisdom "if you're wrong, admit it quickly." He instructed James A. Farley, the new Postmaster General (Brown had been hounded from office) to call for new bids for the contracts. With unethical haste almost as reprehensible as Brown's had been, these were quickly awarded before further damage was done.

Considering the magnitude of indignation that had swept across the nation, the reviews of the Air Corps' record during those fateful two months were strangely low keyed. Much emphasis was placed on the $3,767,000 calculated to have been spent, but the individual accidents were forgotten. The report from the War Department's files submitted to Farley was not made generally available. Not that it was necessary to suppress it; the public was simply lulled into forgetting about it, its mind having been made up for it by the interested parties and the media.

More than half a century later, with the increasing objectivity that the passage of time can sometimes bring, a dispassionate recapitulation of the facts is interesting. They reveal, for example, that tremendous credit should be given to the Army Air Corps for having achieved a minor masterpiece of operational ingenuity, extracting the greatest productivity from the slenderest of resources: a motley collection of pursuit 'planes and ponderous bombers, flown by pilots whose training had not anticipated a pending emergency and had not therefore been in a state of readiness for a ruthlessly severe test.

A close study of the Army Air Corps operation shows that almost all long-distance obligations were fulfilled. The routes flown (see map) were un-cannily similar to those of the original system mapped out for the first dozen important contract air mail routes in 1926-27. It was arguably more efficient. Necessity being the mother of invention, it employed the hub system, all too

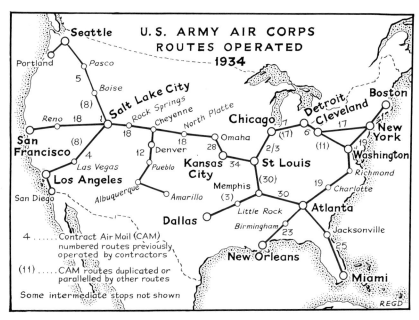

By a system of traffic hubs, the U.S. Army Air Corps was able to economize on the number of routes that it needed to fly to reach all the most important centers of population in the U.S.A. Other cities, such as Minneapolis, Buffalo, or Cincinnati, were connected by excellent rail service.

familiar today as the competitive and operational answer to maximizing loads. In 1934, the Army was given no credit for that.

The outstanding feature of the Air Corps' map was that it excluded many short routes, such as Minneapolis-Chicago or Cincinnati-Chicago, and several routes of low traffic density such as Salt Lake City-Great Falls. On most of these, overnight rail services were excellent. The only long-distance routes of any consequence that were omitted were the west coast link from Seattle to San Francisco and Los Angeles—and this was neatly taken care of by the Salt Lake City hub; and the southern transcontinental route, then generating only a fraction of the traffic that it does today, and served competitively by the Southern Pacific and Santa Fe railroads.

Had the Air Corps chosen to include these short and easy-to-fly routes as part of its mission, it could have improved on its statistical record. In the event, it faced up to its responsibilities, accepted the challenge of flying old crates across the Alleghenies and the Rockies, and got down to work. It took over the trunkline frameworks of the General Motors, AVCO, and United groups, and modified them into three operating zones, Eastern, Central, and Western. Each had its own hub, New York, Chicago, and Salt Lake City, respectively, with Atlanta emerging as a fourth hub, by chance if not by design.

The 86-page *Final Report of the War Department Special Committee on Army Air Corps,* published on 18 July 1934, was signed by none other than James H. Doolittle. It examined the efficiency of the Air Corps, its relationship with civil aviation, and its general competence, but the commentary and conclusions on the air mail experience were conspicuous almost by their absence. Much attention was given to defense policy, the separation of Army and Navy air activity, the relationship with civil aviation, pay, promotion, training, equipment, safety, and meteorology. Half a page only was devoted to "Air Mail Lessons." Reiterating the reasons why the Air Corps was neither ready nor able to carry the mail, and emphasizing—justifiably—the atrocious weather, it stated "...the Army fliers met this duty with fidelity which does them great credit as soldiers."

The report contains tables of statistics that bear close examination. Oddly, they do not attempt to draw conclusions that might be expected to show the Army in a better light. Perhaps the Army did not wish to demonstrate that it could perform marvelously with inadequate equipment, otherwise Congress might have taken the view that there was no urgency about re-equipment. One of the problems—as always with statistics—was that it was not possible to compare apples with apples. But the Army tried to be fair, doing no more, perhaps, than to compare Granny Smiths with Golden Delicious.

THE ARMY AIR CORPS OPERATION
February- March 1934

COMPARISON WITH CONTRACT CARRIERS

Period	Operator	Flights Scheduled	Flights Cancelled	Percentage Completed
Feb. 1931	Contract Mail Carriers	1,734	141	92%
Feb. 1932	" "	2,535	199	92%
Feb. 1933	" "	3,045	187	94%
March 1933	" "	3,517	289	92%
19-28 Feb.1934	Army Air Corps	541	148	73%
1-10 March 1934	" "	580	181	69%
19-31 March 1934	" "	416	63	85%

Source: U.S.War Dept. Report,18 July 1934 (Exhibits 5/6)

CAUSES OF DELAY OR CANCELLATION

Causes of Delay or cancellation	Flights delayed but completed	Flights partially completed	Flights cancelled
Weather	446	424	618
Attributed to Air Corps			
Mechanical	39	10	2
Accident	1	1	-
No pilot or 'plane	-	1	2
Miscellaneous	5	56	20
(Sub-total)	45	68	24
Unavoidable			
Mail not ready	111	} 79 {	11
Late trains	16		-
Sequential (awaiting connections)	223	-	2
Route suspended (or combined with other route)	-	-	9
(Sub-total)	350	79	22
TOTALS	841	571	664

Source: U.S. War Dept. Report, 18 July 1934 (Exhibit 7)

Banner headlines in the newspapers proclaimed unmitigated disaster as the unprepared pilots took over Mission Impossible in the worst winter for many decades. But the official statistics tell a different story. The actual results, bearing in mind the inexperience of the aircrew, were commendable.

A little old fashioned arithmetic reveals that the Army Air corps record of performance and reliability, measured by trips completed as a percentage of trips scheduled, was not at all bad (see table). Civilian services had achieved 92% in February 1931 and 1932 and 94% in February 1933. It was also 92% in March 1934. The Army's record was 73% for the period 19-28 February, 69% for 1-20 March, and 85% for 19-31 March, by which time both the weather and the flying experience were improving. The second half of March thus saw the inexperienced Army Air Corps only 7% short of the experienced commercial operators' figures, after only two months of learning-on-the-job.

In another table, a complete analysis of the reasons for flight delay, non-completion, or cancellation, the Air Corps' percentage of trips completed, 64%, is not impressive, and the percentage of trips completed on schedule, 39%, is unacceptable. But if the figures for the extraordinarily bad weather are deducted, (46% of the total) the results are seen in a different perspective.

This latter table also mentions only two accidents, one of which was the cause of a delay, another of non-completion—the details are not revealed. There are brief entries on "late trains," "mail not ready at the post office," "stop order," "no pilot," "no mail," and "waiting connections," Had those factors been taken into account, and (with the possible exception of the "no plane" and "no pilot" entries) been considered to be extenuating circumstances beyond the control of the Air Corps, the figures would even rate as highly commendable. If only the blameworthy incidents, mainly "mechanical," are considered, then the percentage of total delays amounted to only four percent.

The accident record too should be taken in its true perspective. Some of the vociferous critics of the Air Corps should perhaps have cast a few motes out of their own eyes.

On 18 February 1934, right in the middle of the crisis and the day before the air mail contracts were canceled, Jack Frye and Eddie Rickenbacker, both indirectly showing the flag for General Motors, as they were senior executives of airlines under that banner, flew the Douglas DC-1, prototype of a famous line of thoroughbred commercial aircraft, from Burbank to Washington in record time. This was a much publicized event and deservedly so.

Less publicized was the accident record of the commercial airlines during the very same period during which the Army Air Corps came under the harshest scrutiny, with emphasis on the twelve pilots killed. The fact that eight of them were killed on training flights was not given too much prominence in the reports. Equally the airline accidents did not generate a furore as did those of the Air Corps. United, American, and PANAGRA, all experienced commercial airlines at the highest level, had three accidents, killing fifteen people,

FATAL ACCIDENTS BY CONTRACT AIRLINES 1933-1937

(Excluding those by single-engined aircraft, e.g. Lockheed Vega)

Year	Number	Fatalities		Injuries	Airlines involved	Aircraft involved
		Crew	Passengers			
1933	6	12	11	7	Eastern (1) United (4) TWA (1)	Condor (1) Ford (2) B-247 (3)

Interlude: From 19 February to 31 March 1934, the Army Air Corps carried the mail. One report stated that 12 lives were lost in 66 accidents. Official War Dept. records show that on scheduled operations, 4 pilots were killed in 2 accidents

Year	Number	Crew	Passengers	Injuries	Airlines involved	Aircraft involved
1934	2	6	7	4	American (1) PANAGRA (1)	Condor (1) Ford (1)
1935	4	9	14	8	TWA (1) Western (1) United (2)	DC-2 (1) B-247D (3)
1936	8	18	48	2	American (1) TWA (1) United (1) C & S (1) Pan Am (1) Western (1) Northwest (1) Braniff (1)	DC-2 (3) B-247D (2) L-10 (3)
1937	6	15	51	13	Western (1) United (2) TWA (1) PANAGRA (1) Eastern (1)	DC-3 (2) DC-2 (2) B-247D (1) S-43 (1)
*3 month period 15 Dec. 1936 to 25 Mar. 1937	6	15	35	8	Western (2) Northwest (1) United (2) TWA (1)	DC-3 (1) DC-2 (1) B-247D (3) L-10 (3)

* During this eventful period, three accidents occurred on training flights, one of which (by Braniff) had ground staff on board. Five passengers and one crew member were killed, and two were injured. (not included in tabulation)

Sources: Dept. of Commerce records; Kenn C. Rust

Much was made of the fatality list set up by the Army Air Corps during the early months of 1934. But the casualties sustained by the contracted airlines in subsequent years continued to mount in numbers. Most of them were in crashes by modern twin-engined airliners that were far superior to the single-engined aircraft that comprised the main part of the Army Air Corps' fleet.

including nine passengers. The people throwing stones at the Army Air Corps forgot that they lived in glass houses.

Despite the delivery of new, modern aircraft such as the Boeing 247, the Douglas DC-2, and the Lockheed L-10 Electra, the subsequent commercial airline accident record was nothing to boast about. Excluding the incidents involving older aircraft such as Stearmans and Lockheed Vegas, the annual number of people killed was: 23 in 1935, 66 in 1936, and 66 again in 1937. During the three years, 113 passengers were killed. In the three-month 1936-1937 winter, there were six crashes, with modern Boeing, Douglas, and Lockheed machines, in which 15 crew members and 35 passengers were killed. All the crashes were fairly evenly distributed among the modern aircraft and the biggest airlines. **(See Table, page 49)**

The popular condemnation of the U.S. Army Air Corps' record in 1934 needs, therefore, to be re-assessed. Far from being incompetents, the pilots were brave men who faced much adversity, though ill-trained, ill-prepared, and ill-equipped for the specific assignment forced upon them. Almost anonymously, they faced as much danger over the Rockies and the Alleghenies "Hell's Stretch" as Eddie Rickenbacker himself had faced during his incident-prone career. By definition, they never killed a passenger. Their alleged failure to perform has been a long-held fallacy. In truth, they were magnificent men in not very flyable machines.

The Big Flying Boats
(1931–1948)

Many fallacies have been entertained in the appreciation and judgment of flying boats and their contribution to aeronautical progress, especially in commercial aviation. And there have been many fantasies too, mainly of imagined giants, able to carry hundreds of passengers in the style of the great ocean liners, equipped with every amenity, even a ballroom. Both fallacy and fantasy were born during the Golden Age of aviation development between the two World Wars, on what was at the time a reasonable assumption that only large stretches of water could accommodate the enormous machines that were built and the monstrosities that were projected.

Yet despite showing great promise at first, the flying boat's place in history was transient. Only those over the age of 60 can remember the contribution to airline progress that was made in pioneering transoceanic and intercontinental routes during the 1930s. Those who remember do so with a certain affection, because most of the big flying boats possessed an elegance that belied their efficiency but led to romantic images in the eye of the beholder. Most of all, there has been a misconception as to the extent and number of the fleets of the 'ships that had wings'—to use Bill Masland's description—and the magnitude of the flying boat era should be put in its proper perspective.

When Pan American Airways celebrated the 50th Anniversary of its first trans-Pacific air service with the almost legendary *China Clipper,* much popular interest was aroused. The conquest of the world's biggest ocean had been no mean feat, and one manifestation of such interest was a flush of inquiries, by telephone, letter, even visits to the National Air and Space Museum in Washington. The first question was invariably to ask either where one of the Clippers was still operating and where a ticket could be purchased; alternatively did the Museum have one, and if not, where could one be inspected. Answers to the effect that no Pan American flying boat had been in service since 1946 and that none had survived beyond 1951 were often met with undisguised disbelief.

Equally incredible to the inquirer were assurances that Pan Am had only had a grand total of 25 large flying boats, or that only three of the *China Clipper* class were ever built. And to be told that two thirds of the 159 large commercial flying boats ever built were British, albeit inferior to Pan American's Sikorskys, Martins, and Boeings, was regarded as distinctly un-American and tantamount to heresy.

Yet the small numbers belied the magnitude of the achievement. During the whole of air transport's second decade, in fact, from 1931 to 1946, when Pan Am retired or sold its last Boeing 314, flying boats epitomized long-distance commercial aviation. They flew the flag of the United States across the Pacific and Atlantic Oceans, and comprised the bulk of the fleet of Great Britain's Imperial Airways in its role of linking the Empire upon which, it was then said, correctly, that the Sun Never Set.

Pan Am and Imperial were not entirely alone. Smaller flying boats did most of the work on the German and French South Atlantic air mail route, and both countries were experimenting with larger craft to challenge the apparent supremacy of the English-speaking world in the intercontinental skies. Japan developed the Kawanishi H8K 'Emily'—possibly the best flying boat ever built—to link its Greater East Asia Co-Prosperity Sphere with the homeland.

So the big flying boats were a force to be reckoned with. Why then did they not continue to dominate the airways through the process of technical development common to most categories of aircraft?

Certainly, in the pioneering years, they were able to hold their own. The use of water-borne aircraft as load carriers was almost as deeply rooted a tradition as the use of landplanes. Immediately after World War I, few aircraft were much faster than trains, especially when flying against the wind. Commercial aircraft could compete best against relatively slow-moving ships. Thus, the first foreign air mail routes in the United States during the early 1920s were all operated by small floatplanes or flying boats, from Florida to Cuba, from Seattle to Victoria, British Columbia, and from New Orleans to Pilottown. The latter two were neatly scheduled so as to save a day's mailing time and to meet the ships at the first or last port of call. There were also passenger-carrying flying boat operations from Los Angeles to Catalina Island; from New York to Newport, Rhode Island; across some of the Great Lakes; and on prohibition-breaking trips from Miami to the Bahamas, taking thirsty passengers outbound and carrying bootlegged liquor back. At that time, the common thread justifying the operations was convenience. The New York East River dockside or the Miami beachfront were more convenient to the city centers than any airport locality.

A school of aviation thought emerged that appreciated this advantage and suggested, even campaigned for others. Provided that the water was calm, kept free of flotsam, and did not freeze, there was no limit to aircraft weight, and therefore size, as in the case of ships. Airfields, on the other hand, were at the time grass or dirt areas that became muddy in inclement weather, and landplanes could easily get stuck. In most places there was a limit to the size of flat and unimpeded land that could be used as airports, whereas in many cities there were long stretches of water. Flying boats did not need cumbersome landing gears, and the drag-reducing retractable gears had not yet been developed. The first concrete runway, built by Henry Ford at Detroit in 1926, did not inspire a rush to emulate the builder of the Tri-Motor. By the late 1920s, the future of long-distance aircraft seemed, at least in the heavier-than-air category, to lie with the flying boat.

Pan American's interest in this respect had originated in its quest to encircle the Caribbean, as the first stage in Juan Trippe's empire-building program. In the late 1920s, both André Priester, his chief engineer, and Charles Lindbergh, his technical advisor, favored landplanes; but were forced to admit that the construction of adequate airstrips faced severe problems of cost, land shortage, and politics. At every island, however, there was usually a secluded bay where, with little expense, and with no encroachment of land usage, a safe harbor could be found for a versatile little flying boat such as the Sikorsky S-38. Also, when not in use by, say, the twice weekly service, the harbor could still be used by others; and this was not necessarily so in the case of airfields, where the local populace often liked to feed their flocks by day as well as by night.

And so the tradition grew. Pan American acquired larger flying boats. With Consolidated Commodores, taken over from a rival airline, it developed a route all the way to Buenos Aires. At every point along the South American Eastern seaboard, it established flying boat bases and few challenged the wisdom of selecting the boat over the landplane. The same was true throughout the British Empire, served by Imperial Airways as the "chosen instrument." Except when crossing Europe or the Arabian Desert, expanses of water at the seaside, on lakes, or on large rivers, seemed to beckon the boats. In the east the way seemed clear through the Mediterranean, the Persian Gulf, along the Ganges, and down the Malay Peninsula, and beyond through the East Indies. On the route to South Africa, the River Nile provided safe haven for flying boats for half the distance, while the great African lakes seemed to be geographically located by divine intention, although only Lake Victoria was used.

Other factors, a combination of tradition and geography, influenced national choice. British, and to a lesser extent, French aviation inherited a

maritime tradition. British crews serving with Imperial Airways wore uniforms cut in naval styling and like Pan American's, often paraded for inspection before departure. Seeking to control Mediterranean air routes as well as
sea lanes, Italy supported flying boat construction as an apparently obvious
solution, even operating the massive Dornier Do X. The Norwegians, facing
almost insuperable problems of airfield construction along its rugged mountainous coastline, used its fjords as naturally safe harbors for water-borne aircraft.

On the other hand, even with a naval tradition, Germany's viewpoint
was influenced by its geographical separation from direct access to the
oceans. It used flying boats and large seaplanes with marked success in its
praiseworthy experimental programs across the North and South Atlantic during the 1930s. But it kept its options open and was the first to recognize con-
clusively that landplanes provided a better long-term solution to the problems
of trans-oceanic air commerce.

Of the other leading nations, the U.S.S.R. had only a limited interest in
flying boats, because its European waters were frozen solid for parts of the
year. The stolid Dutchmen of K.L.M., relying on Anthony Fokker, master-
builder of reliable landplanes, never operated a flying boat in its entire history,

*Pan American Airways' Sikorsky S-42 of 1934 was five years ahead of its time as
a flying machine. But unless elaborate terminal docks and other installations were
constructed, embarking and disembarking, indicated here by a picture of the*
Bermuda Clipper *at its moorings, were inconvenient for the crew, the passengers,
and the maintenance men. (Pan American Airways)*

and never seriously considered using one. This record can be attributed to the foresight and judgment of Dr. Albert Plesman, who rejected flying boats from the start because he considered them to be uneconomical to operate, compared to landplanes. The world could have listened to him with advantage, and followed K.L.M.'s example.

During the late 1920s and the early 1930s, international air routes developed partly with flying boats and partly with landplanes, in fairly equal numbers. The flying boats were, however, more impressive because they were bigger; they were more handsome, with graceful geometry; and they tended to be better known because they were used as the flagships of the two leading intercontinental airlines of the interwar period, Pan American and Imperial.

Pan American moved progressively from the small Sikorsky S-38 to the much larger S-40, to the superb S-42, then to the Martin 130 *China Clipper* class, and finally to the pre-eminent Boeing 314. The British, trailing badly in technology, introduced the Short S.23 'Empire Boat' in 1937. But these two airlines, instruments of national pride and prestige, chosen to carry their countries' flags, did so with remarkably few aircraft. Pan American never

The Boeing 314, seen here at the La Guardia Marine Air Terminal in 1939, was the greatest flying boat ever to see regular service with the airlines; but its maintenance demanded the use of special equipment. (Pan American Airways)

PAN AMERICAN'S TRANSOCEAN CLIPPERS
YEARS OF SERVICE

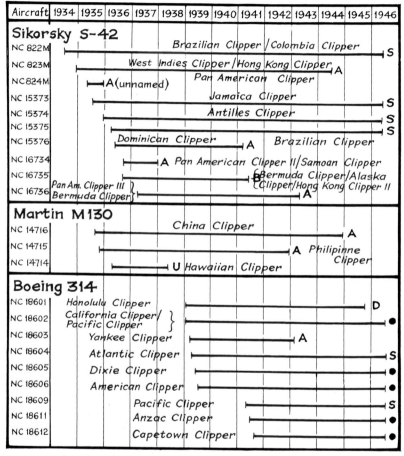

Aircraft	1934	1935	1936	1937	1938	1939	1940	1941	1942	1943	1944	1945	1946

Sikorsky S-42

NC 822M — Brazilian Clipper / Colombia Clipper — S
NC 823M — West Indies Clipper / Hong Kong Clipper — A
NC824M — A (unnamed) — Pan American Clipper
NC 15373 — Jamaica Clipper — S
NC 15374 — Antilles Clipper — S
NC 15375 — S
NC 15376 — Dominican Clipper — A — Brazilian Clipper
NC 16734 — A Pan American Clipper II / Samoan Clipper
NC 16735 — B Bermuda Clipper / Alaska
NC 16736 — Pan Am. Clipper III / Bermuda Clipper — C Clipper / Hong Kong Clipper II — A

Martin M130

NC 14716 — China Clipper — A
NC 14715 — A Philippine Clipper
NC 14714 — U Hawaiian Clipper

Boeing 314

NC 18601 — Honolulu Clipper — D
NC 18602 — California Clipper / Pacific Clipper — ●
NC 18603 — Yankee Clipper — A
NC 18604 — Atlantic Clipper — S
NC 18605 — Dixie Clipper — ●
NC 18606 — American Clipper — ●
NC 18609 — Pacific Clipper — S
NC 18611 — Anzac Clipper — ●
NC 18612 — Capetown Clipper — ●

A = Accident   **B** = Bombed by Japanese
U = Fate Unknown   **D** = Deliberately destroyed
S = Scrapped   **●** = Sold to other operators

The famous fleet of Clipper flying boats that enabled Pan American Airways to conquer both the Pacific and the Atlantic Oceans consisted of a total of only 22 individual aircraft, coming into service progressively from 1934 to 1941. Eight of these were lost in accidents, and three more for other reasons before retirement.

operated more than seventeen individual flying boats simultaneously, and Imperial's record was about the same. But show the flag they did, and were photographed and reported in every corner of the globe, giving rise, perhaps, to the assumption that they were deployed in great numbers.

As time went on during the late 1930s, flying boats began to lose ground as technical advances in landplane construction outpaced those of the flying boats. Landplanes became bigger, faster, and more efficient, and therefore potentially more profitable; and they also showed a tendency to fly longer ranges. The trans-oceanic sphere of operations, hitherto thought to be the regime of the flying boat, for safety reasons associated with its flotation capability, began to look hopeful for landplanes. The round trip flight of the Focke-Wulf Fw200 Condor between Berlin and New York in 1938 must have astonished the aeronautical world as much as did the Sikorsky S-42 in 1934.

The growing evidence of the superior economic potential of the landplane was matched by the experience of the inconvenience often encountered during the flying boat operations. To begin with, Imperial Airways passengers usually had to travel by land to the stretch of water that served as a flying boat base. Europe was badly served. Passengers from London traveled 80 miles by train (from a special platform at Victoria Station) to Southampton *the night before* an early morning departure. From Paris, even with the excellent French trains, the 350-mile journey to Bordeaux would have been a deterrent, had the huge Latécoère flying boats ever operated. Lake and water opportunities at Berlin and Rome were inadequate. Amsterdam, Brussels, Vienna, Copenhagen, and Stockholm would have had severe problems with ice in the winter. Geneva's Lake was dangerously surrounded by mountains. Flying boats at Madrid were out of the question. Only at Lisbon could they be accepted with equanimity, and of all Europe's capital cities, only there could they be seen at their moorings from the city itself.

Elsewhere, facilities for flying boats varied. In the United States, the water areas at New York, San Francisco, and Miami, situated strategically at the three main 'gateway' locations, were acceptable, almost ideal. But Canada was faced with the same winter icing problem as the Soviet Union. In Australia, Sydney Harbour was quite suitable, as long as the ships kept out of the way; but in Japan, where Britain's B.O.A.C., successor to Imperial Airways, perpetuated the flying boat era for a few more years after World War II, the base at Iwakuni, secluded in the Inland Sea, was 200 miles from Osaka and 500 from Tokyo. The patterns could be repeated everywhere. For every major city with reasonable access to water, there were two or three with none.

Then there was the inconvenience of embarking and disembarking, and of servicing the aircraft. Only at a few places such as New York, San Francisco

This series of pictures, taken at Pan American Airways' Dinner Key base at Miami, illustrates an often-forgotten chore that was essential for the maintenance of a flying boat. The specially trained crew of divers first had to maneuver the wheels of the beaching gear down the ramp (top); these then had to be rowed out to the awaiting aircraft (middle); and finally the divers had to attach the towing cables from the aircraft to the tractor, for hauling up the ramp on to dry land. (Dennis Wrynn collection)

(across the Bay at Alameda), and at Southampton or Miami, could passengers step straight on board from the dockside. Normally they had to be ferried to and from the shore by launch. In choppy water, the more sensitive of the clientèle were in danger of being seasick as well as airsick, though, to be fair, the big flying boats were reasonably stable. The aircraft had to be re-fueled by lighter, and engine maintenance and inspection had to be done, often precariously, in the same manner. There were eternal problems with salt water corrosion, and flying boats could attract barnacles which had to be scraped off.

The alighting areas too could be unreliable. While animals or people could stray on to landing strips, there were also potential hazards in the water. Debris on the Nile was not uncommon, while floating objects of uncertain origin or content on the Ganges needed careful watching. And all this was the responsibility of the airline, which could not demand that the local authorities should prevent surface objects from drifting into the flying boat lanes and alighting ares. Inconsistencies of weather were common to all flying machines; but the romance of a flying boat journey was often tarnished by the announcement that flood waters or choppy waves and swells meant a day's delay until conditions improved. On one occasion, the entire complement of a Pan American Boeing 314, passengers and crew alike, spent a Christmas in the Azores because of the notorious 'Horta Swell.'

Delays may have been acceptable at Luxor, where a little more sightseeing could relieve the monotony; but were more tedious at, say, Calcutta, before the days of air-conditioning, and even before international cricket might have been, by a lucky coincidence, a welcome diversion.

As the rate of expansion of long-distance air travel grew, Pan American's North Atlantic triumph in 1939 should have been a powerful stimulant to the traffic growth curve; but another factor intervened that was to toll the flying boat's death knell. For within weeks of Pan American's epoch-making achievement in starting scheduled trans-Atlantic passenger air service with the Boeing 314, the outbreak of World War II put out the lamps of Europe for the second time in a quarter-century.

A besieged Britain badly needed logistics support in the supply of critical materials to the Middle East. Imperial Airways had already recognized the impossibility of serving the West African colonies by flying boat and had started a landplane connecting service across the sub-Sahara savannah from Khartoum. This route now became the focus of an impressive airfield construction and improvement program, as Pan American, under contract to build a chain of modern airfields across Africa, indirectly contributed towards the demise of its own fleet. With good airfields, cargo transport aircraft such as the Douglas C-47 (DC-3) and the Curtiss C-46 could undertake the journey to the beleaguered British forces in Egypt. No thought was ever given to the idea of using flying boats for the purpose.

This was the beginning of the end of the ships that had wings. When the events at Pearl Harbor projected the United States into the war at the end of 1941, the logistics needs intensified beyond all previous imagination. U.S. forces had to be supplied across the Pacific, across the Atlantic, and on to China by the eastbound route; and the U.S. Army Air Force had to deploy its bomber squadrons overseas. An airfield program of unprecedented magnitude was undertaken with equally unprecedented urgency, with conspicuous success. Wherever there was a need, a chain of airfields with concrete or otherwise paved surfaces fashioned a garland around the earth. When the four-engined transports such as the Douglas C-54, and the large bombers such as the B-24 needed them, the airfields were in place, from Wake Island to Khartoum.

When the War ended, the flying boats were eclipsed. The commercial variant of the C-54, the DC-4, had been designed originally as an airliner. Though unpressurized, it was faster, and could carry more passengers over a longer range than any flying boat, with the possible exception of the Japanese 'Emily' of which none were available. The *coup de grace* came quickly in 1946, with the dramatic appearance of the Lockheed Constellation which, in addition to offering pressurized comfort, could carry more people faster and further than the DC-4.

In the three vital elements of the economic and operating envelopes, size, speed, and range, the performance of the 'Connie' outclassed completely any solution that the most ingenious flying boat designer could devise, thanks in no small measure to the worldwide distribution of good airfields that permitted heavyweight aircraft to take off and land with high wing loadings and in no danger of getting stuck in the mud.

The British did make a brave try to perpetuate the flying boat era for a short while. This was dictated partly because the British aircraft manufacturing industry had had to abandon all its promising designs of 1939; and Britain was short of dollars to buy more Constellations than necessary. It operated the post-war developments of the Short Empire Boats for a while and even operated a few larger Solents. Drawing desperately from the depths of its maritime ancestry, Britain also produced a commercial flying boat giant, the 330-seat Saunders-Roe Princess, in 1952. But it never went beyond the prototype stage. It was an anachronism, the last gasp of a dying generation.

There are a few faint reminders today of the former glories of the flying boat era, but curiously these are a distant echo of a remote past in which the idea of using water-borne craft once appeared to have merit. Some visitors to

THE LARGE COMMERCIAL FLYING BOATS
(with 4 or more engines)

Country and Aircraft	Gross Weight (tons)	Max. Seating	Normal Range (miles)	No. Built	Years of Operation	Airlines
U.S.A.						
Sikorsky S-40	17	38	900	3	1931-43	Pan American
Sikorsky S-42	19	32	1,200	10	1932-46	Pan American
Martin M-130	26	32	2,800	3	1935-45	Pan American
Martin M-156	31	30	1,500	1	1940-41	Aeroflot
Boeing B-314	42	70	2,800	12	1939-46	Pan Am, BOAC, World, Universal
Vought-Sikorsky VS-44	29	16	3,000	3	1942-45	American Export, Avalon, Antilles Air Boats
U.K.						
Short S-23	20	24	800	43	1937-47	Imperial-BOAC
Short Sandringham, Hythe, etc.	22	24	1,200	40	1946-75	BOAC, Aero.Argentinas, CAUSA, TEAL, RAI, Ansett
Short S-26	37	12	2,500	3	1940-47	BOAC
Short S-45	40	39	2,000	15	1945-60	BOAC, TEAL
France						
Latécoère 300	25	(mail)	2,000	4	1934-38	Air France
Latécoère 521	40	20	3,500	2	—	— —
Latécoère 621	78	46	3,750	9	1947-48	Air France
Germany						
Dornier DoX	62	66	1,000	3	(1931)	SANA (not on scheduled service)
Japan						
Kawanishi H8K	36	64	2,800	10	1940-45	Japan Naval Air Service
TOTAL				160		

Special Note: over long ranges, seating availability has to be reduced to permit maximum fuel load

Even including those aircraft that were used on quasi-scheduled services, the total number of large commercial flying boats used by the airlines worldwide was only 160. The United States had 25 and the British airline Imperial Airways, later B.O.A.C., had 96 of these.

the Caribbean may have experienced the pleasure of flying around the Virgin Islands in Grumman Gooses or Mallards; and the odd Goose is still to be found in southeast Alaska, which, like Norway, does not offer much opportunity for airfield development; or in the South Pacific, where the notion of obliterating tiny atolls is unattractive.

Former staff of Virgin Islands Seaplane Shuttle still remember, almost with nostalgic affection, the typhoon that almost wiped out the airport at St. Croix and terminated operations there for about two days. The Mallards resumed service immediately after the hurricane had passed on and proudly provided the only air link with St. Thomas in the interim. But this was a rare exception of the flying boat enjoying its proverbial hour of glory in today's world. Unfortunately, another typhoon in 1988 destroyed the Mallard fleet.

And the Grummans are small flying boats, compared to the Sikorskys, Martins, Boeings, and Shorts of yesteryear. To answer the inquirers at the National Air and Space Museum, rare examples are only to be found in museums in London, Paris, Oakland, and Auckland. Two Martin Mars giants, never used in airline service, are to be found on Canada's Vancouver Island, water-bombing the forests. Otherwise, the flying boat era is only a distant memory.

The Commercial Airships (1919–1937)

Of all flying vehicles since the Montgolfier brothers demonstrated their first balloons in 1783, none has identified the realms of fantasy more closely with the reality of practical application than the rigid airship. The fantasy was compounded by more than two decades of endeavor, during which time the advocates of the lighter-than-air rigid airship first achieved plausibility, then general acceptance, and for a while, limited success. But throughout the era during which their sheer size overrode other considerations, including operational problems that were clearly insuperable, the airships were never more than a fantastic pipe-dream.

Before the catastrophic *Hindenburg* disaster in 1937, however, airships had their supporters, and powerful ones too, such as the United States Navy, the British Government, and most emphatically the Third Reich, which viewed the giant dirigibles already in service or projected as evidence of technical achievement that enhanced national prestige. The huge airships were of great propaganda value. Their sheer size was guaranteed to impress during an epoch when the quality of being big was equated with, if it did not exceed all other attributes, except possibly speed. Newspapers throughout the world loved to extol the virtues of big ships such as the *Queen Mary,* big airplanes such as the Dornier Do X, big buildings such as the Empire State Building, and big construction projects such as the Golden Gate Bridge or the Hoover Dam. To praise the *Graf Zeppelin,* the R100, and the *Hindenburg,* in awe-struck admiration and without questioning the wisdom behind their conception, was to follow a well-scripted journalistic course; and the public dutifully absorbed the airship fantasy without too much question. In the early 1930s, the aeronautical world itself was obliged to accept the reality of demonstrated service by the *Graf Zeppelin* until the destruction of the sister-ship *Hindenburg* in 1937 put an end to the rigid airship as a serious contender in the world of air transport.

Yet in the beginning it was a serious mode of aerial travel. Before World War I, during four years of progressive achievement from 1910 to 1914, six

The Schwaben *was one of six airships that carried more than 30,000 people on sight-seeing and inter-city flights in Germany between 1911 and 1914, before the first Great War of 1914–18. These flights created airmindedness throughout the nation and inspired the pride and confidence that gave Germany a head start in commercial aviation after the end of hostilities.*

airships flew around Germany on inter-city and sight-seeing flights with conspicuous success. During this time they carried about 34,000 people, of whom about 10,000 paid for the simple thrill of emulating the birds and being able to see their own cities, even their homes, literally with a bird's eye view. During this pre-war period this was the only way, short of rather hazardous and unpredictable balloon flights. The heavier-than-air airplanes had not progressed beyond the stage of carrying any load, other than its pilot, and even then only for a limited time, seldom more than an hour or two. The airplane, in fact, was viewed as useful for sporting purposes, or aerial photography or reconnaissance, but for very little else.

The airship seemed to be the answer for carrying groups of people and for flying long distances reliably. Such recognition can be attributed to the faith and determination of one man, Count Ferdinand von Zeppelin, and his team of engineers whose activities on the shores of the Bodensee (Lake Constance, or Constanz) were to give to the little town of Friedrichshafen a recognizable identity exceeding that of any other small community of comparable size anywhere in the world, with the possible exception of Cooperstown. Even today, aviation devotees are known to visit the site of the great airship sheds as a pilgrimage to pay tribute to the astonishing development of the rigid airship.

Zeppelin persevered in his self-appointed task of proving the feasibility of his idea to the extent that, when he died in 1917, he had good reason to believe that he had succeeded. Before the Great 1914-1918 War, his airships had carried bigger loads much farther and more safely than had any airplane. During the War, they had been a powerful force, threatening the morale if not the productive effort of wartime Britain. One of the Afrika-Zeppelins, LZ 59, had flown from Bulgaria to Khartoum and back nonstop. The round-trip distance was 4,200 miles, beyond the wildest dreams of airplane designers at the time, and not surpassed for a decade.

After the war ended, harsh conditions imposed on the Germans by the 1919 Peace Treaties terminated scheduled service started by the Zeppelin airship *Bodensee;* and such circumstance may well have obscured or restrained any rational analysis. For the sustained operations of the wartime Zeppelins had revealed shortcomings as well as noteworthy advantages over the airplane.

However awe-inspiring their size, the great airships were unwieldy in the air, cumbersome to maneuver, and vulnerable in high winds. To be fair, during the first decade of aviation, airplanes were not too manageable either, nor significantly faster. But on the ground the disadvantages of the airship were discernible as substantial, and comparing most unfavorably with the requirements of the airplane. Airships had either to be housed in huge sheds or tethered to mooring masts. In both cases the airships were difficult to maneuver, demanding a small army of ground handlers to man the landlines dropped from above.

As many as 250 men were required in 1936 to secure the *Hindenburg* and one regular routine task marking every arrival at Frankfurt was the round-up of sufficient manpower to bring the airship safely in. Once secured, and provided the weather was calm, it could be steered carefully into the shed, where it would be protected from the elements. But if the wind was too high—an airship could never be taken into a shed in anything approaching a cross-wind—then it would have to be tethered to a mast, around which it would need to swing as the wind changed, thus demanding a large area that encompassed a radius from the mast of at least the length of the ship—no modest piece of real estate, say half a square mile.

Construction techniques also posed problems. With lighter-than-air craft, the only way to progress to greater load-carrying ability was to increase the capacity—and therefore the size—of the gasbags that enclosed the source of lift, namely lighter-than-air gas, normally hydrogen, but if available, the non-flammable but rarer and therefore more expensive helium. By definition, this meant bigger airships and therefore bigger airship construction sheds. As each larger generation of airship succeeded another, so did a larger shed have to supplement or supersede another. While to a certain extent, this was also the case with airplanes, the magnitude of the problem bore no comparison. A whole production line of four-engined airplanes could be built in the same space as that required to build one dirigible.

The construction of a rigid airship itself was a masterpiece of engineering efficiency, somewhat comparable with that of a well-designed bridge, and from an engineers's viewpoint, a thing of beauty. An intricate framework of longitudinal girders and cross-frames was fashioned of light-weight duralumin alloy in triangular lengths of delicate yet structurally sound truss design. The real problem was in the fabrication of the gasbags. During the early years, the only material that could be found to combine light weight, strength, and gas-proof properties (because of an inherent adhesive quality) was goldbeater's skin, an animal product that was actually the membrane from cattle intestines. During the height of World War I, the entire slaughterhouse industry of Germany was committed to supply this material to the Zeppelin works as an essential contribution to the war effort. Fortunately for the cattle industry and airship builders alike, rubber technology produced a composite rubberized fabric that could do the job even better.

The apparent superiority of the airship as a load-carrier had continued throughout World War I. The German Zeppelins were a menace and the first to demonstrate the military device of strategic bombing. The Zeppelin raiders' record of destruction was not very impressive, measured by the number of factories or installations put out of action; but their effect was detrimental to the morale of the British people, especially in the target cities of the east coast that had to bear the brunt of the raids. Only towards the end of the war could multi-engined airplanes carry comparable loads.

With hostilities at an end, interest in the idea of large airships as airborne load-carriers was alive and well during the 1920s. German wartime activity had been impressive enough to arouse considerable interest in and support for airships among the victorious powers. Great Britain, the United States, France, and Italy all received German airships as part of the enormous reparations program, while in Great Britain and the U.S. (but only to a minor extent in France and Italy) large airship construction was undertaken, drawing almost entirely from German technology and experience.

In the United States, the airship was adopted with great enthusiasm by the Navy. In 1923 it built one of its own, after having ordered one from Great Britain in 1921. The British one, the R38, broke up with great loss of life while on trials, and the U.S. one, the *Shenandoah*, was destroyed in a storm in Ohio, also with loss of life, in 1925. By this time, In October, 1924, the Germans had delivered the LZ126 as the *Los Angeles,* on a 5,060-mile transatlantic voyage. Two more, the *Akron* and the *Macon* were built by Goodyear Tire at Akron in 1931 and 1933 respectively. Of all these U.S. rigid airships, none was ever used commercially, partly because the Postmaster General, Walter Folger Brown, demanded further sustained proof of their operational aptitude. This was not forthcoming. Only one airship, the German-built one, survived beyond 1935.

The British took the opposite course. The R34, British-built but of German design, had made a successful round trip to Canada in 1919, carrying a large crew in both directions. Confidence in airships was subsequently sufficient to encourage the British Government to pursue the idea of linking the faraway dominions of the British Empire with commercial airship services, and grandiose plans were made. Two great airships, the R100 and the R101, were laid down, a large airship shed was built at Karachi and a mooring mast erected at Ismailia, Egypt. The high hopes of starting a service to India, however, were shattered when, on its maiden voyage to India in 1930, the R-101 crashed at Beauvais, France, killing everyone on board, including the Minister for Air and the Director General of Civil Aviation. The British promptly abandoned its airship program.

In Germany, the disastrous experiences of the U.S. and British ventures were ignored. The Zeppelin company was convinced that its ships were superior to all others. Certainly, the survival of the *Los Angeles* suggested they were right. Under the leadership of Dr. Eckener, the LZ127 *Graf Zeppelin* was built as a symbol of national pride and resurgent German technical expertise. It completed a dramatic round-the-world flight in 1929, stopping only at Tokyo, Los Angeles, and New York; and went into regular commercial service to Brazil in 1932, increasing the service frequency with each succeeding year.

Such was the success of the now-famous German dirigible that a larger, longer-ranged partner ship, the LZ129 *Hindenburg* was built specifically for the North Atlantic route. During 1936, the year when the Olympic Games were held in Berlin, the great airship made 16 round trips between New York and Frankfurt. The *Hindenburg* displayed both the Olympic symbol and the swastika, a curious combination in the light of subsequent history, the one symbolizing brotherhood between nations, the other quite the reverse.

With American Airlines including special DC-3 connecting schedules to the New York airship base at Lakehurst, New Jersey, this was the high point in the commercial airship's career. It had reached thus far only because, in the early 1930s, the airplane designers were still struggling to find a successful formula that would enable them to produce a machine that could lift enough

The Graf Zeppelin *operated scheduled services from Germany to South America from 1932 to 1937. Of all the big dirigibles, it was the only one that succeeded in fulfilling its assigned missions without disaster or interruption; and the only one that ever came close to repaying its investment. (Lufthansa)*

The Hindenburg *was the finest airship ever to operate a commercial airline service; but its destruction by fire in May 1937 put an abrupt and dramatic end to the era of lighter-than-air aircraft, except for relatively minor activities in general aviation. (Lufthansa)*

total load to permit it to carry a substantial number of passengers, as well as to fly a long enough distance, to cross the world's oceans. Until 1935, Pan American's best flying boat, the Sikorsky S-42, could cross the oceans only when equipped with extra tankage and by dispensing with passengers. The larger Martin 130s could fly from San Francisco to Hawaii with only a few passengers as well as the fuel necessary to maintain a margin of safety. Veteran Pan Am crew members remember arrivals at Alameda with almost dry tanks, not to mention sweaty palms. The *Graf Zeppelin,* on the other hand, had a range of 5,000 miles, with 25 passengers, while the *Hindenburg* could fly 8,000 miles with 50, and had been modified to carry 72 before Fate took a hand.

As the aviation world entered 1937, the German airships appeared to have a place in the grand scheme of intercontinental air commerce, with their long range capability a trump card, albeit the heavy crew demands posing a practical handicap, as well as the special ground areas needed. Alas, there was a malevolent joker in the pack. With the historic *Hindenburg* holocaust at

GERMAN SCHEDULED AIRSHIP ROUTES 1931-37

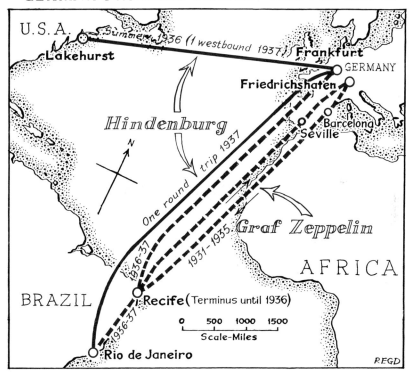

During the 1930s, many aviation authorities clung to the belief that airships pro-vided the answer to long distance scheduled air service. The performance of the Graf Zeppelin *every summer seemed to support this view, but the notorious* Hindenburg *disaster put an end to such aspirations.*

Lakehurst on 6 May 1937, German airship pride was transformed abruptly to despair. The ever-present danger of fire had literally shot down an industry in flames. The case for the airship collapsed overnight.

The reasons causing the spectacular disaster have never been satisfactorily resolved. Sabotage and spontaneous static electricity discharge have been popular explanations. Some crew members who survived the conflagration—and amazingly no less than 62 on board the *Hindenburg* survived, compared with the 36 who were killed—believe that the cause was the snapping of a steel wire, one of the many that provided extra strength to the structure, when the airship made a fairly tight turn before descending at Lakehurst, incurring unacceptable stress loads on the enormous area presenting itself to the wind. This would have had the instantaneous effect of generating a spark and simultaneously rupturing one of the hydrogen-filled gasbags, as the wire whip-lashed within the airship's interior.

The controversy raged, and still resurfaces occasionally, as to whether the U.S.A. should have supplied helium to Germany. This only emphasized the risk that was being taken, with the known flashpoint characteristics of hydrogen. But the *Hindenburg* was primarily a vehicle of national pride rather than a serious contender for mass air transport, and its operation was dictated more by politics than economics.

High construction costs and high operating costs would have restricted the big airships to a limited market. To break even, very high fares would always have been necessary. To cover the expense of the 55 air crew and a battalion of ground handlers, not to mention the cost of the installations themselves, the fares had to be set at a level beyond the pocket of all but the very rich. The *Hindenburg's* transatlantic fare, equated to present levels of monetary value, would be equivalent to that of the Concorde, itself out of reach to all but a tiny minority of travelers.

Even had generous subsidies provided an artificially economic basis for operations, the practical problems would have been insuperable. Had, for instance, the *Hindenburg* been supplemented by other airships, to provide a frequent schedule, the demands on precious real estate would have been quite unacceptable; and the prospect of two big airships requiring ground handling at the same place at the same time in a high wind and perhaps at night are unthinkable.

The operational record of the big airships was deplorable, as was the number of fatalities. Of the U.S. Navy's five, only the German-built one survived for the scrap yard in 1939. Meanwhile, 134 people had been killed. Of the two big British ships, 47 were killed on the R101's maiden flight; and the R100 was scrapped. The *Hindenburg* debacle occurred at the beginning of only its second year of operation, adding 36 to the death toll. Only the *Graf*

NOTABLE LARGE RIGID AIRSHIPS
OPERATED AFTER WORLD WAR I

Name and Number	Place Built, Manufacturer	Crew	Pass. Accom	Date of First Flight	Date of Last Flight	Remarks	Killed	Survived
U.S.A.								
ZR-1 Shenandoah	Philadelphia Navy Yard (assembled at Lakehurst)	23	–	4 Sept.1923	3 Sept. 1923	Destroyed in storm at Marietta, Ohio	14	29
R-38 ZR-2	Cardington, England	30	-	23 June 1921	24 Aug. 1921	Broke up on trials	44	-
LZ 126 ZR-3 Los Ángeles	Friedrichshafen Germany, Zeppelin Works	28	-	27 Aug. 1924	1939	Delivered 12-14 Oct. 1924; retired 1932; re-commissioned 1933; scrapped 1939	-	-
ZR-4 Akron	Akron, Ohio, Goodyear Zeppelin Co.	60	-	27 Oct. 1931	4 April 1933	Lost at sea during storm	73	3
ZR-5 Macon	Akron, Ohio, Goodyear Zeppelin Co.	60	-	23 June 1933	12 Feb. 1935	Lost off California coast	2	81
Great Britain								
R-33 (G-FAAG)	Barlow, England Armstrong-Whitworth	23	–	6 March 1919	16 April 1926	Copied from LZ-76(L-33) Used intermittently; Broken up 1928	-	-
R-34	Inchinnan, Scotland, Beardmore	33	–	14 March 1919	28 Jan. 1921	Copied from LZ-76 (L-33) brought down in 1916. Made round trip to Canada, 1919. Crashed in Yorkshire	-	-
R-100 (G-FAAV)	Howden, England, Airship Guarantee Co. (Vickers)	37	–	16 Dec. 1929	Aug. 1930	Made round trip to Canada, 1930; scrapped after R-101 disaster	-	-
R-101 (G-FAAW)	Cardington, England, Royal Airship Works	48		14 Oct. 1929	5 Oct.1930	Crashed at Beauvais, France	48	-
Germany								
LZ-120 Bodensee	Friedrichshafen Zeppelin Works	16	21	20 Aug. 1919	1928	Operated scheduled service, Friedrichshafen-Berlin, 24 Aug.-5 Dec 1919 To Italy (war reparations) July 1921, renamed Esperia. Dismantled	-	-
LZ-121 Nordstern	Friedrichshafen Zeppelin Works	16	–	8 June 1921	3 Nov. 1925	To France (reparations) June 1921, renamed Mediterranée. Dismantled	-	-
LZ-127 Graf Zeppelin	Friedrichshafen Zeppelin Works	36	20	18 Sept. 1928	18 June 1937	Operated South Atlantic service, 1931-1937, scrapped March 1940	-	-
LZ-129 Hindenburg	Friedrichshafen Zeppelin Works	40	50	4 March 1936	6 May 1937	Operated Atlantic service 1936. Destroyed, Lakehurst New Jersey	35	61
France								
LZ-114 (L-72) Dixmude	Friedrichshafen Zeppelin Works	30	–	3 July 1920	18 Dec. 1923	To France (reparations) Exploded over Mediterranean	50	-

Note: Three large non-rigid Italian airships, built after World War I, deserve
mention. All were built by the Stablimento di Costruzione Aeronautiche.
The T34 *Roma*, built in 1919, was purchased by the U.S. Army, but was burned
at Langley Field on 21 Feb. 1922, killing 34 people. The *Norge*, built in 1924, flew
from Spitzbergen over the North Pole (Amundsen-Ellsworth-Nobile) to Teller, Alaska,
on 14 May 1926. The *Italia*, built in 1927, crashed near Spitzbergen on 26 May,
1928. Nine crew and rescue party members, inc. Amundsen, died. 15 survived.

Devotees of the romance of the commercial airships can reflect that the standard of passenger amenities on board the great German airships, such as this dining room in the Hindenburg, *has never been surpassed, even today. But few could enjoy the privilege, as the fares were, in equivalent monetary value, twice as high as today's Concorde's which, in turn, is about ten times as high as the average economy class passenger is accustomed to pay. (Lufthansa)*

Zeppelin's record was unblemished, and the great airship that carried its progenitor's name retired honorably, to be broken up for scrap and Messerschmitts when World War II erupted.

For a brief period, the airships were no fantasy. During World War I, Germany had about 80 airship stations, some equipped with sheds that revolved on tracks so as to cope with any wind direction. The statistical record of strategic bombing effectiveness was hardly a threat to the British war production; but the citizens of Hull or Sunderland may have disagreed at the time.

The airship has never been a serious means of air transport. It can be used for special purposes in ideal weather, for sight-seeing, observation, aerial photography, and advertising, for which purposes its slow speed is an advantage. But weather is an ever-present factor. Even at the pinnacle of their success, the *Graf Zeppelin* and the *Hindenburg* never operated during the winter.

They could never have competed with the Boeing 314 flying boat and the generation of long-range landplanes that were developed during the early 1940s. They were aviation's dinosaurs, doomed to extinction, because, in the words of the great K.L.M. pilot, Ivan Smirnoff, they were "too slow, too dear, too unmanageable."

The Mayo Composite Aircraft (1938)

The most extraordinary aspect of the Mayo Composite aircraft idea was that it was ever done at all. It was a text-book example of the perceived, if not demonstrated, reputation of its originator outweighing all other considerations, including common sense. Even when the remarkable scheme was leaked to the press late in 1934, the eminent British aviation magazine, *Flight,* always prepared to wave the Union Jack for any good cause, was a little ambiguous: "Were it not for the fact that the "Composite Aircraft" scheme .... been conceived by a man so eminently sane and practical as Major R.H. Mayo, one would be apt to condemn it out of hand." Far from taking this as a warning, perhaps to review other options, the company promoting the scheme used it in support of its product.

The Mayo Composite aircraft, or more strictly pair of aircraft, did indeed have good credentials. Major R.H. Mayo, O.B.E., M.A., Assoc. M. Inst. C.E., F.R. Ae.S., had obtained first class honors in engineering at Cambridge University, and his early experience included spells with the British Royal Aircraft Factory in 1913, as a pilot in the Royal Flying Corps in France early in World War I, and as Head of the Design Section (Aeroplanes) at the Air Ministry from 1917 to 1919. He then became a consultant and was the European Representative of the Guggenheim Fund for the Promotion of Aeronautics. He was an honorary founder member of the Institute of Aeronautical Sciences of America, and had many other foreign connections. By the early 1930s, he was the Technical Adviser to Imperial Airways.

Britain's national airline had been under siege for a while, with criticism from various quarters to the effect that, in fulfilling its mandate to link the British Empire with a network of air services, primarily for the delivery of mail, but with some regard for privileged passenger travel, it had neglected Canada. The reason was fairly obvious. No aircraft in the opening years of the 1930s had the slightest chance of carrying any kind of load across the Atlantic Ocean, and only specially modified aircraft could even carry a pilot or two directly from Europe to North America or vice versa. The swell of opinion had reached a stage whereby "Questions were asked in the House"—meaning that the subject had been raised in Parliament and that the responsible Minister had to defend the situation.

The usual platitudes were uttered to the effect that His Majesty's Government was cognizant of the latest developments and that adequate and necessary steps would be taken when deemed appropriate, and other meaningless phrases of that kind. And to be fair, H.M. Gov. was not entirely idle. When the awful news penetrated English aviation minds that, in 1933 the Boeing 247 was carrying 10 passengers at 160 mph and that in 1934 the Douglas DC-2 was carrying 14 at about the same speed but in much greater comfort, even with sleeping accommodation envisaged, the first reaction had been frank disbelief. This was followed by grudging admission that the Americans had stolen a march on the whole of Europe, but that this would be of concern only to the domestic traffic situation in the United States. Such complacency received, however, a further blow when the Sikorsky S-42 went into service with Pan American in 1934, carrying 38 passengers over 1,000-mile stages in Latin America. And so the British Government, with Imperial Airways as the Chosen Instrument, announced an order for 29 S.23 Empire flying boats 'off the drawing board'—an unprecedented move and nobly courageous in the circumstances; and simultaneously announced the "All-up Empire Air Mail Scheme" that would be progressively introduced with the flying boats. Air mail would be carried throughout the Empire at normal postage rates, with support from the Post Office, and was—correctly—intended to stimulate the development of aircraft, routes, and organization for an airline of which Great Britain and its Dominions could be proud.

Studies of the Sikorsky S-42, however, did reveal that it did not have enough range to cross the Atlantic with a payload. Ignoring the known plans for Martin to build a bigger and better flying boat that would have enough range to cross from Newfoundland to Ireland, and which would be ready by 1935, the British withdrew into a kind of technological cocoon and seemed to have decided that improvements in range and payload would not be made, and that the problems were insuperable. This led to various solutions being put forward, the most prominent of which was Major Mayo's scheme for a Composite Aircraft, that is to say, a device for launching a fast mail-carrying machine from a mother ship—and the four-engined S.23 was ideal—so that extra payload in the form of fuel could be uplifted to provide the necessary trans-Atlantic range. The fast four-engined mail-carrier would be mounted on top of the S.23; both would take off on the power of all eight engines; and the upper aircraft would then be released, having attained sufficient altitude and escaped the handicap of the restrictive drag of the water on take-off.

When, towards the end of 1934, the British newspapers heard about it, it welcomed the idea, and all were full of praise for the brilliance of the scheme. The *Daily Herald* summed up the general opinion that "Britain has produced the first sound ideas for commercial trans-Atlantic flying." Early in 1935, the Mayo Composite Aircraft Company, Ltd., was formed with a capital of £95,000 and began to promote its cause.

Such was the level of antiquated thinking in Great Britain at the time that Mayo's main thrust was to argue that the composite aircraft was far superior to the flight refueling method that was also being promoted, by no less a famous airman than Sir Alan Cobham, of the British pioneering long-distance flying hero. Mayo stressed that the composite aircraft separation could be made in all weathers, even in fog, and that the mother ship could still be used for other commercial operations after the launching. Flight refueling was confined to fair weather, and the refueler was a specialized machine, useful for no other purpose.

No mention was made of the necessity for mother ships to be based at both ends of the route, nor for the possibility that, by flying elsewhere, there would be a chance that they might not be available when wanted. Not too much was said about the distinctly awkward methods that would be required to load passengers into the upper component of the 'piggy-back' combination, a performance somewhat akin to climbing (or clambering) up a fiendishly contrived fire escape. But Mayo did claim that one advantage for passengers would be that "it does not involve any abnormal acceleration." One would hope so.

The engineering involved in the release mechanism was undoubtedly of sound design—approaching what would perhaps qualify as "fail-safe" today. The upper component rested on supports mounted on a strong central keel of the lower component, and the upper component, a floatplane, was also steadied laterally by smaller supports under its floats. The centrally-situated release-hook mechanism included three separate hooks, one released by the pilot of the lower component, the second released by the pilot of the upper component, and finally, a spring-loaded third hook that would disengage when the excess pull of the upper component reached a pre-determined value.

At least it worked. After a private experimental separation a few days earlier, the first publicly demonstrated separation of the Mayo Composite aircraft was made on 23 February 1938. Before an excited bevy of aviation and news reporters clustered in an accompanying aircraft, the upper component *Mercury* climbed smartly away from its mother ship, the *Maia,* with an élan that would become associated with its pilot, D.G.T. Bennett, who later, in World War II, became known as 'Pathfinder' Bennett.

Then on 21 July 1938, *Mercury* showed its true capability. Bennett was launched from Foynes, Ireland, in the estuary of the River Shannon and which was destined to be the key staging point on a flying boat route between Europe and North America. He flew from Foynes non-stop to Montreal and then on to Port Washington, New York. In doing so, he accomplished two goals of the Mayo-Composite project. The unassisted weight of *Mercury* was 14,000 lb; but with *Maia's* help, this had been boosted to 20,800 lb. This included a payload variously reported as 800 lb or 1,000 lb—quite a reasonable load of mail by the standards of the late 1930s, though equivalent to only four or five passengers, if they could clamber in.

The Short-Mayo Maia-Mercury composite aircraft was a ponderous attempt to attain trans-Atlantic range by water-borne craft designed for much shorter ranges. However praiseworthy the technical accomplishment, it would never have been a practical solution for carrying mail, much less passengers. (Short Brothers)

The flight was acclaimed as a tremendous achievement, mainly because it had been the fastest crossing across the North Atlantic so far by any airplane. The 2,860-mile stage from Foynes to Montreal had been covered at an average speed of 141 mph. And so Mayo could claim a double success in demonstrating the ability to carry a payload; and at a competitive speed.

Unfortunately for the Mayo Composite Aircraft Company, but fortunately for the future of British commercial aviation, Imperial Airways did not pin its hopes for the future on the prospect of squadrons of *Mercuries* being launched from matching squadrons of *Maias* scattered at strategic points the length and breadth of the British Empire. Perhaps the thought of passengers suffering from a special kind of vertigo as they ascended the staircases to board the upper component, with the *Maia* rocking gently in a mild swell, may have affected official opinion. In any event, a decision was made with commendable alacrity. The Air Minister rejected the Mayo Composite as Imperial Airways' standard-bearer on 31 March 1939.

No doubt the planners in both the airline and the Ministry had not been blind to what was going on in the rest of the world. They had observed Pan American's Martin Clippers maintaining a regular mail and passenger service across the Pacific Ocean, and were cognizant of that airline's plans to start trans-Atlantic service with the bigger and better Boeing 314 in the summer of

1939. This aircraft could carry 70 passengers over stages of up to about 1,000 miles, and 35 to 40 on a route from New York to Southampton or from New York to Marseilles. They were also conscious of Britain's recalcitrance in allowing the American airline to start trans-Atlantic service earlier, having insisted in a series of reciprocal survey flights in 1937, in which Pan American's vintage Sikorsky S-42s had performed well, carrying better payloads than Imperial's new Short Brothers Empire Boats.

Against such demonstrated technical superiority, the cumbersome Mayo system would have appeared quaint, if not ridiculous, to all but the most dedicated flag-wavers in Britain. The sight of *Mercury* being launched from Port Washington from its mother ship, while the Boeing 314 *Yankee Clipper* was taking off without fuss with a load of passengers would have emphasized only too clearly how far British flying boat technology had fallen behind that of the U.S.A. Some of this differential was later eliminated. The Empire Boat's development, the Sunderland reconnaissance patrol boat and submarine hunter, served well during World War II, more than 700 of them being produced. But in 1939 the United States lead was ominously clearcut.

Considerations of competition from superior flying boats aside (the British were obliged to purchase three of the Boeings in 1940) one of the most baffling aspects of the whole Mayo Composite affair was that the promoters were either unaware of—which was most unlikely—or totally ignored the achievements of the German experimental services across the North Atlantic and the actual regular services across the South Atlantic. As early as 1935, Deutsche Lufthansa was maintaining a regular service across the South Atlantic with the trusty Dornier Wal flying boats, launched from depot ships located at each end of, or in between the African base at Bathurst, Gambia (British territory, no less) and Natal, Brazil. These depot ships, equipped with powerful catapults, could launch the 'Ten Ton' Wals, weighing 22,000 lb, enough to provide adequate fuel and mail load for the crossing.

The Heinkel pneumatic catapults were powerful pieces of apparatus, submitting the Wal pilots to considerable pressure—directly, in the small of the back; and may not have been suitable for passengers. But the mail service was conspicuously successful. Notably, the Germans were launching aircraft weighing 22,000 lb in 1935 and here was Mayo launching aircraft weighing 20,500 in 1938. Compounding the felony, so to speak, the Germans had conducted a series of experimental flights between the Azores and New York during 1937 and 1938, using the superbly elegant Blohm & Voss Ha 139 floatplanes. These aircraft weighed 38,580 lb each, almost exactly the same as the all-up weight of the *Maia*. The Germans were *launching* aircraft that were as heavy as the British mother ship.

TRANSATLANTIC PERFORMANCE
SELECTED FLYING BOATS/FLOATPLANES, 1934-39

Country	Aircraft	First Service	Weights (lb)				Range [1] (st. miles)
			Empty	Disposable	Payload	MTOW	
Great Britain	Short S-23 "Empire Boat" (Atlantic version)	1937	24,000[2]	20,400	2,500	45,000	2,500
	Maia	1938	24,000[2]	3,000	—	27,000	—
	Mercury	1938	14,500	10,500	800	25,000	3,000
	Mayo Composite	1938	38,500	13,500	800	52,000	
Germany	Dornier J II (10-ton)Wal (catapulted)	1935	13,700	8,350	500	22,050	2,000
	Blohm & Voss Ha 139A (catapulted)	1937	22,840[2]	15,740	1,050	38,580	2,500
United States	Sikorsky S-42	1934	24,000	18,000	8,100	42,000	1,200
	Sikorsky S-42B (Atlantic version)	1937	24,300[2]	21,200	4,000	45,500	2,500
	Martin M-130	1935	28,500	23,500	4,380	52,250	3,200[3]
	Boeing B-314	1939	50,270	32,230	8,745	82,500	3,500[4]

1. Approximate effective range with payload and fuel

2. Stripped empty weight; otherwise weights include all furnishings, ready for commercial service (i.e. tare weight

3. The Martin M-130 could carry between five and ten passengers only, plus mail, between San Francisco and Honolulu (2,440 statute miles) on a regular schedule

4. The Boeing B-314 entered trans-Atlantic service in July 1939, carrying up to 24 passengers, plus mail

In a desperate effort to achieve trans-Atlantic performance, the British produced the Mayo composite 'piggy-back' combination. As this tabulation shows, the Germans had already demonstrated that catapult-launched aircraft were effective; while the Americans had produced a series of fine flying boats that could do the job unassisted.

Mayo had followed in the tradition of many other inventors or innovators. Like Alfred Lawson, E.R. Armstrong, and even Count Zeppelin and his devoted followers, he was so convinced of the feasibility and potential of his brainchild that he was oblivious to the possibility of any other solution to Imperial Airways' problems in 1938. At least Lawson was on the right track in visualizing the need for large aircraft for passenger use. Armstrong's idea was a brave, if impossible scheme aimed to solve a problem that, at first, seemed insoluble by any other method known. Zeppelin's airships actually enjoyed some success in wartime and limited success in peacetime.

But Major R.H. Mayo was trying to attack a problem that the Germans had already solved. His saga was an example of the plausibility of the assertion that the publicity given to an ingenious contraption is too often inversely proportional to its usefulness.

The Romance of Early
Air Travel (1919–1940)

I n the recorded history of commercial air transport, there are many claims to firstliness and almost all of them can be substantiated, provided the right combination of qualifications are correctly applied. The St. Petersburg-Tampa Airboat Line was the first to offer scheduled service by airplane, and this claim is never seriously challenged. But it lasted only three months and it carried only about 1,200 passengers across Tampa Bay early in 1914. And what was the nature of this 'service?' Tony Jannus, the pilot, carried them, one at a time, in an open cockpit, at an altitude of about ten feet. It was more of a sporting challenge than a way of traveling from one place to another.

Before this historic episode, however, seven German airships of the DELAG company had already carried 34,000 people over the skies of Germany. Two thirds of these were crew members, but more than 10,000 passengers paid for the thrill of flying, mostly on joy rides of an hour or so, but also on inter-city flights. They traveled in comfort in the airship gondolas and were even served refreshments on board. The airships were far ahead of their heavier-than-air airplane rivals in terms of passenger satisfaction, and at the time just as safe; but, as related in Chapter 7, they were doomed to oblivion after a succession of disasters.

After the nations had put World War I behind them and applied their resources to using airplanes commercially, the United States was curiously apathetic to the idea of using them to carry people. Until 1927, the effort was concentrated only on the carriage of mail. The few isolated examples of airlines trying to start air passenger service received no encouragement, either from business investors or from the government, and these attempts were consequently short-lived.

Europe was first on the scene with a widespread network and organization of passenger travel by air, a decade ahead of the United States. It forged ahead in the 1920s for a combination of reasons: a massive surplus of warplanes was converted or modified for commercial use; the disruption of surface communications, because of the devastation of the 1914–1918 War, encouraged the use of an alternative transport mode; and there was a strong spirit of competition for aviation progress in the larger countries.

In the case of Germany, technical talents, suppressed for a few years by the Allied Peace Treaty restrictions, were shrewdly supported by government, state, city, and industrial interests alike, in the furtherance of a perceived technological leadership. All over Europe, airlines were formed and people were carried. By 1920, half a dozen countries had airline service. By 1927, almost every country in Europe had at least one airline, and many were making impressive strides. But the actual creation of a new form of travel, as we know as air transport today, was more imagined than real. The publicity of the airlines, with enlightened poster art and well-designed literature, gave a false impression that Europe was taking wings. But such achievement could in truth be claimed only by special pleading, even self-deception, rather than by operational results.

Measured by the statistics themselves,during the post-World War I period, only a privileged few people in Europe, and hardly any in the United States, took an air trip. Until well into the 1930s, it was expensive, it was uncomfortable, and, by the standards of today, it was dangerous. Except in special circumstances, it did not save much time. Not until the late 1920s were air services offered over distances that were long enough to provide some advantage over surface transport. Airplanes customarily flew at about 100 mph, twice as fast as the average express trains; but these latter invariably took their passengers into the city centers rather than deposit them on the edge of town. Road transport was not a factor. The pioneer super-highways, the German autobahnen, were still generations away for the fast motorists. Yet curiously, the same members of the more affluent levels of society who could afford both the time and the money to drive expensive cars from, say, northern Europe to the French Riviera, were the same people who could afford to take the *Golden Ray* or *Silver Wing* services between London and Paris, where part of the competition, across the Channel, could average only 20 mph.

In the early years, on both sides of the Atlantic, there was much justifiable concern for safety. Airplanes were still crashing quite frequently, mainly because of the unreliability of the engines. The failure of an engine in the customarily single-engined machines was too often fatal, and the primitive instruments did not help. In the early 1920s, if a pilot accidentally found himself in an area of poor visibility, he was often, quite literally, lost. Compasses and altimeters were notoriously unreliable and the introduction of a turn-and-bank indicator was a major breakthrough. In conditions of impenetrable fog, not only did the unfortunate pilot lose his sense of position, direction, or height; he could not orient himself either, and could not even know if he was flying the right way up.

With the honorable exception of those who flew in the Junkers-F 13, passengers who ventured into the single-engined aircraft of the early 1920s were thus putting their trust in flimsy craft, at best built of wood and fabric wrapped around a thin tubular steel frame, and flown by pilots who were so ill-equipped that they had to rely partly on intuition. Such was the standard of aircraft construction that few machines lasted more than a few years. Aside from the en route crashes or those on take-off and landing, there were many write-offs and cases of "damaged beyond repair"—a euphemism for airframe senility. For the first few postwar years, the situation was chronic, and was barely satisfactory even at the end of the first postwar decade.

In the United States, in fact, the popular idea that flying was dangerous was actually encouraged by the new kind of circus act that swept the nation. This became popularly known as barnstorming, a dangerous aerial ritual launched by pilots who had learned to fly during the closing stages of the war, and had come to enjoy the experience, but had no opportunity to deploy their talents. They therefore developed a catalog of stunts, almost all of them ostensibly hair-raising, in which the daredevil fliers transcended the exploits of the acrobats in the traditional circus ring. There may have been some romance about the flying machines, but the American public tended to view the prospect of taking an airplane ride with about the same degree of enthusiasm as of volunteering to swing on the flying trapeze or to walk the tight rope.

In Europe, however, air travel was slowly getting under way. For the privileged few passengers, there were special amenities. Ground transport was frequently provided at no cost to and from the airport, door-to-door. Little booklets were handed out, with intriguing supplements for keeping a diary of the journey, as a rare souvenir to display to friends. From the airlines' viewpoint, every passenger as a Very Important Person. Flying was still a novelty. Except possibly in Germany, where air travel was subsidized to the extent that senior businessmen were able to fly, only about one European in a thousand ever took an air trip in the 1920s; and until the last years of the decade, only one in ten thousand in the United States.

Even the motivation to fly was often not so much to travel from one place to another more quickly but simply to savor the pleasures of flight itself. Of the major inter-city routes of Europe, only the cross-Channel ones from London to Paris, Brussels, and Amsterdam could justify air travel on the grounds of speed alone. A survey of the brochures and timetables and promotional literature, in fact, reveals that, until the mid-1920s at least, one of the incentives to take an air trip was simply for the novelty of taking a bird's eye view of the ground, and especially, with luck, to observe famous places such as London's Trafalgar Square or Paris's Place de la Concorde from the air.

The airline literature contained more pictures of aerial views than it did of the airplanes.

Attitudes began to change towards the latter 1920s, when the airlines improved the safety factor by introducing tri-motored equipment, and took advantage of new innovations in navigational aids, improved instrumentation, introduced radio for communications and for direction-finding, and adopted a more disciplined approach to maintenance and the business of operating an airline on a commercial basis.

Even when the U.S. surged ahead of the rest of the world after Charles Lindbergh's epic trans-Atlantic flight had changed American attitudes almost overnight, the romance of air travel for ordinary folk was derived more from the public perception based on magazine articles and color supplements than from actual experience. The simple inescapable fact was that air travel in the late 1920s and early 1930s was prodigiously expensive. When, with Lindbergh's assistance, the first transcontinental air service began in 1929, and a fanfare of publicity—and still recalled, correctly, as a milestone of achievement—the record books passed lightly over the statistics. Very few people paid to take the service which, when inaugurated, charged a minimum of $338.00 for the one-way coast-to-coast air-rail journey; and with reasonable amenities such as a place to lay one's head during the night, the fare was $403.00.

At this time, such a sum came close, if not completely, to the annual pay for an office worker and half that for a manager. It was beyond the imagination of the blue-collar worker. It was roughly the same price as a small saloon car. Predictably, few people took the trip, and the airline, T.A.T., promptly reduced the fares in a desperate attempt to attract more traffic and increase revenues so as to offset the enormous investment costs of several millions of dollars—equivalent to several hundreds of millions today. The prospect of ever making ends meet in the airline business was not even a remote possibility; and that of challenging the long distance railroads on a economic basis was a myth.

The romantic perception of the standard aircraft of the period, the Ford Tri-Motor, is also one of today's myths. It is now a revered aviation museum piece and rightly epitomizes a definable era in the development of U.S. air transport. In 1990 the enterprising Al Chaney could still barnstorm his incredible way around the country with one of the surviving Fords, giving joy-rides at $20.00 a time. But in 1930 the 'Tin Goose' was not exactly a desirable way to cross the continent. The experience was literally deafening, and passengers were provided with earplugs; and Mr. Wrigley did a roaring trade as a contributor to deafness relief. Onboard catering was frugal, so that Harvey House

TRANSCONTINENTAL AIR TRAVEL, 1929

The schedule and meal arrangements from New York, N. Y., Philadelphia, Pa., Washington, D. C., and Baltimore, Md., to Los Angeles, Cal., and San Francisco, Cal., are as follows:

WESTBOUND

FIRST DAY
Pennsylvania Railroad
The Airway Limited

Lv. New York, N. Y.	6.05 P. M.	E. T.
Lv. North Philadelphia, Pa.	7.50 P. M.	E. T.
Lv. Washington, D. C.	6.30 P. M.	E. T.
Lv. Baltimore, Md.	7.30 P. M.	E. T.

Dinner in Pennsylvania Railroad Dining Car.

SECOND DAY
Breakfast in Pennsylvania Railroad Dining Car.

Ar. Port Columbus, O. (A new station stop seven miles east of Columbus, O.)	7.55 A. M.	E. T.

Transcontinental Air Transport, Inc.

Lv. Port Columbus, O.	8.15 A. M.	E. T.
Ar. Indianapolis, Ind.	9.13 A. M.	C. T.
Lv. Indianapolis, Ind.	9.28 A. M.	C. T.
Ar. St. Louis, Mo.	12.03 P. M.	C. T.
Lv. St. Louis, Mo.	12.18 P. M.	C. T.

Luncheon on plane—Fred Harvey Service.

Ar. Kansas City, Mo.	2.47 P. M.	C. T.
Lv. Kansas City, Mo.	3.02 P. M.	C. T.
Ar. Wichita, Kans.	4.56 P. M.	C. T.
Lv. Wichita, Kans.	5.11 P. M.	C. T.
Ar. Airport, Okla. (Landing field four and one-half miles east of Waynoka.)	6.24 P. M.	C. T.

Transfer by aero Car to Harvey House, Waynoka, for dinner.

Atchison, Topeka & Santa Fe Railway

Lv. Waynoka, Okla. (Sleeping Car ready for occupancy 8.00 P. M.)	11.00 P. M.	C. T.

THIRD DAY

Ar. Clovis, N. M.	8.20 A. M.	C. T.

Breakfast in Harvey House. Transfer by aero Car to Portair.

Transcontinental Air Transport, Inc.

Lv. Portair, N. M. (Landing field five miles west of Clovis.)	8.10 A. M.	M. T.
Ar. Albuquerque, N. M.	10.17 A. M.	M. T.
Lv. Albuquerque, N. M.	10.32 A. M.	M. T.
Ar. Winslow, Ariz.	1.12 P. M.	M. T.
Lv. Winslow, Ariz.	1.27 P. M.	M. T.

Luncheon on plane—Fred Harvey Service.

Ar. Kingman, Ariz.	2.31 P. M.	P. T.
Lv. Kingman, Ariz.	2.46 P. M.	P. T.
Ar. Los Angeles, Cal.	5.52 P. M.	P. T.

Grand Central Air Terminal, Glendale, Cal., about five miles from the center of Los Angeles.
Passengers will be transferred by aero Car to central section of Los Angeles.

San Francisco passengers, upon arrival at Los Angeles, will be given the option of using overnight train from either Los Angeles or Glendale, or they may remain overnight in Los Angeles and proceed by Maddux Air Line plane from Glendale Airport, morning service for San Francisco. Tickets for whichever plan is selected by passenger will be furnished by the Transcontinental Air Transport, Inc.

All meals on planes are included in the ticket. All other meals at passengers' expense.

TOTAL CHARGE FOR EACH PERSON USING COMBINATION OF ONE-WAY FARES
NEW YORK, N. Y., TO LOS ANGELES, CAL., OR SAN FRANCISCO, CAL.

New York, N. Y., to Port Columbus, O.:

Via Pennsylvania Railroad (one passage ticket)	$22.45
Train No. 65 (one extra fare ticket)	3.60
Pullman—Lower berth, including surcharge	6.38

Waynoka, Okla., to Clovis, N. M.:

Via Atchison, Topeka & Santa Fe Ry. (one whole and one half passage ticket)	16.76
Pullman—Compartment, including surcharge	12.75

Port Columbus, O., to Airport, Okla., and Portair, N. M., to destination:

Via Transcontinental Air Transport, Inc., including seat	290.00

Total charge	{Lower berth New York to Port Columbus / Compartment Waynoka to Clovis}	When occupied by one person	$351.94

			Total Charge per Passenger
LOWER BERTH	{New York to Port Columbus / Waynoka to Clovis}	When occupied by one person	$338.10
SECTION	{New York to Port Columbus / Waynoka to Clovis}	When occupied by one person / When occupied by two persons	346.80 / 337.01
SECTION **COMPARTMENT**	New York to Port Columbus / Waynoka to Clovis	When occupied by one person / When occupied by two persons	357.04 / 339.34
COMPARTMENT	{New York to Port Columbus / Waynoka to Clovis}	When occupied by one person / When occupied by two persons	389.61 / 342.60
DRAWING ROOM	{New York to Port Columbus / Waynoka to Clovis}	When occupied by one person / When occupied by two persons / When occupied by three persons	403.44 / 346.72 / 340.22

While not exactly a pioneering adventure, to cross the United States in 1929 was an undertaking demanding a little fortitude. Four changes of transport mode were involved, from rail to airplane and vice versa. Passengers were issued earplugs and chewing gum to relieve the noise effect on the eardrums; and, as this extract from the contemporary airline literature shows, the journey was no bargain. Such a fare in those days, measured in real earning power, was equivalent to that of a Concorde flight today.

The Ford Tri-Motor's cabin was advertised as the last word in comfort in the late 1920s. But the photographs did not reveal that the passengers were issued with ear-plugs and chewing gum, so loud was the noise. (National Air and Space Museum, Smithsonian Institution)

pitstop meals were welcome. And aircraft toilets were primitive affairs. The railroad Pullman cars, with their efficient amenities, easily resisted any inroads to their supremacy. That transition came two full decades later.

The answer to the economic problem, of course, was subsidy, and this was the basis on which the U.S. air transport system had been built. Every air passenger in the United States was heavily subsidized by generous mail payments, right up until the 1950s. Indeed, in the early 1930s, so much of the taxpayers' money was going in this direction that a major scandal erupted in 1934 that was the then Postmaster General's Watergate.

Improved modern aircraft such as the Boeing 247, the Douglas DC-2 and -3, and the Lockheed 10 replaced the bone-shakers and eardrum-splitters in the mid-1930s, and the situation improved slightly. When American Airlines trumped T.W.A.'s DC-2 ace in 1936 by bringing in the DC-3, President C.R. Smith claimed that it was the first aircraft that could make a profit by carrying passengers alone, without mail payments. But 'C.R.' did not confirm this by volunteering to give up the subsidy payments. The truth was that his statement was true only if the aircraft was full up and everyone on board paid the full fare.

Only in the latter 1930s did U.S. air traffic surge and airline efficiency improve enough to bring fares down far enough to become acceptable at levels of the income pyramid lower than the absolute pinnacle. By the outbreak of World War II, a one-way transcontinental air ticket would cost about two or three months' pay for the average wage-earner. Today, even the minimum wage, mandated by law, would provide the funds, all else aside, for the same trip in about two or three weeks.

Much of the romance popularly attached to early long-distance intercontinental or trans-oceanic air travel is related to the flying boats, whose aesthetic appeal was almost inversely proportional to their ability to provide a reasonable service. The technical aspects of the shortcomings of the flying boat have been reviewed in Chapter 6 of this book, but there are other aspects that have been distorted by most historians. Juan Trippe and Pan American Airways deserve full credit for having come close to putting an airline girdle around the earth by 1939, but once again, the reality was very far from the imagined romance of trans-ocean travel.

Pan American's love affair with the flying boat began with a successful flirtation in the Caribbean, and quickly exploded into a torrid infatuation in South America. Epitomizing the sophisticated life of ease and pleasure, 'flying down to Rio'—an idea popularized in a film of that name—was portrayed

This picture illustrates the typical Pan American flying-boat passenger cabin of the 1930s. The Sikorsky S-40 that went into service in 1931 offered a high standard of amenities and comfort compared with those of the land planes.

almost as though anyone could take the trip. The harsh fact was, once again, that, in the 1930s, the New York-Rio de Janeiro and New York-Buenos Aires fare was beyond the pockets of all but the oilmen, cattle barons, film stars, and diplomats of the flying boat era.

Pan Am pioneered trans-oceanic air travel, first by the conquest of the Pacific and later of the North Atlantic. The Martin 130 *China Clipper* became one of the most famous airliners of all time. But few realize that there were only three of these fine ships of the air. In fact, the total number of large four-engined flying boats owned by Pan American, all the Sikorskys, Martins, and Boeings, was only 25; and the maximum number operated at one time was 16.

The reason why this total was so small was because the traffic demand—directly related to the fares charged—was low, so that frequencies were equally low. Neither the trans-Pacific nor the trans-Atlantic frequencies ever reached the dizzy heights of a daily service. On the critical San Francisco-Honolulu segment, even the miraculous Martins, fine ships though they were, were payload-limited to nine passengers, that is to say, less than half the load of an average commuter airliner today. The fare, true to form, was $799.00 one way to Manila. Not many made the trip, and many of those were millionaires, or close to being so; or friends of Juan Trippe, which amounted to more or less the same thing.

If Clippers had to fly against a mild headwind it was touch and go if they reached landfall. Less publicized than the champagne bottle-breaking at the inaugural ceremony were those flights that had to turn back before reaching the point of no return, or those that had to be nursed into Alameda on a wing and a prayer, with the dipstick coming out dry from the fuel tanks on inspection. Official records show that the average load to Hawaii was between four and five; and there were occasions when the eight crew members had only the sacks of mail for company.

On the other side of the globe, the romance of the flying boat era was similarly more in the imagined perception than in the reality of experience. The staunchest support came from those who were not obliged to make a long journey in one, but who enjoyed the vicarious pleasure of the promotional literature of Imperial Airways, Great Britain's flying boat flag-waver of the Thirties. Imperial was Britain's Chosen Instrument, much in the same role as Pan Am, and was charged with the task of linking the home country with its dominion outposts of its globe-encircling empire. Except for Canada, these were located in Asia, Africa, and the Pacific rim, and with the exception of Australia, were on land masses contiguous with Europe. In contrast with Pan American's critical 2,400-mile San Francisco-Honolulu segment, Imperial's was the 500 miles across the Timor Sea, from Koepang to Darwin. The chal-

TRANSPACIFIC TRAVEL, 1936
VIA SAN FRANCISCO GATEWAY

TABLE **12**   U.S.A.-HAWAII-GUAM-PHILIPPINES

Daily	3:00	Lv. BOSTON, Mass., U.S.A. (AMA)...E.S.T. Ar.	11:48	Daily
"	5:00	Lv. NEW YORK, N. Y., U.S.A. (UAL) " Ar.	9:00	"
"	4:45	Lv. WASHING'N, D. C., U.S.A. (PAL) " Ar.	10:45	"
"	9:30	Lv. CHICAGO, Ill., U.S.A. (UAL).....C.S.T. Ar.	3:29	"
"	9:15	Ar. SAN FRANCISCO, U.S.A. (UAL) ..P.S.T. Lv.	1:15	"
Orient Express(z)		Pan American Airways Co. (PAAP)		Orient Express(z)
Wed.	3:00	Lv. SAN FRANCISCO (Alameda), U.S.A.P.S.T. Ar.	10:30	Tues.
Thur.	8:30	Ar. HONOLULU (Pearl Harbor), H.I....H.L.T.Lv.	12:00N	Mon.
Fri.	6:30	Lv. HONOLULU (Pearl Harbor), H.I....H.L.T. Ar.	5:30	Sun.
"	3:00	Ar. MIDWAY ISLAND................M.L.T.Lv.	6:00	"
Sat.	6:00	Lv. MIDWAY ISLAND................M.L.T.Ar.	5:00	Sat.
		(International Date Line)		
Sun.	3:00	Ar. WAKE ISLANDS....................165° Lv.	6:00	Sun.
Mon.	6:00	Lv. WAKE ISLANDS...................." Ar.	7:00	Sat.
"	5:00	Ar. GUAM ISLAND.....................150° Lv.	6:00	"
Tue.	6:00	Lv. GUAM ISLAND...................." Ar.	6:30	Fri.
"	5:00	Ar. MANILA (Cavite), P.I................120° Lv.	4:00*	"

*Departures from Manila subject to advancement to previous afternoon as occasion demands.

All times are approximate other than at San Francisco Westbound and at Honolulu Eastbound.

Light Face Type - A. M.— Bold Face - P. M.

U. S. Cy. PASSENGER TARIFF

Fares quoted below are One Way fares. Round Trip fares are twice one-way less 10%

TABLE **12**	San Francisco Cal., U.S.A.	Honolulu H. I.	Midway Isl.	Wake Isls.	Guam Isl.	Manila P. I.
San Francisco, Cal., U.S.A.	....	$360	$445	$587	$704	$799
Honolulu, H. I...........	$360	....	157	299	480	614
Midway Isl..............	445	157	....	142	323	514
Wake Isls..............	587	299	142	....	181	372
Guam Isl...............	704	480	323	181	....	191
Manila, P. I............	799	614	514	372	191	....

Fares Include: Ground transportation at all stations except San Francisco, meals aloft, berth San Francisco-Honolulu and overnight hotel expenses at Midway, Wake and Guam.

AIR-STEAMER TARIFF

Matson and Dollar Lines may be used advantageously between San Francisco and Honolulu or vice versa in connection with Pan American services west of Honolulu, or in connection with round-trip tickets sold one way by air and one way by steamer.

Air-Steamer fares will be the sum of the fares for the air and steamer services used.

While Pan American's achievement in opening an air route across the Pacific Ocean in 1936 was a landmark in the annals of airline history, few people were able to take advantage of the experience, which involved overnight stops at four islands en route to Manila. The fare was equivalent to at least six months' wages for the average working man.

American's critical 2,400-mile San Francisco-Honolulu segment, Imperial's was the 500 miles across the Timor Sea, from Koepang to Darwin. The challenge of the North Atlantic was to come later, and by the time the British had developed a flying boat that could even approach, much less surpass, the Martins and the Boeings of Pan Am, the era was over, and the landplanes ruled the commercial aviation skies.

Under such circumstances, and in retrospect, Imperial's choice of the flying boat seems to have been a little odd. The reasons have been reviewed in Chapter 6. Essentially, the absence of good airfields and the enormous cost of building them at, say, 200-mile intervals, all along the routes to Australia, Hong Kong, and South Africa, in inhospitable climates and terrain, often in foreign territories, must have influenced the decision against a large landplane as the flagship of the fleet. Here an element of a romantic notion, if not romance, may have crept into the decision-making process, with its origins in Britain's great maritime tradition. The vision of British flying boats as the modern ships of twentieth century Merchant Venturers, evoking distant memories of their eighteenth and nineteenth Century seaborne counterparts, must have been attractive to those steeped in the traditions of the sea- and water-borne craft.

The Short S-23 'Empire Boat' was ordered 'off the drawing board' by Imperial Airways in 1934, and was the British airline's flagship during the pre-war period of development throughout the Eastern Hemisphere. Its double-decked layout permitted the luxury of a promenade deck so that passengers could stretch their legs on long flights.

called, were reported in the commerce pages of the *Daily Telegraph,* along-side those of the Cunard, P. & O., and Union Pacific luxury ocean liners. Only too often, however, the entry would reveal that delays in remote corners of the British Empire could be measured in days, not hours.

The Short boats were undoubtedly elegant, and they made a pretty sight when pictured at anchor on the Nile, or taxiing along the Ganges, or posing gracefully under the Sydney Harbour Bridge. But the journey itself was not as elegant, even with the advantage of the S.23's distinguishing feature, the upper or 'promenade' deck—the marine tradition creeping in again—where bored or stiff-limbed passengers could stretch their legs. Their journey was long, three to four days to India, and eight to ten days to Australia. They left London early in the evening by train and stopped overnight at Southampton, with an early wake-up call for the 5:30 a.m. departure from the dockside. This crack-of-dawn departure regimen was to be repeated nine more times before reaching Sydney.

At most of these overnight stops, as on the trunk route to South Africa, the boarding and disembarking was conducted by launch to and from the dock, while refueling was usually carried out by lighters. In a strong breeze, with choppy water, a certain agility came in useful For this romantic adventure—romantic for the exotic sights to be seen and the wonder of it all; and adventurous because few of the ten-day flights to Australia were completed with absolutely no incident of some kind—the passengers paid £160. At the then current rate of exchange that was about $675.00, the price of a family car, or about forty weeks' pay for the average worker.

While trans-oceanic fare levels remained high right up to the outbreak of World War II, the amenities did undergo a distinct improvement. The air service across the North Atlantic was not launched by Pan American until the superb Boeing 314 flying boats were available. They were faster, smoother, more comfortable, and altogether more reliable than their predecessor types. Simultaneously, the dockside installations were transformed from the sometimes near-primitive jetties into edifices that could symbolize progress and expansion, a departure from the romance and adventure towards air transport as a travel mode in its own right. The Marine Air Terminal at New York's La Guardia Airport was a model of adaptation of contemporary architecture to a utilitarian purpose—and surprisingly still functions today as the terminal building for Delta's (formerly Pan Am's) landplane Shuttle. But in 1939, the fares were still a formidable obstacle to the prospect of mass air travel. Not too many discretionary income levels could cope with a one-way New York-Southampton or New York-Marseilles fare of $375.00.

EMPIRE TRAVEL, 1936 EMPIRE TRAVEL, 1936
AFRICAN SERVICE

ENGLAND—EGYPT, EAST AFRICA, SOUTH AFRICA
Service in force from 1 Mar. 1933 until further notice

Place		Departure and Arrival Times (Local Standard)		Miles Port to Port	Miles from London
Airway Terminus, Victoria, London, S.W.1 †	dep.	Wed.	11.45		
Air Port of London, Croydon, England	dep.	,,	12.30		
Paris, Gare de Lyon, France	dep.	,,	*21.30	225	225
Paris to Brindisi		Thurs.			
Brindisi, Italy	arr.	Fri.	Morn.	1147	1372
,, ,,	dep.	,,	11.30		
Athens, Greece	arr.	,,	Aftn.	380	1752
,, ,,	dep.	Sat.	07.00		
Alexandria, Egypt	arr.	,,	Aftn.	580	2332
Cairo ,,	arr.	,,	Even.	125	2457
,, ,,	dep.	Sun.	07.30		
Assiut ,,	dep.	,,	10.30	205	2662
Assuan ,,	dep.	,,	14.15	265	2927
Wadi Halfa, Anglo-Egypt-Sudan	arr.	,,	Even.	190	3117
,,	dep.	Mon.	05.00		
Atbara ,,	dep.	,,	10.20	344	3461
Khartoum ,,	arr.	,,	Aftn.	177	3638
,, ,,	dep.	Tues.	05.00		
Kosti ,,	dep.	,,	07.45	180	3818
Malakal ,,	dep.	,,	11.45	270	4088
Juba ,,	arr.	,,	Even.	375	4463
,, ,,	dep.	Wed.	05.00		
Entebbe, Uganda ‡	dep.	,,	10.40	370	4833
Kisumu, Kenya Colony	dep.	,,	14.30	150	4983
Nairobi ,,	arr.	,,	Even.	185	5168
,, ,,	dep.	Thurs.	07.30		
Moshi, Tanganyika Territory†	dep.	,,	10.05	160	5328
Dodoma ,,	dep.	,,	13.35	230	5558
Mbeya ,,	arr.	,,	Even.	250	5808
,, ,,	dep.	Fri.	07.10		
Mpika, N. Rhodesia	dep.	,,	09.30	255	6063
Broken Hill ,,	dep.	,,	13.15	270	6333
Salisbury, S. Rhodesia	arr.	,,	Even.	300	6633
,, ,,	dep.	Sat.	07.00		
Bulawayo ,,	dep.	,,	10.25	240	6873
Pietersburg, Transvaal	dep.	,,	14.25	270	7143
Johannesburg ,,	arr.	,,	Even.	270	7323
,, ,,	dep.	Sun.	06.00		
Kimberley, Cape Province	dep.	,,	09.40	270	7593
Victoria West ,,	dep.	,,	12.40	215	7808
Cape Town ,,	arr.	,,	Even.	340	8148

SOUTH AFRICA, EAST AFRICA, EGYPT—ENGLAND
Service in force from 1 Mar. 1933 until further notice

Place		Departure and Arrival Times (Local Standard)		Miles Port to Port	Miles from C.Town
Cape Town, Cape Province	dep.	Wed.	06.30		
Victoria West ,,	dep.	,,	11.20	340	340
Kimberley ,,	dep.	,,	14.35	215	555
Johannesburg, T'svaal	arr.	,,	Even.	270	825
,, ,,	dep.	Thurs.	07.00		
Pietersburg ,,	dep.	,,	09.55	180	1005
Bulawayo, S. Rhodesia	dep.	,,	13.55	270	1275
Salisbury ,,	arr.	,,	Even.	240	1515
,, ,,	dep.	Fri.	05.45		
Broken Hill, N. Rhodesia	dep.	,,	09.55	300	1815
Mpika ,,	dep.	,,	13.40	270	2085
Mbeya, Tanganyika T.	arr.	,,	Even.	255	2340
,,	dep.	Sat.	07.30		
Dodoma ,,	dep.	,,	11.25	250	2590
Moshi ,, †	dep.	,,	14.45	230	2820
Nairobi, Kenya Colony	arr.	,,	Even.	160	2980
,,	dep.	Sun.	06.45		
Kisumu ,,	dep.	,,	10.30	185	3165
Entebbe, Uganda ‡	dep.	,,	12.45	150	3315
Juba, A.-E.-Sudan	arr.	,,	Even.	370	3685
,,	dep.	Mon.	07.30		
Malakal ,,	dep.	,,	11.10	375	4060
Kosti ,,	dep.	,,	15.45	270	4330
Khartoum ,,	arr.	,,	Even.	180	4510
,, ,,	dep.	Tues.	07.30		
Atbara ,,	dep.	,,	11.00	177	4687
Wadi Halfa ,,	arr.	,,	Morn.	344	5031
,,	dep.	Wed.	06.00		
Assuan, Egypt	dep.	,,	09.15	190	5221
Assiut ,,	dep.	,,	13.15	265	5486
Cairo ,,	arr.	,,	Aftn.	205	5691
,, ,,	dep.	Thurs.	06.30		
Alexandria ,,	dep.	,,	08.30	125	5816
Athens, Greece	arr.	,,	Aftn.	580	6396
,, ,,	dep.	Fri.	07.30		
Brindisi, Italy	arr.	,,	Morn.	380	6776
,, ,,	dep.	,,	Even.		
,, to Paris		Sat.			
Paris, Gare de Lyon, France	arr.	Sun.	Morn.	1147	7923
Air Port of Paris, Le Bourget	dep.	,,	09.00		
Air Port of London, Croydon	arr.	,,	Morn.	225	8148
Airway Terminus, Victoria, London, S.W.1	arr.	,,	,,		

= A passenger spends the night in bed at this port or in the train
= by rail
† = This call may be made alternatively at Arusha, according to the prevailing circumstances
* = On and after 29 March this train will leave at 22.25 hours
‡ = This call may be made alternatively at Kampala according to the prevailing circumstances

N.B. Passengers for destinations on the Empire routes may travel by any of the Company's services to Paris, leaving the Air Port of London, Croydon, before 16.30 hours on the day for which their ticket is valid. Passengers should not travel by the evening service as connexion with the train leaving Paris cannot be guaranteed

Great Britain's Imperial Airways pioneered a network of air routes to link London with its far-flung empire. As this timetable extract shows, this was not easy. In the early 1930s, neither water-based nor land-based aircraft were equal to the task, and much ingenuity was required to ensure a service that could be defined as either regular or scheduled. On the route to Johannesburg, for example, 33 individual segments and six changes of vehicle (including the use of trains and ships) were involved.

This elegant Pan American Boeing 314, just after docking at New York's La Guardia Marine Air Terminal in 1939, evokes the glamour of the flying boat era, with the aircrew marching smartly, in naval tradition, along the floating pier to the briefing room; and a welcoming party greeting the emerging passengers. But efficient installations such as this were seldom available elsewhere in the world. (Pan American)

income levels could cope with a one-way New York-Southampton or New York-Marseilles fare of $375.00.

The romantic era of the airlines did not, as would have happened with normal peacetime evolution, give way gradually to a more materialistic and more practical age. World War II erupted with devastating suddenness in European 1939 and for the U.S.A. in 1941. It served to separate abruptly the Old Order from the New as much, and possibly more, in aviation, as in any other field of endeavor. There was no transition period of calculated gradualness, just a six-year-long hiatus. A new era supplanted the old almost as though some all-powerful world aviation controller had ordained "stop the romance, let commerce begin."

With the cessation of hostilities in 1945, a new airline breed emerged, barely recognizable from the old. 300-mph Constellation landplanes superseded the 130-mph flying boats; handsome airport terminal buildings fronted miles of concrete runways (most of them built during the war for military use) to offer unsurpassed convenience, compared with waterside flying boat bases. Technical improvements had reduced the operating costs, and therefore the fares, to levels that the middle classes of the world's industrial nations, at least, could afford.

The human memory, fortunately, tends to retain the pleasant and to erase the distasteful. The veterans recall the joys of watching the sunrise at Lake Victoria or of sipping a Singapore Sling at the Raffles Hotel. But they forget the times when they wetted more than their feet when stepping off the launch at Basra or when they arrived four days late at Sydney and missed the England-Australia Test Match.

They remember too the symbols of the maritime tradition: the pennants and ensigns on the flying boats' prows, the naval cut of the crew uniforms, Pan American's crew inspection before each flight. They remember the proud Clipper names, every one related to the seafaring tradition and the sea, and still perpetuated on almost every Boeing 747 that flew Pan Am's colors. But they forget the sometimes endless days of delay because of rough seas, and when an entire Boeing 314-load, passengers and crew alike, spent Christmas in the Azores rather than at home, because of the notorious Horta Swell.

Bill Masland, veteran flying boat captain, recalled sadly that, when the last of the great Boeing 314s taxied into Baltimore late one night in 1946, to bring to a close the Atlantic flying boat era, the romance and adventure of the formative years of air travel were already forgotten. These memories were no more than a fleeting vision, an imagined charade. For there was no fanfare, no reception committee, no speeches, no commemorative dinner. Just the night watchman.

The First Comet
(1952–1954)

I n the United States particularly, with pardonable pride in its own resources of mechanical and scientific achievement, the aviation fraternity has tended to dismiss the British Comet airliner as a failure. At the other extreme, in the United Kingdom, with emotions stirred by patriotism, its fame is exceeded only by that of the Concorde. The true assessment lies somewhere between the two; but in the interests of objective reporting on the technical development of commercial aircraft, the wealth of positive advances, innovations, even inventions, made by the de Havilland team in Hatfield, England, during more than a decade of dedicated toil and tribulation, substantially outweigh the shortcomings that caused the dramatic disasters—from which, paradoxically, the world's aircraft manufacturing industry has benefited, largely at de Havilland's expense.

The two crashes that, in 1954, put an end to the momentum of a spectacular aircraft's career, and what might have changed completely the worldwide balance of commercial aircraft manufacturing output, were devastating as tragic events in themselves. Even more devastating was the revelation that the cause of the crashes was structural failure. Apart from reflecting adversely upon the integrity of a highly respected company, it meant that to rectify the problem was no easy matter. Failures of systems, or of controls, or in performance, can often be put right by modification, re-design, or by the exercise of improved quality control. With structural failure, the manufacturer has to go back to square one.

Until the first of the critical crashes, the Comet's service record since British Overseas Airways Corporation's (B.O.A.C.'s) dramatic inauguration on 2 May 1952 had been excellent. True, there had been crashes. One by a B.O.A.C. Comet 1 at Rome on 26 October of that year and another by a Canadian Pacific Airways Comet 1A at Karachi on 2 March 1953 were diagnosed as ground stalls caused by an aerofoil section not designed for high angles of attack. Both aircraft scraped their tails on take-off and ground stalled. This defect was quickly put right by chief designer Ron Bishop's pencilled drawing. The result was a new leading edge, still holding up perfectly

The British de Havilland D.H. Comet 1 took the world by storm when, in 1952, it halved the time between London and Johannesburg, South Africa. De Havilland paid a heavy price for its pioneering innovation, for it never fully recovered from the tragic crashes of 1954, even though its enterprise had transformed the commercial aviation world and set it on a new course. (De Havilland)

as the Royal Air Force Nimrods leap off the runways at Kinloss and St. Mawgan airfields today. And still holding up too, incidentally, is John Cunningham, the test pilot who deliberately scraped the tail of test airplane to examine the characteristics of this particular kind of stall, which could not be reproduced in a wind tunnel or, in those days, be fed into a computer.

The other crash was by a B.O.A.C. Comet 1 at Calcutta on 2 May 1953. It broke up in the air in a violent thunderstorm. This led to revising operating procedures at the then unprecedented altitudes of between six and eight miles, far above that of the piston-engined Constellations and DC-6Bs chugging along four miles below. The Calcutta crash advanced the case for installing storm radar, led to stricter rough-air speed control, and resulted in the installation of G-feel, so that stick forces would be proportional to the control loads. In these developments the Comet was ahead of the industry, which took due note of the vital lessons.

Early in 1954, however, there was complete confidence in the Comet. There had been no mystery about the three crashes. The record of safety and punctuality had been satisfactory. The Comet was making news wherever it went. Orders were pouring in. The airline world was descending on Hatfield and chief salesman Frank Lloyd was having problems in accommodating the distinguished visitors—though, it has to be said, he had few problems in entertaining them. Even the great Pan American, the Chosen Instrument of the United States, had placed an order on 20 October 1952 for a developed version, the Comet 3, for the Atlantic run.

On 19 February 1953, the French independent airline, U.A.T., had put the Comet into service on its routes to West Africa; Air France followed with Comet service to Beirut on 26 August, and South African Airways, stung by B.O.A.C.'s jet competition, introduced the Comet on 4 October, leasing aircraft from its rival. Panair do Brasil had ordered four Comets in March for the

Often forgotten, in the face of the drama of the 1954 Comet crashes, is the fact that, for almost two years, the de Havilland jets had been operating throughout the eastern hemisphere: Europe, Asia, and Africa, in the colors of four airlines, including Air France, one of whose Comet 1As is pictured here. (Air France)

South Atlantic. B.O.A.C. meanwhile had expanded the Comet network throughout most of the Commonwealth, and had introduced jet airline service to Tokyo on 3 April 1953. By the end of the year, thirty cities in the world were privileged to receive jet airline service (see **Map**).

With such a record of achievement, therefore, the inexplicable disintegration of a London-bound Comet near Rome on 10 January 1954 came as a distinct shock. Nevertheless, such was the confidence in the Comet that the cause was presumed to be a technical problem of the same order of magnitude as those experienced by all new commercial airliners during the early months or years of service. B.O.A.C. took all its Comets out of service and inspected them carefully. No defect was found and services were resumed on 23 March 1954, with many convinced that sabotage was the most likely explanation.

But if the Rome crash had been disastrous, the next B.O.A.C. crash, occurring only sixteen days after the resumption of service, was catastrophic. A South African Airways Comet disappeared in almost identical circumstances

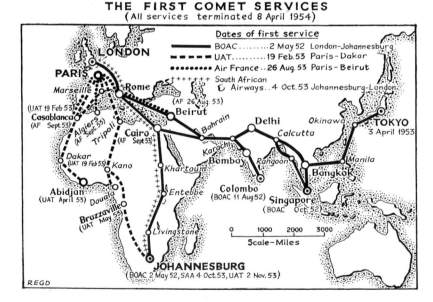

THE FIRST COMET SERVICES
(All services terminated 8 April 1954)

While the world's first scheduled jet airline services were tragically short-lived, the record of the early de Havilland Comets was much better than is sometimes remembered in the aftermath of the inexplicable (at the time) crashes of 1954. Four airlines operated Comets for almost two years, serving thirty cities throughout three continents.

near Stromboli, off the coast of Sicily, on 8 April 1954. Clearly there was a serious fundamental problem, as the coincidence of the circumstances of the Rome and the Sicily crashes, both occurring on the initial climb at about the same altitude, and with both aircraft at about the same airframe life, was too close to ignore. The Comet's Certificate of Airworthiness was withdrawn on 12 April and the agonizing reappraisal began.

This involved a thorough investigation by the Royal Aeronautical Establishment at Farnborough, under the direction of Sir Arnold Hall. The salvage teams of the Royal Navy, who had been trying to recover the remains of the 10 January crash from the bottom of the Mediterranean off the coast of Elba, redoubled their efforts. They put the pieces together like a jigsaw puzzle, to reveal tell-tale traces that led to the conclusion that the cabin had suffered an abrupt failure. The cause was metal fatigue, under the stress of repeated pressurization cycles, and which had never heretofore been experienced by any airliner, simply because none had ever flown so high or had been subjected to such high pressure.

The critical fracture was identified at an inspection hatch on top of the fuselage, where a tiny crack had spread at the corner of the rectangular-shaped aperture. This led to a simplistic conclusion that the sharply rounded corners were a design error. This was not so. All jet transport windows since the Comet have had rounded corners.

The irony was that the much-publicized—and much-praised—inquiry was not quite correct in its findings. By chance, in 1955, an Italian fishing vessel trawled up a window that proved that the failure had started there, not at the ADF hatch on top of the fuselage. The investigation was not re-opened. There was no need. As Bishop commented: "Once you know *what* happened, it doesn't matter *where* it happened."

One of the biggest lessons was that no amount of ground testing or test flying, however conscientious and meticulous, can reproduce the rigors of airline service. To their credit, de Havilland had already set new standards of excellence in the strict discipline of structural testing. The engineers and designers knew they were reaching beyond the horizons of known experience, beyond the threshold of the conventional airline operations envelope; and had been doubly conservative. In the pressure rig, the windows had been cycled 2,000 times from zero to 8lb/inch and back. One window had even been subjected to 100 lb/inch. The forward section of the fuselage had been tested in the water tank—another de Havilland innovation—at 8 lb/inch over 16,000 cycles, equivalent to 40,000 hours of flying. At this time, this was equivalent to about eighteen or twenty years of airline service life, twice that of contemporary airliners. To make sure, Bishop fixed the pressure level at 11 lb/inch, and 12 at the windows.

The whole world of aircraft manufacturing learned vital lessons from de Havilland's dreadful experience. Structural strength and material strength were no longer safeguards against metal fatigue. The service life of metal clothes hangers and paper clips declined with enthusiastic demonstrations to the lay public of the newly discovered metallurgical property. A new vocabulary came into use in top-level debates at Long Beach, Burbank, Seattle, and Toulouse. Terminology such as fail-safe, multi-path load, and damage tolerance came into daily parlance in the design offices, while stressmen and draftsmen concentrated on crack-stoppers.

To be fair, the more objective of those aeronautical analysts with a respect for development problems and a sense of history have recognized the incomparable contribution that de Havilland made in pushing the Comet 1 beyond the frontiers of known aviation technology during the mid-1950s. A company can take out world-wide patent rights to protect itself from blatant reproduction and copying of an invention or design. But unfortunately there is no compensation for making a mistake for all to see and from which all can learn.

The single contribution to aeronautical progress made by de Havilland in exposing the perils of metal fatigue led to the fail-safe approach that has become standard throughout the industry. This, however, had tended to obscure many other de Havilland achievements, perhaps not so spectacular in their perception but nevertheless very important. Almost forgotten is the wide variety of threshold-crossing innovations pursued by de Havilland for eleven years before the first B.O.A.C. Comet went into service. This in itself deserves a brief review.

As early as 1941, when Great Britain was mainly concerned with building an air force to match the might of the Luftwaffe, de Havilland's chief designer, Ron Bishop, and his assistant, David Newman, were scribbling on table napkins at the teabreaks during their work on the Mosquito. They toyed with the idea of putting two Halford H-1 engines (Goblins) into the D.H. 95 Flamingo, an all-metal airliner that had entered service just before the outbreak of World War II in 1939. Then when the D.H. Vampire jet fighter first flew in 1943, C.C. Walker, one of Sir Geoffrey de Havilland's lifetime associates, remarked: "you know, you could have all that in a transport aircraft."

During the war, the British Government had, with remarkable vision, formed the Brabazon Committee, to fashion a manufacturing pattern for postwar civil aviation. Its Type IV specification called for a mailplane that could cruise at 400 mph and carry a ton of payload. Only the cockpit was to have cabin pressure.

De Havilland tried various design ideas, one with three Halford H-2 (Ghost) engines, one with two propeller-turbines, one with a canard wing, one even without a tail. The one that eventually qualified for the de Havilland numerical series as the D.H. 106 was drawn up on 13 October 1944, changed many times and took final shape in July 1946. It had four Halford H-2 engines, with conventional tail and elevators, moderate sweepback, simple flaps, and single-wheel landing gear—although this last would later be changed to a four-wheel gear. The exclusively mail mission requirement was forgotten. The fuselage could seat four abreast.

In September 1946, the Ministry of Supply, at that time charged by the Labour Government with the task of overseeing and ordering all commercial aircraft, ordered two prototypes. On 21 January 1947, B.O.A.C. ordered, through the M.O.S., eight aircraft, and British South American Airways later ordered six. Still regarded by many as a pipedream, this great undertaking, the world's first commercial jet airliner, was under way.

While the Comet was not a closely-guarded secret—many aviation people in Britain knew that 'something was going on' at Hatfield—de Havilland itself, no slouches at dignified promotion under Martin Sharpe, just did not say much. Bishop himself kept an odd-looking tailless swept-wing airliner on his desk for visitors to draw their own, incorrect, conclusions. The first prototype just happened to be assembled behind some large ground-test rigs, cloaking if not camouflaging what was going on. When the D.H.106 ventured out of the hangar on 2 April 1949 for engine runs, a fortuitous mist shielded its unusual shape. In the *De Havilland Gazette* of that month, an introductory statement confined itself to generalities, but stressed that the Comet would be able to operate from normal airports along all the world's trunk air routes. This was not, incidentally, the case when the Boeing 707 entered service almost a decade later.

On 27 July 1949 the London press corps swarmed around the new aircraft as it was unveiled for all to see. After the usual hospitality and briefing, the reporters were told that the aircraft would fly when it was ready and not before, and they all went home. That evening, de Havilland chief pilot, John Cunningham, decided that it was ready and took off on the first flight, which lasted for 31 minutes, and ascended to 10,000 feet. John saluted the de Havilland staff with a flypast at 100 feet. The press took a long time to forgive the folks at Hatfield. *The Times* air correspondent never mentioned the name de Havilland again.

From then on, however, the Comet was the talk of the aviation world, as systematic testing and flying proceeded according to plan, and followed by the public with eager expectation. I was at a meeting at the Ministry of Civil Aviation on 25 October 1949 when a messenger slipped a note to the chairman at the head of the table. He paraphrased the words aloud: "Gentlemen, he said, the D.H.106 has just flown to Castel Benito (the airfield at Tripoli, North Africa) in 3 hours 23 minutes." This was a five-hour flight for a Constellation, which could only have reached Rome in the same time. The meeting broke up, and I think someone produced the sherry.

And so the Comet moved on to its debut as a working airliner. After receiving its Certificate of Airworthiness on 22 January 1952, and with the Avon-powered Comet 2 making its first flight on 16 February, the great day came on 2 May, when, fitted with 36 seats, it went into regular service with B.O.A.C. on the Johannesburg route. Within a few months, as the records of the operations accumulated, it became clear that the Comet's superiority did not lie simply with its speed. The substantial time-savings were translated into economic figures that were startling. The trouble-free regularity impressed the airline world. The doubters were shamed, the critics were silent, de Havilland had the world at its feet.

The biggest doubt was concerned with the operating costs, particularly because of high fuel consumption, always the source of skepticism. But the Comet's higher fuel consumption was largely offset by the lower price of the kerosene used by the jet engines, compared with that of gasoline. The jet engines were lighter, and such weight-saving could be transferred to add payload. The engines required little attention and maintenance costs plummeted. The Ghost engines started with a T.B.O. (Time Between Overhaul) of 375 hours. Within a year it was 1,000 hours, an unprecedented increase in such a short time, and the harbinger of future jet engine overhaul lives beyond the dreams of piston-engined maintenance men. The smooth-running turbine engines eliminated the airframe vibration imposed by reciprocating engines, and airframe maintenance time and costs were reduced as a consequence.

On the revenue side of the economic equation, the benefits were substantial. The attraction of the Comet's speed gave a new dimension to the term airline competition. An outbound DC-6B, leaving London at the same time, met the Comet when it was halfway *back* from Johannesburg. Five Comets could do the work of eight piston-engined airplanes of the same size, and this revenue-generating capability offset much of the higher costs.

But the Comet's success did not, as some commentators deduced, depend solely on its speed. As with the subsequent generations of even bigger and better airliners that were to follow in its trail-blazing footsteps, the success depended upon all of the elements summarized above: the engine efficiency and the consequent effect on lower costs, combined with the benefits of higher utilization and productivity. Airline analysts quickly recognized the break-through in operating economics and translated this into lower fares. The Comet 1 itself did not survive to see the introduction of economy fares; but the new thinking that its revolutionary performance set in motion can be traced back to those first few months of service in 1952.

The breadth of the pioneering work of the de Havilland team in breaking new frontiers of aviation knowledge has too often been forgotten. It settled the long-standing argument as to whether or not the turboprop engine was more economical for long ranges; and arguably killed the chances of the four-engined turboprop Britannias, Electras, or Ilyushin Il-18s from ever breaking sales records. Yet in the 1940s the arguments against the jet seemed to be too convincing, with doubts on fuel consumption, fuselage pressure, and high-speed compressibility causing real concern. Richard M. Clarkson, de Havilland's visionary technical director in charge of the aerodynamics of all D.H. jet aircraft, reviewed the contemporary skepticism expressed by the technical adviser to the Brabazon Committee: " We studied Roxbee-Cox's findings with gloomy concurrence." Doubts there may have been, but to put it bluntly, de Havilland had the intuitive conviction, the courage, the sheer guts to keep going.

Other engineering features, now standard, were first introduced in the Comet; and work done in relation to the Comet had long-standing effects on the subsequent course of airliner development. When Bishop and Clarkson visited Germany in October 1945 to study the revelations in swept wing design, they fully recognized the speed advantage that would be derived therefrom; but they also took account of the consequential payload penalty. The final Comet wing was only modestly swept but its large area gave it superb airfield performance. Flight refuelling, which had its articulate supporters, was rejected, especially when John Cunningham said "I'll do it if ordered to, but not otherwise."

The great leap forward in the technique of cabin pressure, pioneered by the Comet, has never been fully appreciated by the Comet detractors. Back in the 1940s, de Havilland faced daunting challenges. The team was venturing into the unknown frigidity and semi-vacuum of the tropopause altitudes of 40,000 feet. Writer-historian Mike Ramsden, delivering the 1989 de Havilland Memorial Lecture of the Royal Aeronautical Society at Hatfield, to commemorate simultaneously the 40th anniversary of the Comet's first flight, remembered: "Robinson now had to process tons rather than pounds of air per flight, conditioning it and regulating it so perfectly that grannies and babies would not notice the difference." Robinson's achievement in maintaining 8,000-feet pressure inside the cabin at 40,000 feet outside was the prototype of every jet airliner's cabin air system today. Chief designer Bishop cut through much discussion by instructing his team to bleed hot air directly from the engine compressors, cooling it and regulating it, and incidentally using it for airframe de-icing. Again, these principles, first explored by de Havilland, have been used by every jetliner since.

The list goes on. The bonding of metals by the use of Redux, an extremely powerful metal glue, to reinforce or even supersede riveting, was first used extensively in the Comet. Invented by Aero Research at Duxford, England—hence the name—it was employed to save weight as well as to strengthen. Redux also helped in the design of integral fuel tanks in the wing—another Comet first. For the control system, Bishop had to fight a battle with his own associates, including Sir Geoffrey de Havilland himself, to insist on full power, without manual backup. The Comet's power controls, with its built-in safeguards, have never failed. The same basic system is used in today's Airbus generation and in the Concorde. The Comet also incorporated, after the prototype stage, multiple-wheeled landing gear; and it was the aircraft for which pressure refueling was first developed.

All these innovations enabled the Comet to survive the traumatic experience of the catastrophic crashes, albeit at enormous sacrifice; because the precious technical lead had been lost and the other manufacturers had got the message and had jumped on the jet bandwagon. The Boeing 707 and the Douglas DC-8 were on their way. De Havilland picked itself up, with much burning of midnight oil, and decided to go on with the Comet and correct the structural deficiency. In due course, the Comet 4 had the honor of inaugurating the world's first trans-Atlantic jet airline service, when B.O.A.C. supplemented its Britannias on 4 October 1958 and proceeded to deploy Comets throughout its worldwide network. De Havilland had the satisfaction of winning more orders overseas and of seeing its product lead the way in the jet conquest of most of the world's intercontinental trunk routes. Developed as a military version, the Nimrod variant started operations in 1970 to patrol the NATO skies, a responsibility that it will hold for many years to come.

The Nimrod's wing is exactly the same as the first Comet's. It was designed by Bill Tamblin and his team to accommodate the large-diameter Ghost engines which necessitated the solving of a large problem, expressed by Bishop: "The more you know about fatigue the more you know it starts from holes, and here were four of the biggest holes in the wing business." Tamblin got it right without a computer and without even a pocket calculator, and the Nimrods go on flying impressively today.

Certainly the Comet was outclassed in 1958 by the Boeing 707 and, more than a year later, by the Douglas DC-8. But often forgotten is the hard fact (no pun intended) that, when the big American jets were launched, with Pan American's dramatic order for 45 of them in 1955, the airport authorities all over the world had to start pouring concrete in vast quantities. The 707 needed $1\frac{1}{2}$ miles of runway and in the late 1950s almost all the main airports of the world had to be upgraded to accept them—a hidden subsidy that the Comet did not need.

Sometimes forgotten also is that the Comet, smaller than the 707 or DC-8, was better suited to the lower traffic density on some long-distance routes, especially on a number of segments on the trans-Asian and trans-African B.O.A.C. network. Before traffic grew in the late 1960s, higher load factors and fewer empty seats gave the Comet an economic advantage over the Boeing 707 on these routes. Statistics in the B.O.A.C. annual reports at the time revealed this apparent contradiction, but when de Havilland drew the airline's attention to it, the relevant figures were quietly eliminated from future reports.

The de Havilland Comet had originally gone into service eleven years after the idea was first touched upon in 1941 with the Goblin-engined Flamingo. Sadly, all the inspired imagination, all the laborious years of effort, all the trial and error that led to the right decisions: all these memories of pioneering achievement have been all but obliterated by the memories of the heartaches and agonizing re-appraisals that followed the two 1954 crashes.

But to describe the Comet as a failure, as too many writers have done, or at least implied, is ridiculous. Constantly pointing to the structural failure and the square windows, is, with the advantage of hindsight, like condemning the Wright brothers for warping the wings instead of inventing ailerons.

In my book about the world's airline history I described the Comet's career as The Magnificent False Start. It was just that. The Comet jumped the gun, and gave faster sprinters, learning from de Havilland's impetuosity, but who had hitherto stood aside, a chance to join in the race. De Havilland's audacity, however, had accelerated the debut of jet air travel in the western world by about five years.

No single stage in airline progress has been so important as the introduction of jet travel. Yet none was made with such sacrifice by its creator. The aviation world should beat a pathway to Hatfield's main gate, not to buy aircraft, but to pay homage to the place where an inspired team of visionaries laid the foundations of the Jet Age, and, with the Comet, transformed the world by making it, for good or for bad, a much smaller place.

The Concorde (1976–   )

O f all the fallacies and fantasies reviewed so far in this book, the greatest is the much-quoted claim that the Anglo-French Concorde is a profit-making commercial airliner. The Mach 2 supersonic Concorde is without challenge a technical miracle. Its solid achievement of accident-free service since 1976 is just that. Equally, however, it has been an economic disaster, clear for all to see, from the earliest years of its embryo stage of development. Great Britain has had to pay a terrible price for its indulgent favoritism for the Concorde which, from the start, should have been recognized as the Cuckoo in the British Aviation Nest, gobbling up precious resources, and offering no return on the investment. In cosseting the Concorde, many promising aircraft projects were criminally neglected, much in the same way that infant hedgesparrows are ejected by the usurping glutton.

After all the emotional squabbling during the Concorde's development and production was finally over, only 20 were built, and 6 of these were never put into service. The two national airlines of the joint constructing countries, Britain and France, were frogmarched into buying the other fourteen, evenly shared. By extracting unprecedented concessions as the condition of accepting them with good grace, British Airways and Air France were able to operate the aircraft without paying for them, and to be able to maintain them without having to buy the normal allocation of spare parts. They then operated them at fares far higher than normal first-class levels, and proceeded to cover the purely marginal expenses of buying the fuel and paying the crew. Hence the so-called "profit".

No other airline was hoodwinked by the sometimes ludicrous claims made by the salesmen who had to try to convince a cynical and skeptical clientèle who had to make money the hard way. Any market analyst could have told the perpetrators of the hoax that the market was very small, negligible, or nil. But the views of the market analysts were seldom asked for, and if asked, their opinions were either rejected out of hand or they were covered up.

The British Treasury itself—the ultimate source of the development funding—was kept in the dark as to the true facts. Cost figures were falsified and estimates of the potential market were wildly exaggerated without the slightest attempt to approach the problem in a rational manner. If ever there was a case of "Don't confuse me with the facts, my mind is made up" it was the approach made by the Concorde protagonists in the 1950s.

Putting all its commercial aircraft eggs into this particular basket, Great Britain effectively withdrew support from aircraft projects that could have secured at least a respectable share of the world's commercial airliner market, given half a chance. If £1 had been allocated to the Trident for every £100 thrown at the Concorde, de Havilland could have snatched about a third of the Boeing 727's market. France, at least, kept its options open by full support for the Airbus, the A300, whereas Britain turned its back on this potential world-beater, except as a sub-contractor.

Why did the two leading aircraft manufacturing nations of Europe persevere with this high-tech aviation cuckoo? Certainly it was a thing of rare beauty. Just to watch a Concorde on the final approach to land is to excite a sense of awe, rather like the first glimpse of an exquisite Modigliani, that engineers and designers could fashion such a wondrous shape. But the aviation theorists and aerodynamicists and the engineers who so strenuously promoted the Concorde; and the politicians who so unethically used it as a bargaining chip in international in-fighting, were less concerned with beauty then with an almost paranoid obsession with Speed—for its own sake and at any price — and with the prestige and pride of being able to claim the privilege of having built the first supersonic airliner in the world.

To achieve this was a long struggle. If determination to proceed against all the odds of common sense and logic was the sole criterion of excellence, then the Concorde team and its supporters deserve full marks. For press on they did. The Concorde flew, and flew spectacularly and impeccably; and went into service, with fanfares of trumpets. But after the feast of celebration and flag-waving came the reckoning.

And what a reckoning! About four billion U.S. dollars were spent in development costs alone, excluding production costs. This worked out at about $250 million per Concorde. And this was in the 1960s. In today's money the figures would be equivalent to about double that amount. Production costs would be an added expense of no mean proportions, while high operating costs would have to be added by the airlines that put them into service.

In some respects, the Concorde's fanatical protagonists, deceived by the ludicrous supply of disinformation on which they based their assumptions, had a case. The enormity of the technical and cost problems aside, there was a certain rationale for building a supersonic airliner. For in the early 1950s, just as the Concorde promotion was beginning to gain momentum, the British were suffering from an acute sense of frustration. The prospect of a substan-

substantial penetration into the world's commercial airliner market, hitherto dominated by the United States, had just been plucked from its grasp.

In 1951, the year when Arnold (later Sir Arnold) Hall took over as director of the Royal Aeronautical Establishment at Farnborough, England, Britain's aircraft industry was setting a cracking pace, threatening to leave the rest of the world behind in some categories of aircraft. The de Havilland Comet entered service in 1952 to toll the death knell of piston-engined airliners. The Vickers Viscount followed in 1953 to capture a handsome share of the short-haul market, and to sell in respectable numbers in the bastion of aviation technology and production, the United States. The English Electric Canberra multi-purpose military aircraft was even to be built in the States, a technology transfer that had not happened since the de Havilland D.H.4 U.S.-licensed production in 1918.

The standard-bearer of these hopes and dreams had been cruelly dashed with the Comet 1 disasters early in 1954. The Americans were reprieved. Pan American ordered 25 Douglas DC-8s and 20 Boeing 707s in 1955, to reverse the direction of the cash flow back to the West Coast. The Viscount did reasonably well. The huge Saunders-Roe flying boat and the giant Bristol Brabazon had already been consigned to the breaker's yard. The Bristol Britannia, which had had to play second fiddle to the Comet, was suddenly Britain's last hope with conventional airliners. But its makers, ill-prepared for the sudden responsibility thrust upon them, had to toil against irritating engine teething problems, and a world airline market that was becoming suspicious about Britain's ability to deliver the goods.

Almost simultaneously with the catastrophic Comet crashes in the Mediterranean, Dr. Morien (later Sir Morien) Morgan was, on 25 February 1954, appointed as Hall's deputy, and he it was who first raised the idea of a supersonic airliner as a solution to Britain's problems in this competitive arena. Just as the Comet had spearheaded a giant leapfrogging movement to take the airline world by storm, he argued, so could a supersonic airliner. So if the Americans built 600-mph 707s and DC-8s, Britain would build 1,200 mph airliners and leave the others trailing in their wake. The sheer magnitude of the idea was breathtaking; and it attracted many supporters.

Unfortunately, when the talents of Morgan's working party were charged with studying the feasibility of such an ambition, the answers were hardly encouraging. The best they could come up with at first was a design that could carry 50 people at about five times the cost of subsonic airliners, and which would have to stop to refuel on the critical London-New York route. To be fair to the visionaries, there was a good precedent: the first Comet design was just as far removed from the aircraft that was unveiled in 1949.

Undaunted, the protagonists pressed their case. On 1 November 1956, at the Ministry of Supply, then still in charge of all research, development, and production of British aircraft, a high-level meeting took place, chaired by Sir Cyril Musgrave. It was attended by the heads of many British airframe and engine companies, and by the Farnborough chief. The conclusion was drawn from an over-riding unpalatable fact: Britain's aircraft industry was in such a state of disarray when it came to having a viable program for the future that the choice was supersonic or nothing. Accordingly, the first meeting of the Supersonic Transport Aircraft Committee (S.T.A.C.) assembled on 4 November, under the chairmanship of Morien Morgan, now determined that his supersonic decision had nationwide support.

But for some brilliant work in advanced aerodynamics, involving the behavior of wingtip vortex patterns and their positive contribution to lift on a sharp-edged delta wing, the Concorde might never have happened. This work was conducted mainly under the direction of Dietrich Kuchemann, a German aerodynamicist who had come to England at the end of World War II. The S.T.A.C. report was kept secret for many years because, among other revelations, it distorted the development cost estimates, which were optimistically thought to be about £150 million.

The project snowballed from then on. The Minister of Supply, Aubrey Jones, used the supersonic project for political ends in seeking a rapprochement with the French, and discussed it with the French Transport Minister at the Paris Air Show in June 1959. After the October general election of that year, Duncan Sandys took over from Jones and strengthened the French Connection. His Parliamentary Secretary, Geoffrey Rippon, passed on the key S.T.A.C. report to the French and from then on an Anglo-French concordat was inescapable.

At least nobody tried to break the agreement. It was backed by the Macmillan Government as a ticket of entry into the Common Market. The Wilson Government tried to escape in 1964, when it discovered new estimates of £835 million, but Charles de Gaulle said No. Wilson could have risked a negative vote at the International Court and cut its losses to less than 200 million; and the verdict might not even have been negative. But to abandon Concorde would have prompted banner headlines accusing the Labour Party of treason or worse. To criticize Concorde in Britain at that time would have been like stamping on the Stars and Stripes in front of the White House.

By the time Labour lost office in 1970, there was still a slender chance for Britain to escape from the Supersonic Agreement, which applied only to development costs, not production. During the mid-1960s, even Farnborough had had to concede that the Sonic Boom was a physical phenomenon that no

slight of aerodynamic hand could eliminate. This admission meant that the
Concorde could not fly over land, except possibly over deserts or uninhabited
tundra. The market was thus suddenly reduced to transoceanic routes.

The U.S. airlines, Eastern, American, Continental, and T.W.A., as well
as Japan Air Lines, hastily asked for their deposits to be returned. Then, on 31
January 1973, Pan American, past conqueror of the world's transoceanic air
lanes, withdrew. Pan Am had launched three of the five main eras of intercontinental air transport. Now it effectively caused another to be stillborn. With
the U.S. Chosen Instrument on its order book, the Concorde might just have
stood a chance. Without Pan Am, it was dead, except for the two prototypes,
four for B.O.A.C., three for Air France, and five for sale. These last were never sold, but were taken up by the two indigenous airlines.

The Concorde went into service on 21 January 1976, when British Airways flew to Bahrain, to attract the oil magnates of the Middle East; and Air
France, more flamboyantly, to Rio de Janeiro. U.S. authorities would not permit the Concorde to land in New York on scheduled services until 22 Novem-

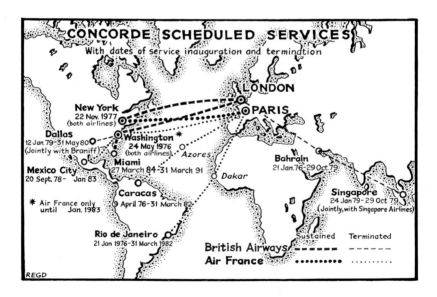

*Many Concorde routes were inaugurated during the late 1970s, in a wave of su-
personic optimism. But the realities of operating economics forced the two airlines, Air France and British Airways, to terminate most of them. Only three
routes remain in operation today, the high fares acting as a severe deterrent to
ticket sales.*

The Anglo-French Concorde, pictured here at Washington's Dulles Internatioal Airport, is a thing of beauty; but its operating costs are hopelessly high, so that the fares are set at a level that is affordable only to the very wealthy. For every passenger carried across the Atlantic, the Concorde carries a ton of fuel. (British Airways)

ember 1977. Both airlines tried to expand their supersonic networks but there were simply not enough passengers to pay the high fares. The Concorde's disappointing service record, which had little impact on world airline affairs, is chronicled in the accompanying map.

The sheer magnitude of the Concorde's technical achievement obscured its market and economic problems. From the first flight onwards, there was much to admire, even to marvel at. Though its seating capacity had had to be reduced from 135 to 100, a trade-off to provide more fuel for trans-Atlantic range, it did everything that its designers said it would. It takes off like a dragster out of the starting gate (and with the same earsplitting noise) and then accelerates nonchalantly through the sound barrier to Mach 2 with as much apparent fuss as the Boeing 727 reaches 600 mph. The transition through the barrier is so smooth that passengers need a special indicator to make them aware of their unusual experience. Admittedly they tolerate cramped quarters in a cabin only inches wider than that of a 1936 DC-3. The windows are only the size of small plates; but, in compensation, the large plates that are part of the Concorde meal service are in use for most of the trans-Atlantic journey time.

The Concorde has demonstrated a truly impressive record of reliability and regularity. Even at the severely curtailed level of service frequency and route deployment today, British Airways and Air France Concordes may possibly fly more supersonic hours annually than the combined fleets of all the air forces of the world. Statistics aside, Concorde has given the European aircraft manufacturing industry a technical achievement and a consequent spiritual uplift almost comparable with those earned in the United States and the Soviet Union by their space efforts.

But airline sales are not based on pride and patriotism. Most airlines, even the state-operated and -subsidized ones, have to show a return on their investment; and the Concorde's cost figures (even those that could be admitted) were so outrageously high that they could not be countenanced. Independent expressions of incredulity were summarily dismissed. Mary Goldring of the *Economist* and Andrew Wilson and Peter Eglin of the *Observer* (not to mention backstage grumbling from this writer) were lone voices of dissent in a cacophony of mindless Concorde-worship. Normally intelligent aviation magazines, led by *Flight International*, waved the Union Jack vigorously, and, in describing potential success for Britain's last hope, ran the gamut of phrases like "There can be no doubt that...." and "All the indications are that ...." There was an understanding that operating costs would not be revealed, as they were too horrific to contemplate, but the good old standby "comparable" was dangerously overworked by the hundreds of journalists and writers who were sumptuously wined and dined on free flights. Adverse comment would have been ungentlemanly and ungracious.

The salesmen had to admit that the sonic boom applied to Concorde as well as to other lesser aircraft and that even the combined genius of Farnborough, Bristol, Weybridge, and Toulouse couldn't fool with Mother Nature. They also had to explain away the noise of the Bristol Olympus engines which were more than deafening on takeoff. Bystanders could *feel* as well as hear the Concorde take off—little wonder as the 100-decibel (normal busy street noise level) footprint area of the Concorde was close to 50 square miles, compared with the three square miles of the Boeing 747.

Most of the wilder advocacy fell on deaf ears as the practical operational procedures, the ones that mean success or failure to a commercial airline, had been investigated and found wanting. The claimed advantages for a busi-

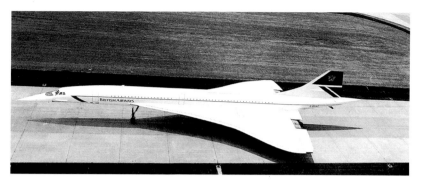

The Concorde's elegant exterior disguises the fact that its fuselage is only a few inches wider than the DC-3's, and there is less headroom. The windows are the size of a small plate or large saucer. (British Airways)

nessman who could arrive by Concorde hours ahead of his subsonic rival and thereby clinch a deal were ridiculed by the businessmen themselves who knew that deals are not made that way. Assertions that the Concorde eliminated jet lag were dispelled by experienced travelers who knew that the circadian rhythm had nothing to do with the speed of travel. Eyes still drooped at 7 p.m. in New York. In the reverse direction, those who arrived in London, bright-eyed and bushy-tailed in the late evening, found their hosts markedly unenthusiastic at the prospect of going home with the milkman. The theoretical idea of two flights a day with one Concorde had to be abandoned because departure and arrival times just did not fit with the patterns of daily life on both sides of the Atlantic.

The Concorde's costs were always so impossibly high that commercial sales were never a prospect. By all the normal criteria of economic evaluation, the odds against them were overwhelming. One reliable rule-of-thumb is the cost per seat. In 1973, a $23 million 360-seat Boeing 747 cost $70,000 per seat. A $36 million (grossly underpriced) 100-seat Concorde cost $360,000 per seat, five times as much. Boeing's price was calculated by astute accountants with eyes on a breakeven number of at least 400 aircraft. Concorde's price was based on the product of wishful thinking and special pleading and was completely artificial. The cost per seat based on the real market potential would have been astronomical.

Aircraft price is only one ingredient in the formula used to calculate unit operating costs. The fixed basic cost of ownership can be reduced only by spreading it out over many years and by intensive use of the aircraft. The Concorde's utilization, measured in hours flown per year, is less than half that of subsonic airliners. British Airways and Air France paid almost nothing for their Concordes and thus the fixed cost element was zero. But that privilege would not have been given to other foreign customers.

No-one has ever begrudged the high salaries earned by the Concorde crews. They fly at margins outside the scope of subsonic mortals, having to think, for instance, of the approach pattern to John F. Kennedy Airport at New York while still 1,000 miles away, and ticking off the miles at the rate of one every three seconds. As the elite of the flight deck world, they draw elitist pay, but this has little effect on the costs, as the crew numbers are small—the same as for any other airliner.

More important as an element of cost is the fuel. The Concorde has to carry 100 tons of it on every flight, one ton for every passenger in a full load, more if there are empty seats.

Such high operating costs were frightening. At first, some hopes were entertained that these could be partially offset by charging higher fares. Elaborate charts were drawn up to suggest that the world's first-class air passengers would travel by Concorde, while the other ranks would fly subsonically. Nobody seemed to question, much less bother to analyze or calculate, the traffic by class of travel. The brochures seemed to portray the first-class percentage at about 30. The actual percentage is about five. Studies were concentrated on the North Atlantic route, and did not take into account the fact that this premium long-distance air corridor accounts for no less than about a quarter of the world's intercontinental air routes, and about a third of all transoceanic air travel.

Validated by comprehensive statistical data, these facts permit the expression of of the Davies Law of the Supersonic Market (D.L.S.M.) which states that this market can never, even theoretically, be more than about 40 aircraft; and practically even less. And this applies to Mach 2 Concordes, Mach 3 U.S. SSTs, or Mach 5, Mach 8, or Mach 58 HST (hypersonic) airliners.

This Law is derived from the simple equation $T/P = M$ where T is the first-class traffic, P is the aircraft productivity, and M is the resultant aircraft market number. The calculation is set out in the table opposite and will remain valid until the invention of a new *and more economic* method of propulsion than that of the present-day turbojets.

In defiance of the Davies Law, Concorde salesmen optimistically hoped that the first-class market would be augmented by some of the people flying in business class. This was a myth. Businessmen of high caliber, working for firms whose success depended upon sensible book-keeping, were not even allowed to fly first-class, much less by Concorde, on penalty of severe reprimand, deductions from salary, or worse. With today's New York-London

THE DAVIES LAW
OF THE SUPERSONIC MARKET
(D.L.S.M.—Mach 2 version)

Total North Atlantic Passengers (one way)

Assume 20,000,000 per year
x 5% First Class........................1,000,000
x 40% on top city pairs..............400,000[1]
x 150% to include upgrading
   first and business class.........600,000[2].....T_{NA}

Concorde Passengers (one way) (per aircraft)

Assume one round trip per day .....200 seats
x 70% load factor ....140 passengers
x 365 days in year...................50,000 .... P_{NA}

North Atlantic Concorde Market

$$\frac{T_{NA}}{P_{NA}} = \frac{600,000}{50,000} \quad \ldots\ldots\ldots\ldots\ldots\ldots\ldots 12 \ldots\ldots\ldots M_{NA}$$

World Concorde Market

Assume North Atlantic to be one third of total
   transocean (or equivalent) market[3]
                12 x 3 ....36 .... M_W

Note: In the above calculation, there are three distinct elements of compounded optimism, indicated by
1. Concorde range limitation and inability to fly supersonically over land would almost certainly reduce this percentage to less than 40%.
2. High Concorde fares and good first and business class comfort standards suggest that the upgrading percentage is much less than the assumed figure.
3. Trans-Pacific market much smaller than North Atlantic and Concorde would have range problems; other operationally acceptable intercontinental markets very small. North Atlantic market could be half the total.

Concorde fare well in excess of $3,500, arguments about the advantage of getting to London or Paris three hours sooner than by 747 fall on deaf ears. Few business meetings start in Paris in the late afternoon or early evening.

The other great fallacy was that, dazzled by the glamour of the Concorde, all the elitist traffic would be channeled through the Concorde co-termini, i.e. from Pittsburgh or Boston or Philadelphia through New York; or from Amsterdam or Brussels through London; or from Frankfurt or Zurich through Paris, by connecting flights. There are not enough Swiss bankers to fill a daily, or even thrice weekly Concorde from Zurich to New York, but no Swiss banker is going to risk a weather-delayed tight connection at Paris, just to save three hours over a Swissair Boeing 747. And if the connection is not a tight one, there is no point in making it.

Restricted to operating only those routes on which enough people could be found to pay a *one-way* fare of about $3,500 (1990) to cross the Atlantic, and comforted by the knowledge that no progress payments were due on the purchase of the aircraft, British Airways and Air France adopted the habit of announcing that the Concorde was making a profit. This did not exactly lead to a stream of inquires by jealous airlines as to how they too could acquire such profitable airplanes. To make an earthbound analogy, this would be like asking someone to donate a free Rolls-Royce, plus a supply of spare parts, finding four or five people to pay a dollar a mile each to join a car pool, and then claiming that a Rolls-Royce-based car pool was a money-making investment.

The Concorde did pay untold dividends in promoting the fashionable image of its operators as leading the world in airline operating technology. The Concorde persuaded prospective travelers to ask for them first. The glamour was reflected on the 747s, DC-10s, and Tristars in a halo effect. In a previous generation, the British had a fine airliner, the Vickers VC 10 which, like the Concorde, was more expensive per seat-mile than the rival aircraft. But only slightly so. It was well promoted, with catch-phrases like "Try a Little VC-Tenderness" and with pictures of Marlene Dietrich's legs to emphasize the legroom. Yet B.O.A.C. never capitalized on this airliner, which pulled in at least 10 percent more revenue per equivalent flight than did the Boeing 707s.

Careful economic analysis could have proved the VC 10's worth, but the airline concentrated solely upon the marginally higher seat-mile costs, almost as an obsession, ignoring the revenue-earning capability of the airplane itself and its halo effect. In the case of the Concorde, speed was the obsession. The God of Speed was epitomized by the Concorde, which became the Deity to whom the nation worshipped.

Herein lay the worst aspect of the Concorde's role in Britain's manufacturing industry. Such devotion did not wholly destroy British efforts to maintain parity with the United States in the science of producing commercial aircraft; but it came close. The British Treasury, encouraged, persuaded, blackmailed, and deceived, was led to put all its financially supportive eggs into the Concorde basket. Many other projects were abandoned or, at the very least, neglected. The VC 10 and the Trident fell by the wayside, and—the biggest error of all—equal participation in the Airbus and design leadership of the entire project was handed over to France, with Germany offered an opportunity which would never have come its way, but for the Concorde. Britain's choice had really been: Airbus or nothing, at any cost.

The British aircraft industry, once a thriving and energetic, even inspirational component of the industrial strength of Britain, and of Europe, has been reduced to a shadow of its former self. Against all common sense, engineers, civil servants, and politicians cynically used the Concorde to further their own ends; while misguided journalists mesmerized the public in its appreciation of what was going on. While the British waved their Concorde flags, the French shrewdly switched their attention to the Airbus, and Boeing and Douglas laughed all the way to the bank.

The British and French taxpayers footed the bill for $4 billion, for which they received fourteen operational Concordes. Never has so much been paid by so many for so few.

The U.S. SST (1958–1971)

Compared to the British aircraft industry, which was irrevocably disabled by the misguided belief that, in the commercial use of its products, speed was automatically equated to success, the United States manufacturers were saved from making fools of themselves by the far-sighted judgment of a few clear-thinking individuals in the concerned government agencies and by supportive sanity from certain members of Congress. But for such D.O.D. stalwarts as Joseph Califano, later a presidential adviser, and Harvard physicist William Shurcliff, who founded the Citizens League against the Sonic Boom, Boeing might easily have been persuaded to build the Model 2707, which would have gone into the record books as having beaten the speed record in reaching premature extinction. The Seattle giant would have squandered its resources in building perhaps a dozen short-lived Mach 3 SSTs instead of a thousand Boeing 747s, a type which seems destined to stay in production until the next century. In the event, the United States aircraft industry was saved from ignominy by the close vote in the Senate which, on 24 March 1971, finally turned down the U.S. SST by refusing to spend any more of the taxpayers' money on it.

The entire story in the United States had provided the arena for formidable gladiators as the arguments raged and the contests were fought over various aspects of the issues involved. First and foremost, chronologically, psychologically, politically, and industrially, was the element of competition, interwoven with a powerful sense of national pride. Accustomed to being the technical leader in almost every field of mechanical and constructional enterprise, the U.S.A. was not about to surrender this status to Great Britain and its Concorde, nor to the Soviet Union and its Tupolev Tu-144.

By May 1958—five months before Pan American Airways put the Boeing 707, the first U.S. commercial subsonic jet airliner, into service—Douglas and Lockheed had both announced Mach 2 supersonic designs. General Dynamics came in with a Mach 3 proposal earlier in 1959, and soon afterwards Boeing joined the fray with designs that would eventually crystallize into the Boeing 2707. The subject of supersonic travel was uppermost in the minds of

118

everyone in the aviation industry at the time. *Aviation Week,* that reliable barometer of contemporary opinion, devoted more space to the SST in 1959 than to any other air transport subject. With a long history of conservative thinking in future design projects (contrasting with inspired initiative in developing known and tried products) Douglas dropped out of the running in August 1963. This left the other three to submit proposals to the F.A.A. in 1964. After endless wrangling, during which North American also became disenchanted with the SST, Boeing emerged as the winner early in 1967, in a fierce no-holds-barred battle with Lockheed. After an abortive attempt at a complex swing-wing design, Boeing incorporated a fixed delta wing, with a tail and canard foreplane, and would be built primarily of titanium so as to permit a speed of Mach 2.7, between 250 and 300 seats (the Concorde and the Tupolev could manage only a maximum of 120), 4,000 miles range (Concorde and Tupolev were only marginally trans-Atlantic at the time), and a gross weight, even with titanium, of more than 300 tons.

All this would have been fine, had the SST been just another airplane. But, as in Britain and the Soviet Union, the technicians were arrogant enough to assume that they could mitigate the effects of the sonic boom, make it go away, or persuade the general public that it would not affect everyday life. On all three counts they failed. The sonic boom resulted from basic laws of physics, and the manufacturers could not mitigate a basic law, much less make it go away. As to persuasion of the public, this was compounded by a program of deception that was as unethical as it was surreptitious. The public was left with the impression—because the facts were never carefully explained—that an airplane created a sonic boom only at the time and place when and where it pierced the sound barrier at Mach 1. Few realized that, having exceeded Mach 1, a supersonic airplane carried its boom along with it, creating a swathe of frightening sound, equivalent to a perpetual thunderclap, up to about 60 miles wide, as long as and wherever it went.

At least there was a body of concerned citizens, administrators, and politicians who showed enough interest to challenge the bland assumption that the sonic boom was simply a technical problem that could be taken care of, if enough research money was thrown at it. The skeptical assertions of Bo Lundberg, a noted aeronautics specialist and Director of the Swedish Aeronautical Institute, were supported by the International Air Transport Association (IATA) and could not, therefore, be totally ignored. In March 1963, the National Operations Research Center echoed the international sentiments. By this time, the politicians and the manufacturers knew that the problem was real and could not be brushed off with wishful theoretical thinking. At first they resisted the idea of conducting tests but only managed to postpone them.

This full scale model of the Boeing B-2707 supersonic airliner is as far as the United States ever reached in this direction of aviation technology. The expectations of this ceremonious occasion were never fulfilled; and the 25 airline badges on the model represented only speculative deposit money, not firm orders. (The Boeing Company)

The complexity of the Boeing B-2707 supersonic airliner project included provision for a 'drooped snoot' nose flexibility (as in the Concorde) and also a wing whose angle of sweep could be changed to adapt to varying speeds up to Mach 3. This multi-exposure photograph of the full-scale mockup illustrates this revolutionary development. (The Boeing Company)

Between February and July 1964, tests were held in Oklahoma City and the results, even in edited form, were grim. On 2 December of the same year, tests were made at the White Sands proving grounds. These results were devastating.

The SST protagonists reluctantly accepted the awful prospect of restricting supersonic airliner operations only to areas of water (and far enough away from land to eliminate the boom effect) and over uninhabited or sparsely populated areas. This view, incidentally, had been held by the Commerce Department right from the start, but the department had had to defer to what were considered to be more authoritative sources of knowledge. Acceptance of the restriction was inescapable. It effectively cut the potential SST market by a margin that varied from 50 percent to 75 percent, depending upon operational criteria yet to be decided. Astoundingly, so little had been done to assess the market in a realistic and systematic manner that nobody really knew the facts, and worse, did not know how to calculate them. Worse still, there were those who preferred not to know them, in a classic "don't confuse me with the facts, my mind is made up" attitude. The SST project should have been killed right then. Yet so influential were the SST protagonists that the F.A.A. directive on the sonic boom was not promulgated until April 1970, a full six years after the facts were known.

Consequently an aura of quiet confidence still continued to pervade the industry, which continued to spend a lot of money on the SST Concurrently with the controversy over the sonic boom, however, the approach to, and the assessment of the costs involved in developing and building the SST were either unbelievably naïve or were criminally deceptive in their optimism. In the fall of 1960, the expenditure on the program was estimated to be no more than $450 million for the next eight years. Two years later, this was increased to $750 million, of which $100 million would be spent in the first year. The figures were beginning to approach Pentagon proportions.

Many knowledgeable people in the administration covertly thought that these figures too were under-estimates, and overtly introduced the idea of cost-sharing, by which they implied that the costs of the SST programme would be shared, by some measure yet to be determined, by the government (i.e. the taxpayer), the manufacturer, and the airline customers who were expected to produce some upfront money as a display of confidence in the product and an assurance of future orders that would offset the costs.

By the mid-1960s, these had escalated in inverse proportion to the actual cash invested by the airlines or the aircraft industry—which meant that the taxpayer was footing the bill. True, the airlines reserved SST delivery positions, to the extent that, by September 1965, 21 of them, plus a leasing firm, had 'ordered' 96 positions at $100,000 each. In February 1967, the still prestigious Pan American Airways, launch customer for two generations of subsonic jets, gave its stamp of approval with a proposal of $1,000,000, and this was followed by ten airlines that collectively produced $52 million. All this provided wonderful publicity for the airlines involved, and their public relations departments and advertising agencies were ecstatic.

But these amounts were chicken feed, compared to the total expenditures required. When, on 31 December 1966, the Boeing Model 2707 was selected, and on 29 April 1967, President Johnson announced that two prototypes would be built at a cost of $1.44 billion during the next four years, the dreamers had to start to face reality. For clearly $50 or even $100 million in airline deposits was not going to account for very much. Further, Boeing did not meet the design deadline of 30 June 1967 and was given a year's extension to proceed "with all deliberate speed"—a phrase very familiar to those who regarded obfuscation as a desirable expediency. However, the sheer enormity of the task of building a 300-ton titanium Mach 3 airliner was at last beginning to dawn upon those who had been hypnotized by shallow promises from the fountain-heads of technology.

Within a few months of L.B.J.'s announcement, and with level-headed administrators translating $1.44 billion into a realistic $3 or $4 billion; and four years into a realistic six or seven, the first Anglo-French Concorde made its first flight, on 2 March 1969, and the second prototype was airborne on 8 April of the same year, suggesting that the Europeans were getting under way in fine style. Furthermore, to add insult to injury, the Soviet Tupolev Tu-144 had beaten the Concorde into the air on 31 December 1968, albeit at a heavy price in sacrificing a systematic development in exchange for expediency. Dismissed by the most optimistic (or the most conceited) of the U.S. technologists as slow (only Mach 2!) and short of range (only barely trans-Atlantic), the British and French, even the Soviet Union, had nevertheless achieved demonstrable results.

With memories of the colossal project that had been necessary for the U.S. to reassert its lead in space by putting a man on the Moon, the Tupolev SST was regarded as a real threat. The Soviets were even showing signs of aggressive marketing and artificial price-setting, and in Aeroflot, by now the largest single airline in the world, it had a ready-made home market to serve as an operational laboratory and—horror of horrors—to show the hammer and sickle at JFK International Airport in New York long before a Pan Am Boeing 2707 could reciprocate with the Stars and Stripes in Moscow.

Adding to the worries was the knowledge that the only large U.S. military supersonic aircraft had either been failures or of limited use. Only two North American XB-70 Mach 3 bombers had been built, and one of these had

THE DAVIES LAW
OF THE SUPERSONIC MARKET
(D.L.S.M.—Mach 3 version)

Total North Atlantic Passengers (one way)

Assume 30,000,000 per year
x 5% First Class 1,500,000
x 40% on top city pairs .... 600,000[1]
x 150% to include upgrading
    first and business class .... 900,000[2] ..... T_{NA}

U.S. SST Passengers (one way, per aircraft)

Assume one round trip per day .... 300 seats[3]
x 70% load factor......................... 210 passengers
x 365 days in year .... 76,000........... P_{NA}

North Atlantic U.S. SST Market

$$\frac{T_{NA}}{P_{NA}} = \frac{900,000}{76,000} \qquad \dots\dots\dots\dots\dots\dots 12 \dots\dots\dots M_{NA}$$

World U.S. SST Market

Assume North Atlantic to be one third of total
    transocean (or equivalent) market
    (same assumption as with Concorde)
        12 x 3 .... 36........... M_W

Note: As with the Concorde calculation (page 115), there are three distinct elements of compounded optimism, indicated by
1. Substantial increases in the range of long-haul subsonic airliners has led to a proliferation of non-stop city-pair connections, diluting the percentage of traffic in the leading markets.
2. With one way Concorde fares in 1990 of more than $3,000 from New York to London or Paris, upgrading is not widespread.
3. The Boeing 2707 was designed for 250-300 seats.

crashed on 8 July 1966. The other was in the Air Force Museum by the end of 1967. Of the 116 B-58 Hustlers, built by General Dynamics at a cost of $3 billion, thirty were used purely as test aircraft. Although it was a technological masterpiece, pioneered sustained supersonic flight and new construction techniques, and set twelve world speed records, it was never a practical military machine.

Throughout the U.S. SST program, as it dragged on with interminable wrangles over design, sonic booms, noise levels, environmental damage, and costs, the protagonists buoyed up their spirits by producing market studies that ranged from mild misconception to ludicrous optimism. Compiled by aircraft manufacturers' planning departments, prestigious consultants, and government agencies at a steady frequency throughout the 1960s, they all had one thing in common. They were all textbook essays in disinformation. Ignorant of the facts, and therefore with no data base, and compounded by totally unsupported wild assumptions, they produced answers that the SST fanatics obsessively wished to hear. But a close and impartial inspection revealed— although as with the results of the sonic boom, such incredulity was never publicized—that the so-called market forecasters hadn't the slightest knowledge of what they were doing. In particular, the completely imaginary notion that the average airline passenger would pay an exorbitant price to save two or three hours across the Atlantic was a fallacy matched by the almost criminal deception in the apparent ignorance of (or a deliberate avoidance of) the magnitude of world-wide first-class air travel as a proportion of the whole. In short, the SST market forecasts, ranging in their most insane moments to upwards of 300 SSTs, were an insult to the intelligence.

Once again, as in the case of the Concorde (see pages 114 and 115) the application of the D.L.S.M. would have been in order.

Competition by Deregulation (1978—   )

T he Airline Deregulation Act of 1978 went through Congress with surprisingly little demur, considering the far-reaching consequence of the action, and bearing in mind that the existing regulatory authority had been in power—and that word is apt—for forty years. It had kept a dynamic industry on a tight rein, occasionally allowing the airlines to break into a canter for a short while, but holding them in check lest a gallop would result in the loss of control, with the whole apparatus of air transport running amok. The more highly strung of the thoroughbred airlines were anxious for a free rein, and ultimately, under President Carter, they were given their head, when he signed the Act into law on 24 October 1978.

Much was made of the ponderous bureaucratic machinery that characterized most of the Civil Aeronautics Board's deliberations. Long months, sometimes years, and occasionally a whole decade would typically pass before a final decision was made on a hotly-contested issue. Not all of this was the C.A.B.'s fault. The individual airlines all aspired to progress, inevitably identified as growth, and this was often possible only by stealing a march on their competitors by encroaching on traditional marketing areas denied to them because of the strict control of the C.A.B. over routes. The Certificate of Public Convenience and Necessity that constituted the legal authority to operate over any route, or between any two points, was sacrosanct; and many a long battle was fought between incumbent airlines and their potential usurpers on the theoretically neutral ground of the C.A.B. in Washington.

While disputes over routes were the most publicized and the most hotly fought over, these were not the only facets of the C.A.B.'s responsibilities. Competition was specifically included as a factor to be considered when the agency began its work in 1938, but this was always done with great caution, and the Board always had what was broadly termed The Public Interest in

126

mind. It did not include the idea of a free and unfettered market, and throughout the four decades of C.A.B. sovereignty over the airline industry, such competition was strictly controlled.

Before examining what happened to competition with the passing of the 1978 Act, a review of the constituents of competition, and how these were managed under the Civil Aeronautics Board, is relevant and indeed essential; for there have been many misconceptions about the nature of competition in the airline world and the necessity for it. Undoubtedly, had the spirit of free enterprise gone unhindered in the early days of air transport in the U.S., back in the Roaring Twenties and the Depression-affected early Thirties, the result would have been close to chaos. Until 1934 the airlines were at least kept in check because of their need for subsidy, given to them through air mail payments. The Postmaster General thus controlled the airways until he was swept out of office when questionable practices led to the notorious Air Mail Scandals of 1934. After that the mail payments still continued, under conditions of strict control, and the airlines had no choice but to toe the line.

The Civil Aeronautics Act of 1938 regularized the manner in which the control over competition was exercised, and this may be reviewed under specific headings:

Aircraft Airlines were free to operate any aircraft they wished. Curiously, in the year when the C.A.B. was born, almost all the airlines flew the Douglas DC-3 as front-line equipment, and not until T.W.A. introduced the Boeing 307 Stratoliner in 1940 was there any improvement in the performance of the revered Douglas airliner. The pressurized comfort—flying "above the weather" of the 307 was ineffective, because World War II prevented further development. But in the post-war era, one element of competition was paramount, the one that had been dormant since the Boeing 247 had lifted the airlines out of the 100 mph Ford Tri-Motor era in 1933: That element was speed.

From the cessation of hostilities in 1945 until the beginning of the Jet Age in the U.S. in 1958, the airlines and the aircraft manufacturers, working in loose partnerships, played a game of aeronautical leapfrog as they vied for the claim to offer the fastest service. Douglas, Lockheed, and to a lesser extent, Boeing, produced fine airliners that, mainly through engine development to higher power ratings, alternated in giving the airlines the opportunity to reduce journey times, particularly from coast to coast. But this element, so much the darling of the publicity purveyors during the great piston-engined era, evaporated when the Boeing 707 and the Douglas DC-8 jetliners came on the scene in the late 1950s and swept all before them in the decade of the 1960s. Although the third manufacturing competitor, Convair, attempted to prolong the competitive element of speed, it was unsuccessful, because of the enormous technical problems—the notorious 'drag-rise curve'—encountered as the speed approached that of sound; and the industry settled down to accept Mach .85 or about 600 mph as the normal speed above and below which no airline tried to fly, or indeed wished to. And so, by 1960, the element of speed had been removed from the competitive equation, supersonic aspirations by the lunatic fringe notwithstanding.

Routes   The Certificates of Public Conveniences and Necessity mentioned earlier were the chains that either bound or protected the incumbent carriers that had been granted them as the so-called "Grandfather" rights in 1938. Throughout the period of its overlordship, the C.A.B. seldom made a route award that changed the shape or distribution of the individual market shares held by the individual airlines, at least within the 48 States. The three transcontinental airlines linking the populous northeast with California were in every sense protected from incursions; because no other airline was ever permitted to challenge them. The C.A.B. genuinely believed that this would lead to excessive competition (a strange concept in today's environment) and that this was bad for the public interest. When it allowed National to compete with Eastern on the northeast-Florida market in 1944, Eastern regarded the action as decidedly un-American. In general, the Board took the view, one with which many economists would agree, that all the advantages of competition can be gained as long as there are two competitors; and that only a route generating very high traffic volume, such as New York-Chicago, could justify more than two.

Occasionally, the C.A.B. opened up opportunities for an airline here and there. When, in the famous Denver Service Case in 1953, it gave Continental Airlines, hitherto a relatively small airline operating in secondary markets, a route from Chicago to California, it gave Bob Six the big chance he needed to break out of the confines of a restrictive route system, much in the same way that National had done in 1944. But commendable though these route awards were, they made only a small dent in the Big Four's hold on the market share. American Airlines, United Air Lines, T.W.A., and Eastern controlled between them at least half of the passenger-miles flown by all U.S. airlines.

On the other hand, the reluctance to grant routes to aspiring airlines could be damaging, even disastrous. During the latter 1950s, one company, Capital Airlines, led by an innovative president, 'Slim' Carmichael, had challenged the Big Four in those markets where the C.A.B. had, somewhat reluctantly in the face of indignation by the incumbents, allowed it to operate.

Capital had introduced a new element into the aircraft competition, turbine power, when it started service with the Vickers Viscount in 1955. But it needed more routes to be able to make good its advantage; and by the time it obtained them after long arbitration with the C.A.B., it was too late. By acquiring the equipment to apply the competitive edge, Capital had exceeded its capital resources, and was eagerly swallowed up by United Air Lines in 1960.

Scheduling   Theoretically, and even practically, there was no restriction on airlines using all the ingenuity at their command to generate more traffic or to increase market shares by inspired scheduling practices. The most dramatic of these was Eastern's introduction of the no-reservation Air-Shuttle service in the dense Northeast Corridor from Boston to New York and New York to Washington, D.C. On-the-hour, every-hour service had been tried successfully before, notably in California, but the walk-on novelty was an inventive competitive tool. To its credit, the C.A.B. saw nothing wrong with it.

Fares   Although there were those in the C.A.B. who claimed that the agency did not *set* fares, this was a quibble, as effectively it did. It was the clearing house for the airlines that wished to experiment with innovations at what level and under what conditions they charged the public for their services; and because of the procedures established from the start, in 1938, the C.A.B. effectively dampened whatever competitive pressure any individual airline could exert by fare-cutting or fare separation according to the amenities offered. When an airline filed with the Board to introduce a new fare, this advice was circulated among all the other airlines, which would, as often as not, strenuously object; and much time, money, and expense was expended in the litigation, as with the controversies over the route applications.

Normally, if an airline wished to decrease a fare, it was not permitted to do so, as the C.A.B. feared this would start a price war. But more often, if an airline wished to increase a fare—to take care of a wage hike, for example—this was granted across the board. Only occasionally did an airline steal a march on the competition. In 1948, Capital Airlines—always seeking innovation but never given the chance to profit by its initiative—introduced a Night Coach fare, at about half the standard—there was only one—fare. The other airlines ignored it, as they thought Capital had taken leave of its senses; but soon changed their minds when the public informed the industry in no uncertain terms—by flocking to Capital's booking offices—that they actually liked lower fares. Within a year or two, coach class fares had swept the country, but, under the controlled system, the airline that dared to experiment with them was not able to take full advantage of its initiative.

Though rigid, the C.A.B. control over fares did have one great advantage. The fares were, within only a minor degree of deviation, variable with distance, in a descending curve, irrespective of the size, status, or directness of service between any two cities. The fare from New York to Medford, Oregon, for example, was little different from the one to Los Angeles.

On-Board Service   This is one area in which the airlines competed enthusiastically, especially when first-class service became essential, after coach class fares had transformed the public's awareness of what to expect during flight. In some cases, travelers could have been forgiven if they thought that the meal was more important than getting to their destination, such was the inflated emphasis placed upon the standards of catering. But the airlines could not be blamed. Meals and amenities were the one element of competition in which they had comparative freedom. Unlike the international organization, IATA, the C.A.B. did not argue interminably about the definition of a sandwich. But it did try, in some cases, to interfere with what today are termed free market forces. In 1966, in a classic confrontation, Continental Airlines introduced five-abreast seating in place of six-abreast in coach class on its jets; the C.A.B. tried to stop this insidious practice. Western Air Lines also lengthened the seat pitch to provide more leg room on its flights to Hawaii, and this upset the C.A.B. too. Fortunately for the supporters of common sense, both Continental and Western were able to win the day by simply going ahead and challenging the C.A.B. to do anything about it. No doubt fearing ridicule by the public as well as by the industry itself, the matter was allowed to take its own course.

Ground Services   Time was when airlines would provide their own limousines or buses to take passengers to and from the airport from selected downtown areas; but the separation of intermodal control in 1934, intended mainly to dissassociate railroads and manufacturers from airline involvement, prevented airlines from operating any form of surface transport. In foreign countries, this was normal practice, but in the U.S. there was no control by the C.A.B. because it was illegal anyway.

Freedom of Entry   Possibly the biggest blot on the record of the Civil Aeronautics Board during the 40 years of its existence was the way in which it succumbed to the ceaseless pressure of the Air Traffic Association (A.T.A.), the lobbying organization of the airline industry, to prevent any new airline from entering the closed ranks of the incumbent operators, jealously guarding their Grandfather Rights.

The outstanding example was the North American Airlines episode, when an enterprising group of entrepreneurs, led by Stan Weiss, managed to find some loopholes in the regulations, operated a transcontinental air service at half the fares of the certificated carriers, and made a profit in so doing. All this was abhorrent to the A.T.A. and was condemned by the C.A.B. The 'Ninety-Nine-Dollar Airline'—a reference to its transcontinental fare—never did receive a certificate, even though it was clearly fit, willing, and able, with a modern fleet of aircraft purchased new from Douglas. Later on, in 1967, Ed Daly, of World Airways, the largest of the supplemental carriers, tried to do the same, at $75.00 coast-to-coast; but met with the same implacable resistance to innovation from Washington.

Throughout its forty years, the C.A.B. granted a full Certificate to only one airline, Trans-Caribbean Airways, a Washington, D.C., airline operating to Puerto Rico. Orvis Nelson's Transocean Air Lines, on the other hand, which had demonstrated supreme competence in every kind of air transport operation, worldwide and certainly trans-ocean, was denied a chance to show its mettle under circumstances that would not bear too much examination.

Oddly enough, the world outside the U.S. used to look upon the Civil Aeronautics Board as a benevolent agency presiding over, and encouraging the spirit of free enterprise and stimulating competition. As such, it was held up as an example for other countries of like mind to follow. This was not so. Benevolent it may have been, and in many instances, it did its best to encourage; but more often than not, it was buried under the weight of its own ponderous bureaucratic system, and was easily manipulated by vested interests, obeying the wishes of a privileged oligarchy.

With such a formidable array of reasons for dismantling an insidious system, with crippling handicaps for conducting competition except in the narrowest of definitions, the fact that airline deregulation did not come into effect until 1978 was a reflection of a public perception that hitherto the negative aspects of regulation were not severe. When the deed was done, presided over by the ebullient Alfred Kahn, who took over the chairmanship of the C.A.B. on 10 January 1977, it was put into effect with startling speed. The twenty-two months to the passing of the Act was less than it sometimes took the C.A.B. to conduct preliminary hearings on a route case.

But, with a decade and a half of airline deregulation now behind us, what has been achieved? Is the airline industry much different from what it was under rigid regulations; and, most important, are the forces of competition, the keystone element of the free enterprise system, any more effective under deregulation than they were under the Civil Aeronautics Board? One way to try to answer the question is to review the various elements as enumerated above. So let us take them in turn, in the same order.

Aircraft This is almost a non-issue today, and has nothing to do with deregulation. With the technological advances made in the manufacturing of airliners, the accent is on economy, not speed. Few passengers, when booking their seats, take the trouble to find out which type of aircraft they will be flying in. A Plane is a Plane is a Plane; and perhaps that is no bad thing. As with the railroads when they reached maturity, all the main line equipment provides the same speed and the same standards of comfort.

Routes and Scheduling This is theoretically free. Instead of going through an elaborate process with a government agency that frequently seemed in no hurry to reach a decision, and sometimes even appeared to wish not to do so, an airline today can fly almost anywhere it wishes to, and its only obligation is to inform the Department of Transport of its intentions. This does not apply to international routes, any more than it did during the pre-deregulation days, as matters of state are involved, in bilateral agreements, international rights—the Five Freedoms of The Air—and political factors.

But in practical terms, now that the unseemly rush to expand with unfettered freedom, immediately following the passing of the 1978 Act, has run its course, the airlines have settled down to a different kind of status quo, one that reacts to market forces, not to regulations. These forces have taken the shape of a system in which, rather like species of birds or animals, the airlines have laid down territorial rights around their home base and in selected bases—hubs—elsewhere, much in the same way as do birds around their nests and animals around their lairs.

The establishment of the hubs has replaced the old Certificates of Public Necessity and Convenience as the channel by which the Nine Points of the Law, i.e. Possession, is imposed. Across the United States today, and especially in the Midwest, where many cities act as interchange points on transcontinental journeys, the airlines have dug themselves in. And in so doing they have often eliminated the competition, sometimes by purchasing a local operator, sometimes by the default of that operator which was unable to face the onslaught of intensive local expansion by a larger competitor.

The idea of traffic hubs is not new. It was first tried by the Army Air Corps in 1934, then put into practice in the United States by Delta Air Lines, which discovered that its home base in Atlanta was an ideal stopping point for all travelers from the northeast and the Great Lakes region to the resort cities of Florida and the Gulf of Mexico. At first almost a necessity because of range limitations, the pattern became so well established that the northern-based public began to think of Delta instinctively when planning a visit to the South.

By the late 1970s, even before deregulation, and without necessarily assuming that the industry would be deregulated, the airlines turned their eyes and their planning departments towards the hub idea. Then, after 1978, there was a rush to establish them, or, in the case of airlines already flying transcontinental routes, to consolidate strategically-situated points on their routes as hubs. United at Chicago, American at Dallas/Fort Worth, T.W.A. at St. Louis, and Northwest at Minneapolis/St. Paul: all intensified their service patterns. Within a few years several regional airlines such as Ozark at St. Louis and Republic at Minneapolis had been absorbed by the dominant resident airlines, and the larger commuter airlines, as well as the two California intrastate carriers, were also scooped up.

Apart from the continued strong competition for transcontinental traffic by a whole selection of en route one-stop choices, one sequel to the hubbing trend has been that, as destination cities, competition has almost ceased to exist at the hubs. At Pittsburgh, no less than 85 percent of the air travelers fly by USAir, which uses Pittsburgh as its interchange hub and as a springboard from the northeast to and from the Midwest and the West. Similar near-monopoly situations exist at St. Louis (T.W.A. 82 percent), Salt Lake City (Delta, formerly Western, 80 percent), Minneapolis/St. Paul (Northwest, 78 percent), Houston (Continental, 77 percent), and so on.

Under deregulation, therefore, route systems are not more competitive, taken as a whole, as they were under the C.A.B. On heavily-traveled routes there is perhaps even more competition, but the reverse is also true on the thinner routes. The transcontinental routes offer a bigger choice, and the passenger can decide if he or she wishes to change aircraft at St. Louis, Chicago, Denver, Dallas, or even Houston or Minneapolis, not to mention Pittsburgh or Salt Lake City. Nevertheless, most non-stop flights are still being flown by the same carriers as before 1978: American, United, and T.W.A., with Northwest, Delta, and Continental on the fringes, perhaps. But for many cities in the U.S.A., the choice was diminished. Try going to Minneapolis without taking Northwest, or to St. Louis without T.W.A.!

Fares   Before deregulation, the C.A.B. had already become more conciliatory in its attitude towards experimental fares. Under the direction of Frank Lorenzo, Texas International had introduced the 'Peanuts' deep-discount fares program early in 1977, and other airlines had rushed to follow suit:

American, Eastern, and T.W.A., much in the same way in which they had jumped on the Capital Airlines coach fares bandwagon back in 1948. But with deregulation, the flood gates opened, and the airlines, now unrestricted in any way, began a frantic price war, transcontinental one-way at $98.00, New York to Florida $55.00. But the public quickly discovered that such bargains could only be obtained over heavily traveled routes, where high traffic resulted in low unit costs. Elsewhere, on routes of low traffic volume, fares increased and traffic declined in a marketing environment in which airlines were no longer obliged to serve certain points, i.e. to serve the public, if they felt that such service was too costly. In 1980, the cheapest way to fly from Philadelphia to Los Angeles was via New York, even including the taxi fare between airports. The old C.A.B.-supervised system of charging according to distance no longer applied. To those that had was given; to those that had not was taken away.

The aftermath of the competitive price wars, of course, was that they lasted only as long as a temporary advantage could be gained. Then the discounted fares either subsided, or became so difficult to find on complex schedules that they were of little use to anyone who could not, for instance, travel between a Thursday and a Monday, at night, or between the hours of 3 p.m. and 4:30 p.m. and pay for the privilege two months in advance—the example quoted is fictitious hyperbole, but serves to illustrate the point, and many sufferers would allege that truth has been stranger than fiction.

Today, fares are, with certain exceptions (which are not always easy to find) higher than they have ever been. One round of price wars led to severe casualties, with names such as Braniff disappearing from the ranks. Those that survived often did so only by merging—a euphemism for being taken over, lock, stock, and barrel. The dominant survivors are loathe to make the same mistake again of undercutting the price of the product to a suicidal level. Delta—neither an habitual fares slasher nor hiker—charged $152.00 one way day coach, Atlanta-Los Angeles, in 1974. The Standard (regular Economy Class) fare in 1994 was $651 (with a special at $345). In 1974, it was 62 percent higher than Atlanta-Miami, a difference almost exactly proportional to the distance. In 1990 it was only 48 percent. Yet, from time to time, airlines indulged in wildcat price wars, rather like neighbourhood gas stations; and on the whole systematically sold their product—the passenger-mile—more cheaply than it cost to produce. In 1992 alone, the U.S. airline industry lost about $3 billion.

In short, therefore, deregulation has not created as healthy and beneficial a competitive fare structure as was predicted. A *de facto* system has simply replaced a *de jure* one.

On-Board Service   There is little evidence to suggest that this has changed very much under deregulation, and if it has, then deregulation has had little to do with it. The quality of meals, or of amenitites, was the least regulated aspect of air travel in the United States before 1978. Even the C.A.B. did not dare to rule on the size of a hamburger or the meat content of a Salisbury Steak. Most seasoned and frequent travelers would agree that the standards have declined everywhere. Snack, service has become more frequent than meal service, which is now served only on flights of more than two or three hours, and sometimes not even then. Cynics might allege that the only competitive element is in testing the public to judge the level of austerity it will tolerate.

Ground Services   There is still no sign of better ground services, even though, in a deregulated environment, they could be. Air passengers still have to make their own way to the airports on freeways that have become ever more congested, and they have to park their cars in satellite carparks that creep further and further away from the airports. The time taken to go to an airport today is longer than it was in the 1970s, but to be fair, that has nothing to do with airline deregulation. A wise spokesman for the industry, Clement Keys, back in the late 1920s, once said that ninety percent of aviation was on the ground. Under deregulation, the airlines had a great chance to do something about the bottlenecks at each end of the air routes; but they have done nothing.

Freedom of Entry   While the Civil Aeronautics Board should have been roundly criticized from all sides for restricting the entry of such innovative aspirants as North American Airlines, Transocean Air Lines, or World Airways, the freedom of entry bequeathed to prospective airlines under deregulation has not been the cure-all that was originally forecast. The theory was that new, vigorous, energetic companies would give the incumbents a run for their money, by promoting new marketing techniques, and miraculously finding ways of doing things differently so that the public would flock to their booking offices. Alas, the reality did not follow the theory.

The statistics tell their own story, After 1978, 170 new airlines registered with the Department of Transportation, with full intentions of making names for themselves. Of these, about 150 are estimated to have gone bankrupt, or called a halt to their affairs before they did. Most of them never got off the ground—literally. Of all the new entrants, the new group, numbering perhaps a score or two, that, according to the deregulation theorists, was going to usher in a brave new world, only two remain today; and one of these was formerly an intrastate airline that at least was permitted to seek new fields to conquer outside its native Texas. Let us take our hats off to America West, Midway Airlines, and Southwest Airlines. They are to be congratulated for their ingenuity to enter into and to survive in an industry that was not about to open its doors to newcomers with a welcome mat. Each of the three has correctly identified an opportunity and matched its convictions with good planning and good marketing. America West spotted Phoenix as a hub opportunity that had somehow been passed up by the former trunk airlines. Midway built a hub of its own at the old Midway Airport, closer to downtown Chicago than O'Hare. And Southwest did the same at Love Field, in Dallas. These three were the success stories of deregulation; but three out of a 170 is too reminiscent of the old proverb about one swallow not making a summer. [Note: Since this was written, in 1990, America West moved into Chapter 11 bankruptcy, and Midway ceased operations. Only Herb Kelleher's Southwest Airlines has truly succeeded, *magna cum laude*.]

Against these isolated examples of the benefits of Freedom of Entry must, unfortunately, be cited the record of the complementary **Freedom of Exit,** an aspect of deregulation that was never mentioned much by the protagonists of the free market. But the history of the airlines of the United States since the Airline Deregulation Act of 1978 needs to be reviewed to preserve a sense of balance.

For while the C.A.B. could never be accused of opening doors for aspiring new airlines, equally it never shut doors on airlines that were in trouble and it never stood idly by to condone even the threat of a predatory takeover. Of the sixteen domestic trunk airlines that formed the framework of the air transport system of the U.S. when the C.A.B. assumed responsibility in 1938, five had disappeared between 1952 and 1961; but all these were carefully arranged mergers, presided over by an agency that ensured that the due process of the law was observed and that the essential service to the public, route, schedules, fares, and convenience, was preserved.

The course of history has run very differently since the Airline Deregulation Act of 1978. Consider what has happened to the airlines under the different categories recognized by the Civil Aeronautics Board:

The Trunks   Of the eleven remaining in 1978, five (National, Braniff, Eastern, Pan American, and Western) have disappeared altogether.

The Local Service, or Regionals   Of the original 26 that were formed in the immediate post-war era, nine had survived the hazards of operating mainly unprofitable sparsely-traveled route networks until 1978, one of them a former commuter airline (Air New England). Only one, USAir, exists today, having risen in status to join the newly-designated Majors, equivalent to the former trunks. All the others have been engulfed by their larger brethren. Piedmont Airlines was the last, before going to US-Air. Charles Darwin would have recognized the process.

The Intrastates   Recognized by, but not controlled by the C.A.B., three major intrastate airlines (P.S.A., Air California, and Southwest) plus a newcomer, Muse Air, did very well before deregulation. They then burst out beyond their state borders, to compete with other interstate airlines. Only one, Southwest, remains, vigorously successful under the inspired leadership of its flamboyant chief, Herb Kelleher.

The All-Cargo Carriers   They were on their way out before deregulation. Now even Flying Tigers, which for more than forty years epitomized the air freight business, is gone, having been purchased by Federal Express.

The Territorials   This designation had already become redundant when Alaska and Hawaii attained statehood. Ironically, deregulation, that was supposed to encourage competition, has enabled Alaska Airlines to become a near-monopoly in its home state.

The Commuter Airlines   Most of these have become dependents of, if they have not been purchased outright, by the large major airlines, under the code-sharing autocracy of the omnipotent computer reservation system.

The Supplementals   Having unsuccessfully striven to obtain authority to operate scheduled routes under the C.A.B., the larger supplemental airlines such as World, Transamerica, and Capitol, (not Capital, mentioned earlier) leaped into the arena after deregulation. All except World have disappeared, and even World has gone back to its former non-scheduled status.

So much for the airlines as classified under the C.A.B., which in today's world, is arguably irrelevant; but what about the airlines as classified after deregulation—by the C.A.B., incidentally, in its twilight years as its functions were redistributed, mainly into the Department of Transportation? There are eight Majors, but only three of the next-ranking category, the Nationals, remain: Southwest Airways, America West, and Midway Airlines, the last two being the hardy survivors, as reviewed above. With Alaska Airlines, this means that a total of only ten airlines controls the airways of the United States today. This is fewer than the number of Trunk airlines *alone* at the time of the Airline Deregulation Act.

The effect of this piece of legislation has not been, therefore, to encourage competition by the predicted entry of highly-efficient new airlines that would proceed to show the establishment how to do things better; but to create an almost completely unrestricted business environment in which all the medium-sized and small airlines have disappeared off the map. Deregulation has, in fact, introduced the air traveling public to the doubtful joys of an oligopoly which is coming dangerously close to opening the door, in many situations such as the concentrated hubs discussed above, to local monopolies. There is a temptation to coin a new word: monoligopoly.

In the years gone by, fingers used to be pointed (to no avail) to the fact that about 75 percent of the airline business was concentrated in the activities of about eight or nine airlines—the number varied a little up and down within a fairly narrow margin. Today six airlines control about 84 percent of the market share and about 90 percent of the turnover. There are mutterings about a return to a regulated industry as a last resort to avoid the dangers of a near-monopoly. The next cold wind of even a mild recession will almost certainly lead to a reduction in the surviving few. This would be a bitter blow to the advocates of deregulation as an incentive to competition that would benefit the public. But to review the facts, as enumerated in this essay, is to demonstrate that, whatever the advantages of deregulation, competition is not one of them.

Short Take-Off and Landing (STOL)
(and Commercial Helicopters)
(1960s–1980s)

nthusiasm in the aviation community for the idea of developing and operating an aircraft with short take-off and landing capabilities evolved during the 1960s. The era of piston-engined aircraft on the world's trunk air routes was giving way to turbine-powered generations of faster and more economical types. Although the Comet 1's dramatic introduction in 1952, to startle the airline world and provide a glimpse of vast new horizons, had been short-lived, the momentum had begun. The Boeing 707s and Douglas DC-8s particularly, with the new Comets and the Caravelles close behind, ushered in a dynamic new era in 1958, one which, accelerating airline traffic growth as it did during the 1960s, brought with it new problems.

Throughout the 1960s, the annual growth of air traffic world-wide, and including the United States domestic market, increased at an average rate of 15 percent. The world total thus quadrupled in a decade, and one inevitable result was that airports became busier and the ones at the biggest traffic hubs, the larger metropolises, almost burst at the seams. This led to considerable attention being given not only to the expansion of existing airports, but to the construction of additional ones. Many of the big cities laid down plans for secondary airports or new international ones to supersede the old ones; some hitherto neglected airports gained a new lease of life as a solution to the increasing congestion; and many schemes were floated on the idea of laying down small airstrips in suburban areas so as to utilize smaller aircraft with short landing and take-off (STOL) capacity, and thus further relieve the congestion at the main hubs.

One operating factor favored the STOL idea. Most of the demand for relief at the congested airport terminals coincided with short-haul routes,

139

mostly of 300 miles or less. This was because the traffic density on individual city pairs varies broadly according to a formula generally referred to as the gravity model. Although variations from the basic trend occur because of differing levels of wealth or of city function, passenger traffic varies directly with the population and inversely with the stage length, or distance. A simplified formula states that the relationship between traffic volumes on a selected list of city pairs varies according to the product of the populations, divided by the distance—although there are subtle variations on the theme. A tabulation based on this formula invariably reveals that the busiest routes—and therefore the ones most vulnerable to congestion, and coincidentally the ones open to consideration for the application of the short take-off and landing principle—STOL—are relatively short, and between big cities.

An additional incentive to examine STOL closely is to realize that, at such short distances, few city pairs seem worth operating if they are less than 200 miles apart. Except in the United States, the convenience of surface transport outweighs the inconvenience of going to and from the airports, which are normally situated far enough away from the city centers to make the journey by air a tedious one. Occasionally, where airports happen to be, by the fortunate foresight of past generations of airport planners, close to the city center, 200-mile journeys by air are marginally convenient. Examples are the Ponte Aérea between Rio de Janeiro and São Paulo, in Brazil; and between Washington, D.C., and New York. But these are the exceptions to the rule. At most large cities, those of giant stature, say with metropolitan populations exceeding 5 million, the airports tend to be on the fringes of the built-up areas.

In many countries, rail services have been brought to a high standard of speed and comfort, stemming from a revolution in progress when the first Shin Kansen high speed rail line opened in Japan in 1964. Throughout Japan and Europe today, the large cities are linked by 125-mph trains—and some even faster—that have the great advantage of penetrating the suburbs and taking the passengers straight into the downtown railroad stations. The only route in the United States that qualifies to rank among these élite railroad routes is the Amtrak Metroliner track between Washington, D.C., and Pennsylvania Station, in New York's Manhattan. Elsewhere, surface opportunities have been neglected and so, with improved economics available for small aircraft because of the refinements of turboprop engines, the way seemed open for the application of some ingenuity by imaginative project engineers at the aircraft factories, working in conjunction with enterprising airlines.

By definition, the range required of a short-field suburban-located airliner is short, a maximum of perhaps 300 miles. The fuel load necessary is therefore correspondingly small; and this, at least, is a trade-off for the extra

Curiously, these pictures of (top) a Sikorsky S-39 amphibian, and (Bottom) a Cessna C-37 floatplane, illustrate a practical demonstration of the objectives of STOL operations. Able to provide service to a terminus on New York's East River, it brought the advantages of air transport into the center of a big city. (Dennis Wrynn collection)

power and fuel consumption needed for the high-performance take-off characteristics that are essential for short-field use. With such an aircraft, all that was needed, it was popularly thought, was a selection of open spaces, such as large parks, somewhere in the suburbs of large cities; and, more ambitiously, could not use be made of disused sites, such as redundant railroad yards, closer in even to the city centers? In some cities, where an abundant surplus of water areas seemed available, especially in large ports, the gradual decline of shipping suggested that STOL airports might offer waterside access to the downtown business districts, a case of one new transport mode replacing the old. As enthusiasm grew for the STOL concept, the possibilities seemed endless, and in London, for example, one scheme was offered in which the rooftops of railway stations would be converted into STOLports.

One inhibiting factor, in the early days of STOLmania, was the presence of the commercial helicopter, which had shown great promise, leading to the creation of small helicopter networks at the larger cities of the United States, and other applications in Europe. The helicopter, in fact, was more than a short take-off and landing vehicle; it was a vertical take-off and landing vehicle, or VTOL, requiring little more than a patch of land not much bigger than a basketball court. Rooftop convenience was entirely possible, and the most successful demonstration of such obvious convenience was Pan American Airways' helicopter station on the top of the Pan Am Building at Grand Central Station on Park Avenue, New York. As long as the VTOL helicopters prevailed, the protagonists for STOL had their work cut out.

The basic engineering principles of the helicopter had already been worked out and convincingly demonstrated by the distinguished aeronautical engineer, Igor Sikorsky, who was the presiding genius over a group of contemporaries who also made and perfected working helicopters. After two previous careers (as a leading designer in pre-World War I Tzarist Russia, and in building large flying boats, mainly for Pan American Airways) Sikorsky had finally solved the intricate mechanical, transmission, and aerodynamic problems, to produce the world's first practical helicopter, the VS-300, in 1939. Subsequently developed by Sikorsky himself, Bell, and Piasecki in the U.S.; by Westland in the U.K.; and by Mil and Kamov in the Soviet Union, helicopters had grown bigger. Some had dual rotary wings, and with improved operating economics, were beginning to qualify for air transport applications.

At first there were prospects of success. In the U.S.A., Los Angeles Airways began passenger services in the summer of 1951, after a four-year experimental period carrying mail. The network was quite extensive, stretching from the Los Angeles International Airport to the northern suburbs in the San Fernando Valley, along the coast eastwards as far as Newport Beach, and far inland as Riverside and San Bernardino. Other large cities followed suit. New York Airways began passenger helicopter services in July 1952, to serve Trenton, New Jersey, and later to link a terminal on the East River near the Wall Street business district with New York's three airports at La Guardia, J.F. Kennedy on Long Island, and Newark, New Jersey. Helicopter Air Services of Chicago began service in November 1954, and later, San Francisco & Oakland Helicopter Airlines (SFO) became the fourth U.S. passenger helicopter operator, starting in June 1961.

The airline community had been reluctant to start wide-spread helicopter services, mainly because the aircraft were quite small. The Sikorsky S-51 had only four seats, the S-55 had seven, and the S-58 had twelve. The first transport helicopter to have its cabin arranged like that of a conventional airliner was the Vertol (formerly Piasecki) 44B, but even this had only fifteen seats—all on the starboard side of the cabin, with space for baggage on the left. The cost of the technology inherent in helicopter design was high and was reflected in both the purchasing and the operating costs. If the airlines were concerned, the Civil Aeronautics Board and the Congress alike were deeply suspicious, as the total subsidies required to sustain the helicopter airlines mounted each year. Finally, Congress terminated the subsidy altogether, on 11 April 1965. Chicago Helicopter Airways ceased operations at the end of the year, while the New York and Los Angeles companies survived for a few years longer only because they were assisted in different ways from large trunk airlines in partnership arrangements. Even SFO, which had not been subsidized, but had had the advantage of operating the more economical Sikorsky S-61L 28-seat helicopters, had to make similar agreements with the trunk airlines.

One notable exception to the predominantly intra-urban nature of scheduled helicopter services was the prolonged experiment by SABENA, the Belgian national airline. Recognizing the strategically-positioned geographical location of Brussels, epicenter of the assembly of large cities and metropolitan areas in the northwestern part of Europe, SABENA started first mail, then passenger helicopter services in 1953. A passenger could board the flight just outside the Nord Station in the center of Brussels, and fly to Rotterdam, Paris, Dortmund, or Cologne. British European Airways also began helicopter services from the southwestern tip of England to the Scilly Isles, and exceptionally, these have continued to the present day, under other managements. In the Soviet Union too, there are many helicopter services, in regions where airfield standards are often poor, because of extreme conditions of terrain.

In general, however, helicopter services have never paid for themselves. The inherent high costs of manufacture and operation militate against

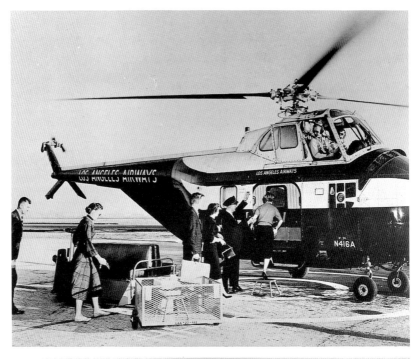

Extensive experience with the commercial helicopter in the major cities of the United States during the 1960s was ultimately unsuccessful. But this was not for want of perseverence. These pictures show a Sikorsky S-55 of Los Angeles Airways, a Sikorsky S-58 of Chicago Helicopter Airways, a Sikorsky S-61, also from Los Angeles, and a Vertol 107 of New York Airways. Both the high operating costs and the disappointing safety record were unacceptable. (United Technologies/ Vertol)

profit-making. Some form of subsidy is always required, directly from a benign government, or indirectly by cross-subsidy. The power requirements needed to lift large aircraft vertically off the ground impose unacceptably costly high fuel consumption. The complex transmission and gearing necessary to ensure perfect rotary wing rotation and control impose heavy maintenance demands. And lurking in the minds of operator and customer alike was always the suspicion that helicopters were dangerous.

The helicopter had been susceptible to the charge of unreliability, because an engine failure could, at best, condemn the aircraft to a high-risk autorotational descent; while, at worst, a rotor-blade failure or fracture would remove even that hope. Well-disciplined maintenance and operational standards had kept the helicopter airlines going for several years, albeit with a generous subsidy to offset the costs; but one crash was bound to be spectacular and well-publicized, simply because it was destined to occur within, or very close to inhabited areas. A helicopter crash in Chicago or New York would attract as much adverse publicity as a mid-air airliner collision in Africa.

Eventually, the laws of probability caught up. Two Los Angeles Airways Sikorsky S-61s crashed in the summer of 1968, killing a total of 44 passengers. This seemed to confirm suspicions about the inherent safety of helicopter operations. Stringent precautions were taken to prevent a recurrence, with additional maintenance checks added to an already severe schedule aimed to produce fail-safe flying. But nine years later came a spectacular incident that heralded the end of intra-city helicopter operations.

With commendable enterprise and imagination, Pan American Airways and T.W.A. supported the New York helicopter operation, after the C.A.B. canceled the subsidy. On 21 December 1965, helicopter service from John F. Kennedy Airport was dramatically inaugurated to the top of the Pan Am Building in New York. This was almost in defiance of the consensus of views about the inherent vulnerability of helicopters, and was preceded by an experimental series of flights to test the feasibility. For the passenger, it was probably the best deal in the airline business anywhere in the world. Seventeen daily flights each took only seven minutes to make the journey from rooftop to ramp. The fare was $7.00 one way, $10.00 round trip. Check-in time at the Pan Am Building was only 45 minutes before take-off.

All went well until one fatal day, 16 May 1977. Another S-61—the same type that crashed in Los Angeles in 1968—tipped over on its side on the Pan Am Building rooftop, just as passengers were boarding. Rotor blades sheered, and the shattered pieces flew off, one straight down to the street below and one into a window, shattering glass. Four of the boarding passengers were killed, and so was a pedestrian two blocks away, hit by the rotor blade.

During the early 1950s, the Belgian airline, SABENA, made a good attempt to introduce helicopter services between the downtown areas of some of the larger cities of the Low Countries and the Ruhr-Rhine region of western Germany. These pictures show (top) a Sikorsky S-55, and (bottom) a Sikorsky S-58, the latter in the middle of Rotterdam. (SABENA)

were killed, and so was a pedestrian two blocks away, hit by the rotor blade. The spectacle of a rain of helicopter parts on the streets of New York was indelibly impregnated into the hearts and minds of the U.S. regulatory agencies and the traveling public alike. When another S-61L crashed on take-off at Newark on 18 April 1979, New York Airways was forced to close down.

During the era of the scheduled service helicopter operations in the United States, lasting from the early 1950s to that time, studies had been made with direct-thrust vertical take-off and landing aircraft (VTOL). These led to the convincing conclusion that such operations would be economically impossible. The power to lift a vehicle vertically off the ground had to exceed the all-up weight by a comfortable margin. The costs of so doing were prohibitive and VTOL applications were confined to military developments, with notable success in the case of the British Hawker Siddeley Harrier fighter, which was further developed in the U.S.A. as the McDonnell Douglas AV-8.

The failure of the commercial helicopter and the irrelevance of VTOL did not deter aeronautical designers and project engineers the world over, who now concentrated their efforts on what appeared to be a sensible compromise between vertical (VTOL) and conventional (C.T.O.L.) take-off and landing aircraft. Matching engine power to aircraft size and weight has always been the prime concern in achieving the ideal specification for a commercial airliner. The minimum power, to obtain maximum economical fuel consumption during the cruising segment of the total flight, can be achieved only at the expense of take-off performance and the consequent need for long take-off runs and therefore long runways. Conventional (C.T.O.L.) aircraft manufacturers tended towards this solution in concentrated and competitive efforts to attain maximum payload capacity (and therefore maximized profitability) combined with maximum fuel capacity, to fly ever further, to achieve ever more stringent targets of range across continents and oceans. The 2,000-mile range of the 40-seat DC-4 of 1945 had become the 4,000-mile range of the 160-seat Boeing 707 as early as 1958, and the 6,000-mile 360-seat Boeing 747 by 1970.

The manufacturers were able to achieve these commendable levels of performance only because of the generosity, even indulgence, of the airport authorities. Countries, states, and municipalities alike cheerfully extended runways by half a mile or more, laying down concrete with great prodigality; and built new airports to cope with successive generations of bigger and more demanding airliners. But these were land-hungry exercises in real-estate development and the land itself was available only outside the city limits, often almost a short airplane ride's distance from the city center. Even if strips of land could be found fairly close to the downtown areas, considerations of safety and noise usually put an end to any serious attempts to place jet airports any nearer than the existing facilities. Indeed, the reverse was the case, as restrictions on jet operations, or at least long-range jet operations, were sometimes placed on otherwise good airports, Washington National being a good example.

A compromise solution, therefore, seemed to be a logical direction for all good project engineers to follow. Why not split the difference, so to speak, between the unacceptable power requirements of VTOL and the land usage demands of C.T.O.L.? If aircraft could be designed especially for a defined need of STOL, could this not fill the gap? Efforts were directed towards advanced lifting devices such as leading edge flaps and spoilers, boundary layer lift, combined with engines that had a wide range of power, for take-off and cruise, so that runway lengths could be shortened without compromising overall economy.

The designers and engineers went to work with great gusto, producing many respectable prototype designs and even occasionally prototype aircraft. The most promising of these was the French Breguet 941S, a four-engined high-winged airliner that could carry 52 passengers over a distance of 250 miles, yet require a take-off distance of only 1,500 feet at sea level on a standard day. This specification seemed so attractive for many of the world's busiest air routes that a close examination was made of the market possibilities. Attention was focused on the Boston-New York-Washington air corridor, about 450 miles long, with a population of more than 40 million, and containing dense concentrations of urban dwellers at New York, Boston, Philadelphia, Baltimore, and Washington. Much to Breguet's satisfaction, no doubt, one of the four 941Ss built was dispatched to New York, under the aegis of an agreement with McDonnell Douglas, the newly merged amalgamation of the military aircraft manufacturer McDonnell and the predominantly commercial manufacturer, Douglas. Under a licensing agreement, the Breguet 941S became the McDonnell Douglas 188.

A series of much-publicized experimental flights were made in the 'Boswash' air corridor, accompanied by the usual brochuremanship, in which, however, like those advocating the SST, the main arguments seemed to be a combination of wishful thinking and special pleading. Certainly, the 188's performance was excellent. Its take-off characteristics at LaGuardia impressed all who witnessed the experimental flights. But the aircraft's take-off in the marketing sense was markedly unimpressive. The combined efforts of manufacturer, journalists, publicity agents, and consultants (always ready to stretch a point or two) did not impress the potential customer—Eastern Air Lines, for instance—even to the stage of signing a non-committal Letter of

Intent. Unable to make either an economic or an operational case with conviction, the Breguet 941S/McDonnell Douglas 188 failed in its campaign to make the case for intercity STOL operations and the prototypes quickly became museum pieces.

Since the mid-1960s, there have been many ingenious projects to discover ways in which the advantages of vertical take-off can be combined with normal cruising aircraft behavior. Conversion from one to the other was—and still is—thought by many to be a feasible solution, using vectored thrust by mechanical means, that is, actually to change the direction of thrust from the vertical to the horizontal. Over the years, there have been the Ryan XV-5A Fan-in-Wing project of the mid-1960s, the Bell XV-3 tilt-rotor aircraft, started in 1952 and finally abandoned in 1966; and the Bell XV-15 tilt-rotor, a $50-million program started in 1971 and funded partly by National Aeronautics and Space Administration (NASA), partly by the Army, which was demonstrated with some success until the early 1980s, but which served only to lay the groundwork for the V-22 Osprey Tilt-Rotor Airplane, the product of a partnership between Bell and Boeing Vertol. This, the latest of the attempts to overcome the difficulties of vectoring the thrust of propellers through an angle of 90°, has also been dropped by the Pentagon.

The development costs of these projects alone have run into hundreds of millions of dollars. Although commercial versions of the essentially military designs have been mooted, no serious attempt has been made to promote or to market them. Underlying all the superficially reasonable arguments to prove their worth is a widespread feeling, stemming from aeronautical engineers to the lay public alike, that these clever constructions are the toys of imaginative minds, and not to be taken seriously as a means of going from A to B.

But the STOL principle still has its backers, encouraged by the partial success of the string of excellent aircraft that have come off the production lines of the de Havilland Canada company, later a division of the all-embracing Boeing Company, and now Bombardier. First the DHC-6 Twin Otter demonstrated a commendable short field performance, able to take-off, if required, from perimeter tracks or taxiways. In 1966, the DHC-5 Buffalo caused a minor sensation when it delivered an 80-piece field hospital, weighing a total of three tons, into a small baseball diamond on New York's East River. Succeeding the ubiquitous DHC-6, which had won worldwide approval for short-haul commuter service as well as the bush operations for which it was designed, the larger, four-engined DHC Dash 7 offered similar STOL performance.

The de Havilland (Canada) DHC-6 Twin Otter came as close as any other small commercial airliner to practical STOL operations during the 1960s and 1970s. It was a familiar sight all over the U.S. This one, of California's Cable Commuter, is pictured at Ontario Airport. (Cable)

One outstanding success story for the STOL idea has seen the marriage of this versatile aircraft with a genuine STOLport. This latter, however, came about as the result of a combination of circumstances that will seldom be repeated. In England, London's dockland area, once the largest port in the world, had become a wasteland, and among the many rebuilding projects was the construction of a STOL runway along one of the fingers of land that was formerly a forest of cranes and warehouses separating the Royal Albert and the King George V Docks. The site is only six miles from the business district of the City of London, and a light rail connection was constructed to link the city center with the new development area.

The London City Airport, as it is called, possesses all the elements necessary for the successful launching of the STOL idea for air transport. The short runway—2,500 feet long—is matched by an aircraft able to use it, the British Aircraft Corporation's BAe 146. No other airport is even half as close to the city center; and there is an excellent ground link between the airport and the center. And here lies the explanation of why STOL arrangements such as in London's docklands have not succeeded elsewhere. A STOL air service is a system, not simply an aircraft. It is not only an aircraft matched to a short runway. It has to be an integrated transport system that provides direct and convenient connection between the STOLport and the city center (or other preferred destination); and furthermore the combination must offer a clear-cut advantage over alternative routes.

In short, STOL service must be a demonstrably superior *system* if it is to succeed. Most of the investment has gone into the design of aircraft that can take off and land at short fields (and achieve the sharp angles of take off and descent) and has been concentrated on that sole objective. Very little has been spent on examining the *practical* problems of dispersing or assembling the passengers, even though schematic diagrams have proliferated in the promotional brochures. Thus, the promising Dash 7, unable to find the practical, as opposed to the theoretical niche, for its deployment, ceased production at the 113th aircraft off the line.

The STOL market researchers should have done a little traveling and familiarized themselves with the hard facts of city life in the world's big cities. In Los Angeles, for example, where arguably there were many tracts of land spacious enough for the construction of a network of STOLports, there were already quite a few airports where orthodox transport aircraft were at home. In addition to Los Angeles International, Burbank, Long Beach, Orange County, and Ontario were only the larger of about a dozen existing fields. But where is the surface transport infrastructure? Los Angeles once had the world's finest urban transit system, the Pacific Electric Railway, affectionately known as the Red Cars, but this precious asset was trashed after World War II in a frenzy of freeway mania designed to ensure that Angelinos were obliged to own and operate at least one automobile to maintain a minimally acceptable life style. And once an air passenger is obliged to drive, there is little incentive to drive to a local STOLport to connect with a main terminal when a few minutes longer drive will take him or her to the terminal itself.

And Los Angeles is exceptionally fortunate in the availability of potential STOLport sites, because of its enormous area. Cities such as New York, Chicago, Philadelphia, or Detroit—to name some of the larger ones in the U.S.—are not so lucky. Even though they have fields close to the city that can be served by standard short-haul airliners, or at a waterside site, say on the Hudson River, attempts to establish STOLports have failed because of apprehension on the grounds of safety. Flying low in heavily populated areas opens up considerably the scope of potential vulnerability.

STOL market studies have also failed to take into account two very important factors. The first is that the dispersal of, say, a passenger market hitherto concentrated at one airport into, say, three STOL airports within a convenient radius, also disperses the supporting infrastructure. The airline has three stations to equip, to staff, and to maintain instead of one; and this costs more money. The second is that by fragmenting the air journey from, say, one 150-seat DC-9 into three 50-seat Dash 7s, the airspace has been further congested by a factor of three; and such situations invariably exist in air corridors where the en route air congestion is already perilously close to the saturation point.

Contrary to accepted theory, the idea that the typical STOL route requirement is from a suburban area to a city center is open to question. Many passengers wish to go from one suburban precinct to another; while some wish to go from one city center to another. And where is the city center? This author's wife once asked the hotel concierge in Los Angeles "Where can I take a bus to the city center?" He replied "Lady, first there ain't no city center, and second, there ain't no bus." Certainly, in some of the newer nuclei of commerce, such as Dallas, Atlanta, and Houston, the business centers seem to be concentrated into a critical mass; but for as many cities such as these, there are as many that are witnessing the dispersal of the city centers into satellite business centers. And as cities become cordilleras of high-rise skyscrapers, the hazards of flying increase and the desire to conserve the few open spaces for parks and recreation overcomes the desire to develop a downtown airport.

The prospects, therefore, for the universal application of STOL aircraft are slim, mainly because the possibilities for providing the essential surface infrastructure are slimmer. The almost complete absence of, or the desire to construct a coordinated urban rail or other public transport system is an astonishing phenomenon of the commercial world in the United States today. The severe shortage of suitable sites has to be faced squarely. The more suitable the site, the more objections, on recreational, safety, pollution, or noise grounds, are likely to be raised. New York's Central Park would be ideal for a STOLport; and so would London's Hyde Park, or Paris's Bois de Boulogne. But to encroach on such precious amenities is unthinkable, as is the prospect of STOL aircraft buzzing into and out of residential areas that cherish their serenity, and for which the residents often paid dearly, is not attractive.

To repeat: STOL must be recognized not as a high performance airplane; it must be developed as an elaborate integrated system. The conditions that permitted the development of the London City Airport are unlikely to be repeated elsewhere, and so the world market potential is low. The elements of performance for an aircraft to qualify as a STOLplane have never been

the problem is, as some cynics have observed, to lay down another 1,000 feet of concrete at an existing airport.

This picture of the London City Airport is a rare example of a large metropolitan area that was able to find sufficient space for an airstrip close to its city center. This was possible only because London's docklands had been abandoned. Such a convenient combination of availability matching a need is unlikely to be widely repeated elsewhere.

The Specialized Commercial Air Freighter (1946–1966)

F or little more than two decades after World War II, or perhaps for about a quarter of a century, from 1956 until 1970, there was a certain enthusiasm in aircraft manufacturing circles, varying from mild interest to fanatical promotion, for the development of commercial aircraft that were designed specifically to carry air freight, to the total exclusion of passengers. This led to the widespread belief that there was an enormous market for the specialized freighter aircraft that would meet the traffic demand often described as the Sleeping Giant of air transport.

The fallacy did not stem entirely from false market forecasts or expectations, although this was part of the problem. There was a large market, though hardly of giant proportions; but the misunderstanding of how to meet the market demand sometimes led aircraft designers into the realms of fantasy.

The self-deception in the aviation community, especially during the 1950s, filtered down throughout the world of commerce, which was often misled by the grandiose forecasts and gave tacit support to the sometimes unrealistic schemes put forward to build freighter aircraft as big as merchant ships. The promotion and publicity also spread to the politicians and the general public, who gained the impression that the world's airways would be congested by freight airliners that would challenge the passenger 'planes for priority. During the 1960s, in fact, some manufacturers, armed with (or hypnotized by) impressive-looking reports from hired consultants, as well as by their own self-serving studies, even went so far as to claim that, within a few years, the Sleeping Giant of air cargo would overtake the passenger market.

Alas, the truth was nowhere near this imaginary pipedream. Even today, with all the increased efficiency of modern fan-jet airliners, air freight comprises only about 15 percent of the total tonnage carried, and only 12 percent of the revenues earned by the world's airlines. The vast majority of this is

During the early years after World War I, some attempts were made to demon-strate practical air freighting. The top picture shows a Junkers-G 31 loading up on the Berlin-London route in the late 1920s. The lower picture is of a more un-orthodox operation, in which a Ford Tri-Motor was modified with a large door so as to accommodate special consignments. These were destined to otherwise inac-cessible locations in jungle and mountainous regions of Central America. (Lufthansa and TACA Airlines)

carried in the belly holds or in specially allocated sections of the main decks of the wide-bodied passenger jets, or in freighter versions of the same types. The world's air cargo has, in fact, settled down to a daily round of hitching a ride with the passengers, or in aircraft designed for passengers.

'Twas not always thus. In the deep, distant past, during the formative years of air transport, there were isolated examples of specialized freighter airplanes performing tasks that could not be achieved by any form of surface transport. One classic case was in New Guinea, where gold had been discovered in substantial quantities in 1926, but unfortunately up an inaccessible creek forty miles from the coast in mountainous jungle. The trek from the coast took eight to ten days, and even poorly paid porters were expensive; and the journey was marked by the presence of hostile tribesmen. The problem was solved by the introduction of a fleet of four metal-built Junkers-G 31s, sturdy aircraft with large freight doors on the side and on the top, which proceeded to provide a superb transport service. Among their efforts was the transport of several enormous gold dredges, a star performance that helped Guinea Airways to claim that, during the fiscal year 1931-32, it carried almost as much freight as the whole of Europe combined, and eight times as much as by all the airlines of the United States put together.

This use of a commercial aircraft as a specialized freighter was echoed in Central America where, during the 1930s, Lowell Yerex, an enterprising New Zealander, built up a network of airlines under the parental title of Transportes Aéreos Centro-Americanos (TACA) and performed some unbelievable feats with Ford Tri-Motors converted to carry bulky loads by having half the side of the fuselage ripped out. But these were isolated examples of special requirements of a temporary nature. Although in Germany Junkers built aircraft that were intended for the carriage of freight, the market was very limited. Deutsche Luft Hansa did attempt to start an all-freight service in the late 1920s but the problem was that the air service was little quicker, but much more expensive than the railroad's.

Sometimes forgotten is the fact that the ubiquitous Douglas DC-3, widely regarded as the jack-of-all-trades because of its wartime and post-war prowess in carrying every kind of commodity to every corner of the globe, was designed as and produced as a passenger airliner, with little or no thought to the freight market. Only when it had demonstrated a level of reliability and versatility as a passenger-carrier with the airlines did the U.S. armed forces recognize its potential and order cargo versions, notably the C-47, to meet the formidable logistics challenges of World War II.

At the end of hostilities, in 1945, huge fleets of war-surplus Douglas C-47s, together with substantial numbers of Curtiss C-46s, able to carry twice

The Curtiss C-46 was a workhorse for carrying freight during the latter years of World War II and the immediate post-World War II era, when thousands of ex-military transports became available for civilian use. (Riddle Air Lines)

the cargo load of a C-47, and augmented by some Douglas four-engined C-54s, plus a few converted Consolidated B-24 and Boeing B-17 bombers, combined to provide an armada of potential commercial air cargo aircraft. They could be obtained very cheaply—even for a few hundred dollars each— and a legion of non-scheduled tramp airlines started business in the U.S. immediately after their pilot-owners were demobilized. To a lesser extent, this happened elsewhere in the world, particularly in regions where surface transport was poor or non-existent, such as in South America or China.

There were also special opportunities, born of special emergencies. During World War II, from 1943 to 1945, a splendid example of rising to the occasion had been set by the U.S.A.A.F. Air Transport Command, aided by China National Aviation Company, in transporting tens of thousands of tons of supplies from India to the China theater in an operation that became known as the "Hump" from the formidable nature of the towering mountain peaks that had to be crossed en route. Douglas C-47s and Consolidated C-87s were used, but the aircraft hero of the hour was the sometimes maligned Curtiss C-46, which by continuous operation against all odds, gave a new dimension to the practice of carrying air freight.

The lessons of the Hump were not forgotten, when, in 1948, in a bitter aftermath of the war, the Soviet authorities abruptly cut off all surface communications from West Berlin to the west, across East Germany. During the second half of the year, the air forces and airlines of the United States and Great Britain combined to perform miracles of air cargo transport, carrying everything from bulk loads of desperately-needed coal, to see the people through the winter, to Christmas presents for the children. Douglas DC-3s and DC-4s (C-47s and C-54s) provided the bulk of the American effort; while the British also used C-47s as well as the Avro Tudor, operated successfully by Freddie Laker, and even Short flying boats, whose hulls were salt-resistant and therefore ideal for carrying that commodity.

Such activity may have given rise to the expectation of a large potential market for air freight and to the thought that, if the market was indeed a large one, then a specialized aircraft should be built for it. Attempts to design and to operate such types had already been made. In the United States, the National Skyway Freight Corporation—later to become the Flying Tiger Line—introduced the Budd Conestoga, which at the time must have appeared strange, even though the general principle was sound, and echoed in later years by the highly successful Lockheed Hercules. The Conestoga had a rear access door that permitted freight to be loaded in a far more convenient manner than through the side. The whole aircraft was built of stainless steel, and was not a success; but it was a brave attempt to break an orthodox trend by an innovative idea.

Another ugly duckling, on the other side of the Atlantic, was the Bristol 170 Wayfarer, or Bristol Freighter. This was an orthodox 'tail-sitter' which ingeniously placed the cockpit on the top of the fuselage, so as to allow a direct access into the square-shaped fuselage through the front. It first went into service in 1945 as a passenger aircraft but was quickly adopted as a freighter, and was so called. But its main claim to fame was in inaugurating the world's first car ferry service, operated by Silver City Airways, from July 1948, and followed by Air Charter (Freddie Laker again) in 1956. For many

Two 'ugly ducklings' specifically designed to carry air freight during the 1940s were (top) in the United States, the stainless steel Budd Conestoga, with rear-end fuselage loading; and (bottom), in Great Britain, the Bristol Freighter, with front-end loading. many of these latter were specially adapted as car-ferries, and did a roaring trade across the English Channel. (Flying Tigers and Bristol Aircraft Company)

years, fleets of Bristol Freighters carried tens of thousands of cars across the English Channel, and reigned supreme until the hovercraft (air cushion vehicles) introduced an even better way for British tourists to reach the routes nationales that led to the French Riviera or the Costa Brava.

Always on the lookout for a new opportunity, Freddie Laker—now of Aviation Traders Ltd.—used the Bristol Freighter design idea to produce a larger aircraft in the same mold. In his own workshops at Southend, England, he converted some old C-54s into ATL 98 Carvairs. These were equipped with the over-deck cockpit, like the Budds and the Bristol 170s, so that the fuselage could accommodate five cars instead of the Bristol's three. The DC-4/C-54 fuselage also made it easier to insert the cars, a tricky operation in the 170, necessitating very small company drivers who, having driven the car in, had to escape through the window.

The Bristol 170 may have been one of the great missed opportunities of the British aircraft industry, which seemed to specialize in such conduct of its affairs. The ugly but eminently practical duckling even had some overseas orders, but Bristol gave little follow-up support, even though it sold about 200 aircraft, no mean achievement for a post-war aircraft in the face of war-surplus availability of DC-3s, converted back to all-purpose civil versions of the C-47.

Bristol's moderate success may have influenced a member of the Hawker-Siddeley Aircraft Corporation to develop a specialized air freighter, based on the same basic principle of eliminating side loading of freight. It combined the rear-end loading of the Budd with the front-end loading of the Bristol, although any direct connection in the thought process behind the Armstrong-Whitworth Argosy and the earlier freighters is unlikely. The Argosy was an original. The front- and end-loading was achieved by mounting the tailplane on twin booms, thus isolating the fuselage. Powered by four Rolls-Royce Dart turbine engines, it was a good performer and a sensible solution to accelerating the time-consuming loading and unloading of freight, which, on the Argosy, could be done simultaneously rather than sequentially. A few aircraft were even sold in 1959 in the United States, to Riddle Airlines, but these were redundant when the airline lost an important military logistics contract. Some saw service with British European Airways and others ended up doing solid work carrying beef in Western Australia and providing an excellent air ferry service between the North and South Islands of New Zealand. Like the Bristol Freighter, the Argosy deserved a better fate, but only a few were sold as the specialized design and the turboprop power were expensive compared to the second- or third-hand DC-3s or C-46s otherwise available at knock-down prices.

In the United States, the development of specialized air freighters was on a different plane. A few of the larger non-scheduled airlines had progressed to be recognized as Large Irregular carriers by the Civil Aeronautics Board and a few had settled down to the precarious life of being certificated all-cargo carriers. Severely restricted by route certificates that hemmed them in to only a few routes, airlines such as Flying Tigers, Slick Airways, Riddle Airlines (which became Airlift International) and Seaboard & Western managed to eke out an existence, even to the point of forcing the major domestic trunk airlines to intensify their attention to the air freight market.

Slick Airways even had the privilege of being the launch customer for one of the best aircraft of the post-war piston-engined era of air transport. The Douglas DC-6A Liftmaster was Douglas's answer to the challenge of the Lockheed Constellation, more powerful, faster, and bigger than the DC-4 Skymaster. Numerically preceding the more famous DC-6B, the freighter version was at first given as much priority as the passenger version, an indication of the growing interest in air cargo at the time. The DC-6A went into service with Slick on 16 April 1951, five days after United. In the event, however, only 74 DC-6As were sold, against 288 DC-6Bs, and Douglas (and every other major commercial airliner builder) never repeated the practice, even though a plethora of optimistic air freight traffic forecasts continued to pour out from the protagonist project engineers, with whom the subject of air cargo often reached the stage of a cult worship.

One boldly-conceived offering to the altar of air freight was the Canadair CL-44, a Canadian-built version of the Bristol Britannia. The CL-44 was more than the usual passenger-to-freight conversion of a standard airliner, i.e. strengthened floor and a large cargo door in the forward end of the fuselage. Canadair made a supreme effort to break the impasse with a remarkable example of engineering ingenuity. The entire back-end section of the fuselage, including the vertical and horizontal stabilizers—the whole tail empennage—was hinged so that it could be swung to one side, to allow for direct loading, as with the old Bristol Freighter, the Budd Conestoga, and the Armstrong Whitworth Argosy. The difference was that the Britannia fuselage was much bigger—wider than a Boeing 707's—and was attractive enough to be described by the Flying Tiger Line as "the first and presently the only uncompromised all-cargo aircraft essential to the development of the air-freight business." The Canadair CL-44 was successful enough to have been operated by all four of the major U.S. all-freight airlines, Tigers, Slick, Seaboard & Western, and Airlift (which took over Slick); and it saw service with a few foreign airlines as well.

Two specially-designed air freighter aircraft of the 1950s/1960s that were inge-niously directed to aid rapid loading of large consignments were (top) the British Armstrong-Whitworth Argosy, that, uniquely, had both front-end and rear-end loading capability; and (bottom) the Canadian Canadair CL-44, a stretched version of the Bristol Britannia. It was modified so that the entire rear section of the fuselage, including the whole tail assembly, could swing outwards to permit access to the cargo hold. (Armstrong-Whitworth and Canadair)

Every now and again, there was a special need for air freight, such as the military airlift emergencies of the Korean and Vietnam wars, or in Brazil, with the sudden political decision to build a new capital in the middle of the country before any railway, and not even a good road, went near the site of what was to become Brasilia. The discovery of oil on the North Slope of Alaska in the early 1960s prompted a massive cargo airlift; but by this time Lockheed had produced one of the best, and one of the most successful freighter aircraft of all time, the C-130 Hercules, as a military cargo and all-purpose maid-of-all-work.

In this case, the developmental roles were reversed. Instead of a military freighter conversion of a standard passenger aircraft being the solution, the

SPECIALIZED AIR FREIGHT AIRCRAFT

(not including passenger types converted for freighting by interior re-design only)

Aircraft Type	Country of Manufacture	Year of First Service	Gross Weight (lb)	Freight Capacity (lb)	Special Design Features	No. Built
Junkers-G 31	Germany	1929	18,750	7,100	Special conversion, with outsize side doors and large roof hatch Spectacular success in New Guinea	3
Budd Conestoga	U.S.A.	1945	33,850	9,500	Stainless steel construction. Rear end ramp loading	14
Bristol Type 170 Freighter Series 32	U.K.	1946 / 1953	37,000 / 44,000	12,500 (2 cars) / (3 cars)	Front end clam-shell loading. Specially adapted as cross-Channel car ferry	80*
Aviation Traders (Freddie Laker) Carvair	U.K.	1962	73,800	18,000 (5 cars)	Adaptation of Douglas DC-4. Flight deck superimposed on fuselage. Front end loading	21
Armstrong Whitworth AW 650 Argosy	U.K.	1962	93,000	31,000	Twin boom tail support. Both front and rear end loading.	53
Canadair CL-44 (CC-106 Yukon)	Canada	1961	210,000	60,000	Stretched version of Bristol Britannia, with unique rear fuselage-hinged swing tail	39
Lockheed L-100 Hercules (C-130)	U.S.A.	1965	155,000	46,500	Civil variant of highly successful military all-purpose transport. Rear end ramp.	81

*Approximately 35 built for passengers only (Wayfarers) and about 100 as military transports

During periodic waves of enthusiasm for the prospects of enormous growth in the air freight market during the two decades following the end of World War II, many promising designs for specialized air freight aircraft were proposed. None of them was successful in building up a substantial order book, although the Bristol Freighter came close and perhaps should have done better, with good marketing; and the Argosy deserved a better fate. The development of cargo versions of standard passenger-carrying airlines met most air freighting requirements.

Lockheed L-100 was a commercial version, intended for civil use, of the standard military freighter. Altogether, more than 2,000 C-130s were sold, to air forces all over the world; but only a few L-100s served the airlines. Delta Air Lines put three of the latter into service in 1966. It was the last specialized freighter aircraft designed to go into service with any of the major trunk airlines, except in the Soviet Union, where the State airline, Aeroflot, combined the roles of civilian airline and military logistics system, and provided an outlet for many workhorse air freighters.

And so the Sleeping Giant continued to slumber, twitching in its sleep occasionally when a special airlift was needed to Berlin, or Brasília, or Prudhoe Bay, but only to resume his steady deep breathing; for two fundamental problems with commercial air freight, constantly preventing any spectacular explosion of growth, both placed a strain on the finances, and no amount of mechanical innovation, on the one hand, or operational and commercial ingenuity on the other, could solve them.

The first of these fundamentals was that cargo has to be handled, either by muscle-power or by mechanical contrivances such as beltloaders, forkedlift trucks, and other contraptions. It also has to transshipped and stored. All these processes are time-consuming and labor-intensive to a greater or lesser degree, depending on the equipment used. And time and labor are money.

The second fundamental is that, by its very nature, freight never comes back. Unlike passengers, who invariably go back home sooner or later, freight stays where it is sent to. Thus, one of the ambitions of every freight-hauler is to try to find a pair of cities where the demand for commercial products from each other is mutual and in balance. Often, the freight airline operators have tried to stimulate this business by offering directional discounts for special commodities. Some of the South American airlines brought its idea almost to a fine art, especially those buccaneer gipsy operators from Colombia that hauled enormous quantities of cut flowers, notably carnations, to Miami; and returned with loads ranging from videos to Volkswagens. Perhaps the most extraordinary item that appeared on the special tariff list was in Australia, where, inbound to Sydney, wombat skins could be shipped at bargain rates.

The directional imbalance was a chronic ailment and the airlines could never solve it, simply because the market patterns were permanent. One enterprising company, Trans-Mediterranean Airlines (T.M.A.) of Beirut, did attempt to demonstrate an inspired solution: it started a round-the-world freight service, so that its fleet returned to base without having to fly the 'dead-heading' empty segments that were normally the fate of the returning freighter aircraft. Alas, T.M.A. became a victim of the terrible fate that was thrust upon Beirut, once the Paris of the Middle East, when it became a battleground for maniacal forces that were an absolute deterrent to commercial activity.

And so, one by one, the great all-freighter airlines disappeared. Slick was obliged to merge with Riddle (which became Airlift International) which, in due course, also had to terminate operations. Seaboard & Western, renamed Seaboard World, had to close down. Finally, Flying Tigers itself, which had come to epitomize everything that was commendable about free-lance private enterprise in a competitive world, was forced into a merger with—to be polite, it was really a takeover by—Federal Express. Here was the supreme irony: the oldest and best-known of the all-freight airlines, was absorbed by a company that, as recently as 1973, had struck a new note in air transport. It had started the world's first exclusive air express service, with guaranteed overnight delivery for small packages and parcels, and the key to the service was the location of the nerve center at Memphis, Tennessee, geographically central in the United States, and ideal for the establishment of a hub-and-spoke network. Federal Express's packages didn't come back, but there was always a two-way flow, as there has always been for mail. In effect, packages and mail are exchanged, and even if there is an imbalance, this is never acute, as with freight.

This is not to assert that freight airlines cannot exist. There are a few left. In Europe, the Luxemburg carrier, Cargolux, now an affiliate of the German national airline Lufthansa, continues to thrive. In Miami, Bill Spohrer, maintaining a tradition of rugged independence that used to characterize pioneers such as Lowell Yerex and C.N. Shelton, actually abandoned a passenger line to Central America in favor of a freight operation. His company, Challenge Air Lines, is appropriately named and will test his resources of initiative and innovation to the limit. Spohrer has already been obliged to hire his own small army of security staff to prevent abuse of his aircraft by ingenious drug-smugglers.

But such airlines as Cargolux and Challenge can only dance around the edges of the world's air cargo market, which is so widely dispersed, and so fragmented, that only those airlines with comprehensive world-wide networks, buttressed by an enormous passenger airline infrastructure, can offer the necessary permutations of origin-destination traffic to justify an all-cargo service. They also have a vast advantage over the specialists. They can meet the requirements with the surplus capacity in the holds of the big airliners, and by operating cargo versions of these airliners, with names such as United Air Lines Air Cargo, British Airways Air Cargo, or Japan Air Cargo painted prominently on the fuselages, they proclaim the importance of the business and remind us of who is moving it.

Summarizing the history of air cargo (or air freight—cargo is presumed to include air mail and air express) four distinct eras can be identified. First there was the pre-World War II period, when no underfloor space was available—it did not exist. Then, in the 1940s and 1950s, underfloor space was available, but was cramped for large shipments; and this led to the peak of demand for the specialized aircraft, from the Bristol Freighter to the Canadair CL-44. Then came the third stage, the debut of the Big Jets, the Boeing 707s and the Douglas DC-8s, whose underfloor holds were spacious, and whose obvious carrying capacity led, first, to the introduction of pallets for speeding the loading process by pre-flight consolidation of loads, and second, to containers, which refined the pallets by adding top and sides to provide form-fitting box structures. With the arrival of the wide-bodied jets, a fourth stage has been reached, in which the capacity for carrying almost any kind of load seems unlimited. The Boeing 747, in fact, with its flight deck already on top of the main passenger deck, was ready to be adapted for front-end loading; and it was.

In short, there will always be a large air cargo market. And there will always be a few specialized air cargo airlines. But the requirement for a specialized freighter aircraft ended long ago, with the arrival of the wide-bodied jets that customarily had enough cargo space to meet any demand, and had big enough freight doors to accept almost any kind of load, short of a Tiger tank.

A a postscript to this essay, which describes the decline of, and analyses the reasons for the absence of, commercial air cargo transports in the western world, reference should be made to the success of air freighters in the former U.S.S.R. To the east of the Ural mountains, this vast area—bigger than the United States—has no form of public transport whatsoever, by land, or water. This unique situation has lent itself to the development of air cargo on a considerable scale.

The Soviet airline, Aeroflot, provided a supply service to about two thousand isolated communities, ranging from new industrial cities like Noriilsk to tiny native villages throughout the length and breadth of Siberia. In addition to the diminutive and ubiquitous Antonov An-2, a maid-of-all-work small biplane, the Soviet industry, led by the Ukrainian Antonov, provided a succession of all-cargo heavy-lift aircraft without equal in the western world.

Smaller types such as the An-12, able to carry 20 tons, were succeeded by the An-22 (88 tons), and the An-124 Ruslan (150 tons), with trans-Siberian or trans-Atlantic range, and equipped with entry doors to the 20-foot wide fuselage at each end. Supplemented by the Ilyushin Il-76, fleets of these great transport aircraft provide incomparable service to a segment of the earth's surface where nothing else can do the job.

Since the disintegration of the Soviet Union, these aircraft are now available to the West, and with commendable enterprise, the Volga-Dnepr company now provides air cargo service of a very specialized nature. The Antonov An-124 can, for example, carry the entire fuselage of most modern airliners, and, somewhat unexpectedly, has partially fulfilled the dreams of the early protagonists of the Sleeping Giant of air transport.

The DC-3 Replacement (1960s–1970s)

O f all the legendary airliners that have punctuated the progress of civil air transport since the resurgence of travel after World War I, none—not even the Ford Tri-Motor, the 'Connie,' the 707, or the 'Jumbo Jet'—has quite surpassed the Douglas DC-3, the immortal 'Gooney Bird,' in lasting fame. It has defied all efforts, including those by the highly respected International Civil Aviation Organization, to have it declared unairworthy for mass transport purposes, and it has defied all attempts by aircraft designers, from the platoons of drawing boards of the great manufacturers to the sketch pads of individual entrepreneurs, to replace it. The combined might of computers, advanced production engineering, improved technology, and inspired aeronautical thinking: all have so far failed to produce what for several decades of the post-World War II era was popularly termed The DC-3 Replacement.

In the euphoria of the late 1940s, when the accelerated wealth of aeronautical knowledge, hard-won benefit of a bitter and bloody war, was thought to be transferable to peaceful purposes, the idea of a new general-purpose airliner, able to do the many things that the DC-3 and its military versions had done, was thought to be simply a matter of making a decision and the emerging result would be a smarter and faster DC-3. Alas, those aircraft that were actually built to such a specification have long since disappeared while the DC-3 lives on.

Their total weight in scrap metal has probably been less than the total weight of paper used in drawings, calculations, and learned project studies that have attempted to emulate the aircraft that first flew on 17 December 1935, on the 32nd anniversary of the Wright brothers' success at Kitty Hawk.

At one stage, it occurred to someone, in fact it occurred to many people wrestling with the problem, to stop trying to re-invent the wheel, and simply set up a production line to build DC-3s. They were astonished at the cost of doing so and the resurrected post-war vintage DC-3s would have constituted a market that nobody could have afforded. And if any minor improvements had been made, such as pressurizing the cabin, or fitting turboprop engines, or—heaven forbid—exchanging the tail wheel for a nose wheel, the cost of doing so would have been hopelessly prohibitive and the cost to the customer quite outrageous. One such experiment was tried, to produce the Super DC-3, but only a few were built as major modifications of existing airframes. Although the performance of the new variant was better, the result was still a DC-3 and the Super element was perceived by the airline world at large not to be super enough to warrant the placement of large orders.

The trouble was that the DC-3 benefited from an accident of events, and but for that accident, it would almost certainly have been consigned to a place in history that, while outstanding, would not have been unique. What made the DC-3 unique was that it was conveniently available as a useful general-purpose transport airplane for the armed forces of the United States and its allies as the war clouds gathered at the beginning of the 1940s. Able to carry up to about 40 troops or about three and a half tons of cargo, able to land in any reasonable area of unprepared surface short of a plowed field, and already in series production, it was ordered in several military versions by the thousands. It was produced not only at the Douglas home factory at Santa Monica, California, but also in Chicago and Tulsa, and by 1944 they were coming off the mass production lines sometimes at a rate approaching one aircraft per hour. A total of 10,645 were built in the United States alone and when the war ended, they were suddenly a glut on the market.

For unlike the thousands of bombers and fighters that had also been built in vast numbers, often exceeding the DC-3 total, the transport airplanes were both durable and usable. Not only did they survive more easily because most of their duties were in logistics and transport duties and were not normally exposed to enemy attack; but also, unlike the bombers and fighters that had outlived their usefulness, the C-47s, C-53s, and the other DC-3 military types were easily converted back to their original civilian roles in life. All over the world, the armed forces set up war-surplus dumps of superfluous airplanes and these were eagerly bought at bargain basement prices, mostly by veteran aviators who wished to stay in the aviation business and who set themselves up as gypsy operators, ready to haul anyone or anything to any destination. The purchase price of the old Gooney Birds was negligible, and the only real expense was the fuel and oil and the maintenance. For the pilots were invariably the owners.

As time went on, passing through the post-war recovery period into the brave new world of the 1950s, the versatility of the airplane that had so conveniently presented itself in the late 1940s began to be questioned. Although it had never been grounded for any technical fault or shortcoming (and has never been so insulted since) its performance—cruising at about 150–160 mph—was seen to be a little passé, and the users and the manufacturers alike had begun to think about improving upon it. The advantage of the bargain-price factor in the cost equations was also being eroded, as the maintenance costs and the cost of spare parts began to rise as the years went by. The thousands of independent DC-3 operators dwindled as the post-war boom in demand for cheap short-haul freight shipments also fell off in the face of a reorganized and highly efficient scheduled airline industry. Nevertheless, when some of the manufacturers, at the beginning of the 1960s, began to ask themselves if the time had come to design a 'DC-3 Replacement,' there were about 2,500 DC-3s, almost all of them converted from military versions, mostly C-47s, still operational throughout the world.

Large numbers of these were to be found in the less developed countries of Asia, Africa, and Latin America, where commercial scheduled airline fleets of 20 or 30 was not unusual. Because of its handling characteristics and especially because of its ability to use poor airfields with grass or dirt strips, it was extremely popular in Australia's Outback and in the U.S.A.'s boondocks. For the pilots it was what is known as a 'forgiving' airplane—one that would help, rather than hinder a rapid correction to a minor (or even major) piloting error; while the ground handling staff loved it because it needed very little looking after. Like a faithful old Chevy that can always be relied upon when the B.M.W. is having an expensive lube job, it gained a justifiable reputation as an airline institution.

One of the problems that the potential builders of a DC-3 Replacement faced was the difficulty of definition and in setting the precise specification for an airplane that could provide the lifting capacity, the performance, the reliability, and, most of all, the challenging airfield performance of the original. Paradoxically, there was no precise specification—and that makes life difficult for engineers and designers who thrive on precision. In fact, there were at least five different specifications, aligned to five different roles that the DC-3 had played, and to find a compromise set of data that would meet the essential criteria for all five was bewilderingly complicated—for what was good for one kind of Gooney Bird was not good for another. The five main roles played by the veteran transport airplane—and there were other minor roles— were derived from its own history of being the maid-of-all-work for twenty-five eventful years. They were: Trunk Route Mainliner, Secondary or Feeder Airliner, All-Purpose Cargo Hauler, Military Transport, and Executive Luxury-Liner. To replace any one of these demanded a separate set of parameters of capacity, performance, and comfort standards.

The first category, the **Trunk Route Mainliner**, was at one end of the demanding design challenge. The DC-3 had started its life as the finest transport airplane of the 1930s, the specialized long-range trans-ocean flying boats excepted. It was introduced in June 1936 by American Airlines as a 21-seat improvement on the 14-seat DC-2, which itself had been a vast improvement on any previous type. Indeed, the two Douglases were the first landplanes that could reasonably be described by the term that is so familiar today: a true passenger-carrier of the air, in fact, an airliner. They were so successful that, by 1941, the year when the United States entered World War II, an estimated 85 percent of all airline passengers in the U.S. were carried by DC-3 or DC-2.

While the post-war years witnessed the relegation of the trusty Douglases to a secondary role, this change of status to a lower rank occurred almost exclusively in the developed industrial countries of North America, Europe, Australia, and Japan. In Brazil, for example, in the late 1950s, one airline alone had 86 DC-3s, and operated them everywhere, partly because the airport construction program was confined only to the major cities. There were also large fleets in such countries as India, Australia, New Zealand, and Mexico; and the problem was that these countries needed a better airplane, befitting the postwar image of modernity, that would be bigger (because the traffic had grown substantially), faster (because, even without direct competition, the public regarded 150 mph as too slow), but—to drive the designers mad—still have the same airfield performance as the DC-3. It was like asking a car manufacturer to build a comfortable, speedy family car, yet have the rough terrain performance of a Land Rover.

The second category, the **Feeder Liner**, was possibly the one with which the designers and engineers could best identify themselves. All over the world, and including the more than a dozen well-subsidized airlines in the local service category in the U.S., there were countless major operators who needed an airliner to fit into a secondary role at a level below that of the trunk airliners; or there were simply secondary level operators. Thus, an airplane with, say 35–40 seats (to take care of the traffic increase), 250–300 mph speed (to take care of the modernity), and a 4,000-foot field length (not too demanding on the airport authorities) should have been easy enough to produce. The problem was that such an airplane, even in the 1950s and 1960s, was priced at around $800,000. The secondary and feeder airlines had to take into consideration the fact that they could buy a whole fleet of DC-3s, well-used but thoroughly reliable, for the same money. And they all knew that the DC-3 would go on flying almost for ever. One is still flying today with almost 94,000 hours on the clock.

The third category, the **All-Purpose Trampship of the Air**, was almost out of reach for replacement by any new airplane, because of the cost. The revenue earned from freight is usually much lower per unit of either weight

This trio of pictures illustrates the way in which the venerable Douglas DC-3 was replaced in what can be termed a mainline air route, in this case the essential air links between Honolulu and the outlying Hawaiian Islands. The piston-engined DC-3 (top) was succeeded first by a turboprop, the Vickers Viscount (middle), which in turn was to give way to the British Aircraft Corporation's BAC One-Eleven (bottom). All three aircraft performed exactly the same function, and the journey time on the short routes differed only by a matter of about twenty minutes or less. (Aloha Airlines)

or capacity, and consequently the operators have to economize in every direction: aircrew salaries, on-board amenities, maintenance, spares replacement. The old DC-3, the 'forgiving' airplane, could be flown by almost any pilot who had checked out on a Piper Cub, had been delivered in flying condition from the U.S. Army war-surplus dump anyway, and would keep going for weeks with little more than a cursory inspection of the bare tires and a squirt or two of oil into the engines' vital parts. And those airplanes could still be bought for a few thousand dollars. To supply this market with new airplanes was almost a contradiction in terms.

The fourth category, a replacement for the DC-3 as a **Military Transport**, was a complete non-starter after World War II, as this was the version of the Douglas transport that was distributed around the world by the U.S. and other nations and had been eagerly acquired by many other air forces. Of the grand total of 17,299 DC-3s built, all except 433 were military types. These included 6,157 produced in the Soviet Union under license as Lisunov Li-2s, and 487 in Japan, built by Nakajima and Showa. Throughout every continent, at every military airfield, the military DC-3s, with their large cargo doors, were standard equipment, performing all the tasks that were asked of them. They were even used as gunships in the Vietnam War.

The fifth category was the **Executive** conversion. Many medium-sized companies or corporations discovered that the fuselage of the DC-3 was big enough to permit a standard of luxury, with cocktail bars, furniture, and other amenities, that the custom-build executive aircraft could not match, simply because of the space limitations. At relatively small cost, the DC-3 could be converted with a handsome interior, and unlike some of the expensive air yachts produced by several specialist aircraft constructors, it could be flown into poor airstrips and would provide few servicing or spare parts problems. You could take a DC-3 anywhere.

These were the five main categories that provided the replacement challenge for the manufacturers. But because of the variety, the specification that would suit one would not suit another. The trunk lines needed bigger and faster types, the feeder lines needed faster aircraft but with stringent field length restrictions. The tramp operators needed anything that was cheap. If a second-hand DC-3 was too expensive, then a third-hand one would do, and the availability of much-used DC-3s was almost unlimited. The military hardly needed them at all, as they already had them. And to build executive types as big as the DC-3, at the same time providing the improved performance sometimes demanded, could be done only at high cost, so that the market was restricted to only the biggest and most affluent corporations.

All these problems did not deter the world's aircraft industry from trying. At least, in the industrialized nations, the DC-3 was clearly outmoded for
mainline inter-city operations. Gone were the days when Eastern's 'Great
Silver Fleet' of DC-2s and DC-3s set the standard of excellence. With the
Lockheed Constellation setting the post-war pace at 300 mph cruising speed
on the long-distance routes, the traveling public demanded something comparable for the shorter hauls too. Over in Europe, the British put the Vickers
Viking into service and the French the Sud-Est 161 Languedoc; but these
were both based on pre-war design criteria, and did not offer significant improvements over the DC-3, which has outlived them handsomely by several
decades of service life. In the United States, however, benefiting particularly
from the increased power from advanced radial piston engines, the Convair
240, a fast (280 mph) pressurized 40-seat twin, made its debut on the airways
when it was introduced by American Airlines in 1948. This set a new pattern,
and a total of 1,086 (including military versions) Convair-Liners were built,
together with 149 Martin twins, of similar performance, to oust the venerable
   DC-3 from the frontline short-haul routes.
      The old Douglas tail-dragger did not give up easily. A United Air Lines
study conducted as late as 1949 showed that, in spite of its apparent obsoles-
cence, it was still operating at an average load factor of 55 percent, more than
three points higher than at the pre-war peak in 1941.
      In the United States, after the Convair-Liners and the Martins, came,
first, the turboprops, with the British Vickers Viscount, a four-engined 320
mph 48-seat smooth-flying challenger, in 1955; followed, at the end of 1965,
by the first of the twin jets, British Aircraft Corporation's BAC One Eleven,
and the 600 mph 80-seat Douglas DC-9. This, in turn, was joined by the tri-
jet Boeing 727, actually introduced a year earlier on medium-haul routes, and
both of these aircraft could, and were, described as the ultimate DC-3 replacement. In one sense they were, in the natural line of succession of improved
technical performance, reflected in better economics, that is the inevitable
sequel to product development.
      When the Convair-Liners and Martins in the U.S.A., and the Viscounts
in Europe, swept the DC-3s from the mainline routes, most of them were
passed down the line on to lesser feeder, or secondary routes of lower traffic
density, either of the trunk airline networks themselves, or of specialized airlines that evolved in the post-war years as the entire airline industry became
diversified. In the United States especially, these local service airlines were
created specifically to perform the task of reaching out to some 400 communities in the 48 States that had previously been deprived of scheduled air service. And the old DC-3 was just right for the task. Acquired cheaply either

Many aircraft manufacturers succeeded in producing aircraft that replaced the 28-seat Douglas DC-3 for feeder, or secondary route networks. Among these were (top left) the piston-engined Martin 4-0-4, with forty seats; (bottom left) the Fokker/Fairchild F-27, also with 40 seats, but with the additional advantage of turboprop engines that replaced the earlier piston-engined Convairliner. This last stalwart was also re-engined with turboprops. The picture (top right) shows the

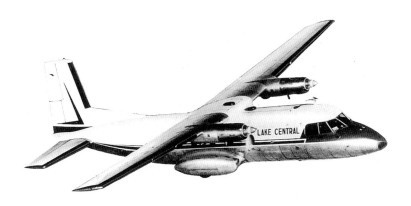

CV580 with Allisons. The final picture shows the French Nord 262, a brave attempt to build a genuine DC-3 replacement, with turboprop power and high wing, and the same size as the DC-3, to serve routes of the same traffic density. For various reasons, mainly the unreliability of the engines, the Nords never succeeded; and the veteran Douglas airliners, that could be obtained cheaply in the used-aircraft market, survived after the Nords had been retired. (Southern Airways, Ozark Airlines, Frontier Airlines, and Lake Central Airlines, respectively)

from the war-surplus stocks, or from the trunk airlines that were eagerly buying the faster, pressurized modern twins, the local service airlines put scores of them to work in the late 1940s and early 1950s. But they too wished to modernize and found the solution in bypassing the Convair-Liner piston-engined generation and going directly to the turboprop, in this case the Fokker F.27 Friendship/Fairchild F-27, a high-winged twin-engined 40-seater that had the same efficient Rolls-Royce Dart power plants as the successful Viscount, and cruised at about 250 mph.

For many years, the Friendships/F-27s operated side-by-side with the DC-3s, as the Local Service industry awaited the arrival of a design proposal that could offer perhaps better performance, possibly a jet; provided that it had good economics; and yet be able to use the same airstrips as the DC-3. They were disappointed. During the 1960s, many manufacturers, especially in Europe, produced designs, and some even built a prototype or a few aircraft; but none were completely successful. The British had built the Avro 748 (later to be renamed the Hawker Siddeley 748 and the British Aerospace 748, with the changing corporate scene) with characteristics similar to those of the Friendship but with even better field performance. In this sense it came closer to being a DC-3 replacement than almost any other airplane, but the head start gained by the successful Friendship—787 were built in a period lasting 27 years—inhibited the market prospects. Nevertheless, more than 250 were sold, mostly to nations in Latin America and Asia, where it was built under license in India.

Of the other contenders, the German VFW 614, a 30-seat turboprop, was not a success; while the most promising project, a small rear-engined jet aircraft, never progressed beyond the drawing boards. At first a 26–30-seat design, the de Havilland D.H.126 became the Hawker Siddeley HS 136 after extensive market surveys revealed a strong demand for a 36–40-seater. It would have had jet performance and excellent field length figures, but was not proceeded with; but ultimately, after many re-designs, it emerged as the British Aerospace BAe 146, an 80–100-seat airliner aimed at a quite different market. In the United States, where, in the 1960s, there had been a healthy demand for aircraft in the 30–50-seat range among the local service airlines, the airlines themselves grew out of such a demand, acquired many more heavily traveled inter-city routes, and moved up into the small feeder jet market represented by the British Aircraft Corporation (BAC) One-Eleven or the Douglas DC-9, both aircraft fitted with 80–90 seats in their earlier versions.

When the Local Service airlines grew out of the DC-3 stage—rather like an adolescent boy growing out of short pants—there was nowhere much for the DC-3s to go, at least not in the scheduled airline field. In the next lower stratum of airline operations, variously termed the scheduled air taxi, the third level, and the commuter airlines, there was, for many years, a strict embargo on their operating any aircraft that weighed more than 12,500 lb, fully loaded. One theory to explain how this figure was arrived at was that it was half the equivalent figure for the DC-3. Whether this rumor was apocryphal or not, the DC-3 was effectively outside the scope of the small airlines of the United States from the 1970s onwards, except where its sheer versatility in operating into places where other aircraft could not made it indispensable, and where, in such cases, the normally rigid Civil Aeronautics Board was prepared to bend the rules a bit. Eventually, with changing attitudes that led to the deregulation of the airline industry, the commuter airlines could operate DC-3s if they wished to. Provincetown-Boston Airline had one that had completed more than 90,000 flying hours, averaging about six hours of service every day for its more than 40 years of a hard-working life. This is not only the highest time record of any DC-3; it is the highest for any kind of aircraft, military or civil, anywhere in the world. Even if the DC-3 is ever replaced, that record seems almost as secure as Henry Aaron's.

With no prospects for passing their advancing years as passenger airliners in some countries, there were still many opportunities for DC-3s in many parts of the world as hardy freighter workhorses. In dozens of circumstances when an airlift of some commodity or work force was required on a temporary basis, DC-3s were always available, either from the resident air force's transport division; or from some of the bush operators whose aircraft could always be found at the back of a hangar in the upper reaches of the Amazon, the outer islands of the Philippines, or the frozen wastes of Siberia. The old Gooney Birds were not simply available. With very little encouragement, the Pratt & Whitney engines would usually start, even after long periods of inactivity. And after perhaps a few hectic months of hauling laborers to a dam site, or vital medical aid to an area struck by an earthquake or flood, one would be returned to its parking spot, with the air crew's salary and the price of the gasoline as the only expense temporarily incurred.

During World War II, one aircraft, the Curtiss C-46, did come very close to challenging the DC-3 in its all-purpose U-Haul role. This aircraft, larger and heavier, and able to carry almost twice the load of a DC-3, came into service towards the end of the war, and did sterling service in the Chinese theater, after a steady stream of them had been flown there via Brazil, the South Atlantic, Africa, and India. Its Hour of Glory came with the great supply route across the precipitous cordilleras in the mountain areas of eastern India and western China, and it even outshone the DC-3 in setting up some impressive load-carrying statistics. The C-46, like the DC-3, was much sought after at the end of the hostilities, and was to be seen performing the same maid-of-all-work duties, especially throughout Latin America.

But the C-46 had one defect that brought it a poor reputation which was not entirely deserved. It was never expected to be as docile an airplane to fly as the DC-3, and the fact that the pilots had less time to relax while at cruising height was not held against it. But its short field and dirt strip capability did not compare with the Douglas veteran's, and its engine-out performance was fraught with hazards for a pilot who could not react within micro-seconds. Any shortfall of power on takeoff was especially dangerous, whereas a DC-3 could usually stagger into the air and soon find a convenient patch of ground on which to make a forced landing if necessary. The C-46 did not have this flexibility.

As a result, the C-46 enjoyed a successful life among the airlines and gypsy operators in the underdeveloped regions of the world but it never replaced the DC-3. As the years passed, and both types of aircraft suffered depletions through accidents of varying degree, more C-46s tended to be written off than the DC-3s, with the familiar 'dbr'—damaged beyond repair—written against their epitaph. The last C-46 in scheduled service was retired in Costa Rica in the early 1980s and not too many of them are left, even in non-scheduled freight service in places like Cochabamba, Bolivia, or Villavicencio, Colombia. But DC-3s are to be seen everywhere still today. About 300 are believed to be still airworthy in the early 1990s, almost 50 years after the majority of them were built during the last two years of World War II; and some of these are even to be found in scheduled service in Central America, South America, and other parts of the world like Canada off the beaten track.

One aircraft came close to matching the DC-3's astonishing ability to use short and unprepared strips as a base for operation. But because of the limited commercial market, such an aircraft was built for military logistics purposes, where the economics of normal airline operating costs and revenue-earning potentials did not apply. The Lockheed C-130 was a much bigger airplane, designed specifically for tactical support, so that it too could bring supplies and material into places where no orthodox aircraft could land. But its sheer size—it could carry 22 tons of cargo—and the purchase price of several millions of dollars, even in the 1960s, when it made its debut: both were prohibitive, and only a few of the L-100 commercial variants were sold to the airlines.

Some of more dramatic demonstrations of the C-130's adaptability and tolerance of poor landing strips were found in Arctic regions. It became the standard vehicle for supplying the North Slope oilfields of Alaska, and for supplying the networks of strategic airfields in northern Canada and Greenland, where the permafrost in the winter could change to marshland during the thaw. It was also a familiar sight in the Antarctic; but although it became the lifeline for the U.S. research stations scattered across the Last Continent's truly formidable icecap, where sub-zero Celsius temperatures were the rule rather than the exception, the DC-3 nevertheless had the honor of being the first aircraft to land at the South Pole, when it made an historic visit on 3 May 1952.

The DC-3's longevity as a survivor in a high-tech era was explained by the manager of an overhaul shop at Biak, in West Irian, the Indonesian half of New Guinea. Here, DC-3s are completely stripped and rebuilt, to give them a new lease of life. "Where else—said the manager—could you find an aircraft that can carry almost four tons of cargo into a 3,000-foot strip at 8,000-foot altitude, with every approach shielded by mountains? The Twin Otter cannot carry the load, and even the C-130 would be restricted and it's far too big for our needs anyway."

At the other end of the aviation social scale, far removed from the time-worn unkempt workhorses of the jungles, the outback, and the tundra, were a few privileged DC-3s that had a face-lift. They were not for trampship operators, with crews in tattered jeans and grimy T-shirts, but for Savile Row-attired businessmen flown by uniformed aircrew. For surprisingly, the lowly DC-3 was used quite widely after the end of World War II by many large corporations that were able to enjoy the luxury of operating their own air fleets. And as one of the main reasons was because their executives frequently had to travel to out-of-the-way places where airfields were not always of the best, the DC-3's versatility was ideal for the purpose.

As time went on, the aircraft manufacturing industry eventually produced aircraft that were especially designed for the corporate executive, luxuriously equipped with every modern convenience, and a cabin layout befitting a chairman of the board. These aircraft were, compared with the DC-3, a little on the small side, and expensive both to buy and to operate. But the corporations were willing to dispense with the DC-3s mainly because the faster and sleeker types became a status symbol. At least part, and often all of the expenses could also be claimed as a tax deduction. Such aircraft as the Aero Commander, a handsome and comfortable small twin piston-engined aircraft; the Grumman Gulfstream, a larger turboprop twin; and the Learjet or the Hawker Siddeley 125, both examples—and there were others—of a fast twin-jet: all these were to be seen at airports in the developed world, where the top executives demanded personalized air travel.

Even so, the old DC-3 still continued to be used by some companies who preferred to aim for more modest corporate aircraft standards, and found that the old Gooney Bird could still serve them well. The old Douglas twins can occasionally been seen taxying in to major hubs, squeezing in between large jet airliners, whose dignity is met with cheerful impudence from the veterans. Such is the DC-3's longevity in this role that at least one firm of aviation engineers, in Wisconsin, does a roaring trade by buying time-worn relics, otherwise doomed to the scrapheap, for a bargain price; spending perhaps $100,000 in refurbishing and cosmetic treatment as well as in complete engineering overhaul; and then selling them for a comfortable quarter of a million dollars.

There have been some other uses to which the DC-3 has been put. Almost every aviation museum in the world has one, and some have two. Some are to be found still in service, dutifully guarding the gate of a military airfield, either mounted on a pylon or tastefully located in its own space, encircled by flowers, lawns, or stonework. Some bring joy to children as centerpieces in playgrounds, and quite a few have been converted into restaurants. And scores of this almost indestructible machine are gradually disintegrating in the corner of an airfield or at the back of an old hangar as they perform the role of a 'Christmas tree' in an ongoing cannibalization process by which the old and decrepit help to keep the more hardy survivors in the air.

In the far north of Siberia, in a tiny community of Yukutia, not far from the Arctic Ocean, a Lisunov Li-2 (the Soviet version of the DC-3) stands on a pedestal in the village square, as a tribute to the veteran aircraft, which for so long was the life-line to the outer world. And at the Moscow Air Show in September 1993, a faithfully restored Li-2 flew past with two Sukhoi 27s, one on each side, escorting the Old Lady as an honour bestowed by representatives of the latest in modern technology, six decades removed from the DC-3's.

The Douglas DC-3 will not be replaced because there never was a single DC-3 Replacement. The DC-3 itself was equivalent to a whole range of different types, and its successors have evolved as a motley assortment of different aircraft types, ranging from the 19-seat de Havilland Canada Twin Otter to the Lockheed C-130 air freighter. And some would argue that, in the logical line of chronological succession, in parallel with air traffic growth, the ultimate replacement has been the Boeing 747—but this is perhaps taking the rationale a little too far.

The Douglas DC-3 was all things to all people. The aviation world will never see the like again, if only because they no longer give airplanes away, as they did after the Second World War.

The Orient Express

I
n the immortal words of a recent president, somewhat paraphrased, there they go again. Not satisfied by seeing the Concorde production line stop at twenty aircraft, with only fourteen going into service; and with the U.S. SST consigned to the archives by an intelligent Congress, the lunatic fringe of the aircraft industry, the hungry industrial consulting firms, and the publicity-seeking airlines are promoting the Hypersonic Transport, or HST, with every meretricious argument they can lay their hands on to mesmerize the eagerly gullible media. Randolph Hearst's famous instruction to his journalists to the effect that the truth should never be allowed to obscure a neat turn of phrase was never abused so much as in the promotion of a supersonic airplane that would be planned to fly from New York to Tokyo—hence the 'Orient Express'—at five times the speed of sound in a journey time of about three hours.

The protagonists of the HST have been able to ride on a wave of instinctive support for any project that reaches out to extend the knowledge of Mankind. Any project engineer who aspires to create a technological breakthrough is always likely to receive encouragement, if only because industrial leaders and image-conscious politicians are reluctant to be identified with the accusation that they are against Progress, and that the Soviet Union (now Russia) and Japan, or Europe and China, will leave America behind in the shaping of the future of the world. The bigger the problem, the bigger the challenge to overcome it; and with the knowledge that we *did* put a Man on the Moon, and that the Concorde *does* fly regularly at Mach 2 on the trans-Atlantic route, the idea has become prevalent that no technological challenge is beyond the wit of science to accept and no problem too difficult to solve.

This basic principle may indeed be true. Given the massive investment and the will to do it, there are certainly many examples in which the challenge of achieving the near-impossible was met with conspicuous success. The Great Pyramid of Cheops would present a massive challenge today if a firm of construction engineers were asked to build it and present their budget estimates to whomever was going to pay for it. But the ancient Egyptians managed it. The Chinese built the Great Wall, which is the only man-made object that can be seen from outer space—although it can not, as many imagine, be seen from the Moon. Those great projects were, to put it mildly, labor-intensive. In the modern world, the problems do not revolve so much in solving labor management techniques as in tackling complex scientific equations and understanding abstruse formulae relating to advanced physics and precision engineering that are beyond the comprehension of all but the most advanced mathematicians and physicists. The design and construction of the Saturn rocket and the Apollo spacecraft that actually enabled Mankind to take its Great Step was little short of miraculous. Little wonder, therefore, that, to any aircraft or space industry project engineer, nothing is impossible; and that includes the HST and the prospect of offering a three-hour ride to Tokyo.

Let us accept, therefore, that, given the injection of almost unlimited capital to support the massive research, development, and production programs that would be needed during the next decade or two, a Mach 5 hypersonic transport vehicle could be built. Let us equally, however, take a look at the other aspects involving the operational feasibility, the economics, and above all, the market for such a machine. But before reviewing these latter items, the technical problems that have to be faced should be mentioned here, if only to put the entire program of any proposed development of a hypersonic airliner into perspective.

In the interests of weight-saving, far beyond the aspirations of the structures departments working on subsonic aircraft, the HST will have to be built of metals or composite materials, or a combination of both, that will combine strength with weight-saving and above all, the ability to retain its strength and stiffness in extremely high temperatures. The skin friction alone will bring the surface temperature up to at least 1,000° C (or about 2,200° F); so that the use of aluminum is out of the question. Typical of the structural materials that might be candidates for the HST is, according to Cornelius Driver, of the NASA-Langley Research Center, "a sandwich of a core or corrugated titanium shaped by superplastic forming joined by diffusion bonding to faceplates of a metal matrix surrounding carbon or metal fibers."

That might just do it, but it will not be cheap.

Accepting that, like building the Great Wall or the Great Pyramids, nothing is impossible, given the resources, and the airframe can be built of a titanium-composite sandwich, the problem then is how to push it along. One of the more startling revelations from all the studies made is that the engines or propulsion units will have to be revolutionary in design, the most important single item of which is the emphasis upon a variable-geometry inlet nozzle, one that could be varied by either a translating or expanding centerbody so as to match the differing requirements of take-off, transonic acceleration, and cruise. At Mach 5, the inlet temperatures will be so high that existing metal alloys could not be used, nor, for that matter, could the engines be powered by conventional fuels that are used today.

One seriously accepted assumption is that the HST would be fueled by liquid hydrogen. Such a liquid is beyond the comprehension of the average layman. It liquefies at a temperature of minus 150° C (-238° F)—not too far from the point of absolute zero, and the problems of carrying it in the air and storing it on the ground are so enormous, they hardly bear thinking about. Liquid hydrogen needs loving care and attention, and for passengers to be accompanied by huge tanks of liquid hydrogen is a daunting prospect. However, some designers have turned necessity into a virtue by proposing that the hydrogen fuel tank can be built within the two shells of a double fuselage, one inside the other, so that the extremely low temperature can be used to keep the skin friction heat down. The passengers inside, of course, would not be able to see what was going on in this fascinating exercise in heat-exchange, as the hypersonic airliner would have no windows. But it is good to know that, for speeds of more than Mach 4, according to Ralph Denning, of Rolls-Royce, cryogenic hydrogen fuel is essential for improvements in fuel consumption and heat sink capability. Other dreamers are promoting a fuel composed of liquid and *solid* hydrogen.

Such factors as those mentioned above, the structure materials, the engine intake design, the fuels, are only some of the staggering challenges that face the engineers; and, as the advertisers of commercial products never fail to tell us, there is much more. But accepting that, formidable though these tasks will be, they can be overcome and the hypersonic airliner can be built, more practical considerations have to be faced squarely. For, in defiance of reality, these are too often glossed over by the advocates of supersonic and hypersonic travel, whatever the cost.

One of the extraordinary features of airline costing with conventional subsonic airliners, using complex formulae to calculate the total operating expense, is that the direct portion is always calculated to several places of decimals to estimate the cost of fuel, crew, and maintenance, even to the point of making allowance for different working rules by the flight deck personnel. Having estimated these direct operating costs with meticulous precision, the indirect costs, or overheads, are then expressed with the broadest of casual assumptions, the most popular of which used to be 'about half the total,' or, after the sudden increments in fuel prices in the 1970s, modified to a lower, but still very broad-brush figure.

This approach has been the same with all the supersonic airliner projects and is still with us today as the scientists dwell on abstruse subjects involving fuel transfer to maintain the center of gravity, or variable intakes,

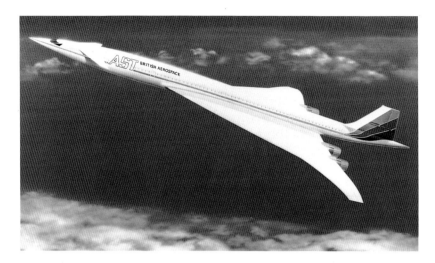

Two contenders for the next generation of supersonic airliners, shown here by imaginative artists' impressions, are the Advanced Supersonic Airliners (ASTs) of (top) British Aerospace, and (bottom) McDonnell Douglas. (British Aerospace, McDonnell Douglas)

or where to put the liquid hydrogen. Yet little attention is given to practical matters such as how to schedule a Mach 5 airliner, how to service it on the ground, and how to cool down an aircraft that has just landed and is practically red hot.

Before enumerating some of these irritants to the hypersonic advocates, credit must, however, be given to one admission on their part. Even James P. Loomis, director of the Center for High Speed Commercial Flight at the Battelle Institute's Columbus Division admitted "it is doubtful that the sonic booms associated with supersonic flight will be reduced to satisfactory levels. Therefore, supersonic transports of this period (AD 2000 to 2010) will have to operate subsonically over land." This is a more pragmatic approach to the boom than that of Cornelius Driver who feels that "further research is urgently needed on that point (of the possibility of reducing the over-pressure coefficient)." He then goes on to say "If the public does not quail, then we can have conventional supersonic flight over land."

Passing over the dismissal of mere 'conventional' supersonic flight, spare a thought for the uncooperative public who have the effrontery to object to sonic booms reverberating around their homes and neighborhoods, not to mention their farms.

To be fair, the whole aircraft research fraternity recognizes that the problem of global ozone depletion, with its protective role in keeping the penetration of ultra-violet light to a level acceptable for the maintenance of tolerable life on earth, is not going to be helped by the operation of hypersonic airliners. And some of the planners, at least, realize that as much work will have to be done on the ground as in the air in maintaining and servicing aircraft whose fuel, systems, and parking and hangarage requirements would bear no resemblance to those of previous generations of subsonic and even supersonic airplanes.

While such recognition of real problems of gigantic proportions is commendable, the glossing over of the colossal costs is less admirable. The Concorde is estimated to have cost the British and French governments some $4 billion in development costs alone, and that was what the HST proponents described as a "conventional" supersonic airliner, cruising at a mere Mach 2. The United States SST, had it been built as a larger and faster Mach 3 transport, would have needed about $10 billion to foot the development bill alone. Even the subsonic Boeing 757 and the Boeing 767 each cost $3 billion in their development. Any estimate for a hypersonic Mach 5 airliner of less that about $25 billion can be viewed as wishful thinking. Fortunately for the enthusiasts, there is no shortage of that abstract commodity.

Nowhere is this more apparent than in the devastating assumptions made about the joys of being able to fly from New York to Tokyo or vice versa in about three hours. With a time zone differential of ten hours, the perceived journey times, according to the local clocks, are minus seven hours (plus one day because of crossing the date line) on westbound flights, and plus thirteen hours (less one day for the same reason). In both cases, to arrange a schedule that makes any sense at all is impossible. For example, a departure from New York on, say, a Monday evening at 7 p.m. would arrive in Tokyo at mid-day on Tuesday, just when, according to New York time, it is ten o'clock: time for bed, not for waiting an hour for the aircraft to cool down to room temperature, nor for a hour going through immigration and customs, followed by two hours in the traffic jam into downtown Tokyo **(see Chart)**.

It is bad enough having to face razor-sharp Japanese businessmen even when bright-eyed and bushy-tailed after a good night's sleep, early morning workout, and bacon and eggs for breakfast. But to do so, fully jet-lagged (for the human constitutional clock does not adjust itself because the body goes hypersonic) at the equivalent of one o'clock in the morning is not the best way to start a negotiating day. If the answer is to take a rest, either before or after the flight, then the whole objective of hypersonic travel is negated.

In both directions, at whatever time is fixed for departure and arrival, the hypersonic candle just cannot be burned at both ends without severely endangering health.

Little wonder that almost every eulogy for the hypersonic cause, listing all the alleged grounds for optimism for engines that burn half the fuel of today's fanjets, materials half the weight but twice as strong as today's alloys and composites, and aerodynamic design challenges that demand a new generation of computers to face them: little wonder that these tracts are punctuated in every paragraph with mights and maybes, shoulds and coulds, and ifs and buts.

Nowhere in the turgid mass of special pleading are the doubts more evident than in estimating the market for the HST, any more than they were for their predecessor Concorde and SST The reason is quite simple: the numbers are usually drawn out of a hat, bearing no relation to market disciplines (and let us not be confused with the facts), yea even by NASA, McDonnell Douglas, Boeing, and the Battelle Center for High Speed Commercial Flight, by people who have not the slightest idea of how to approach the problem; and if they do, then they dare not reveal the truth.

Once again, the dreamers must be brought down to earth from their orbiting flights of fancy, and pay attention to the unpalatable truth that, even more than the Concorde, the hypersonic airliner will, if built, never be able to

LIMITATION OF
TRANSPACIFIC TIME SLOTS

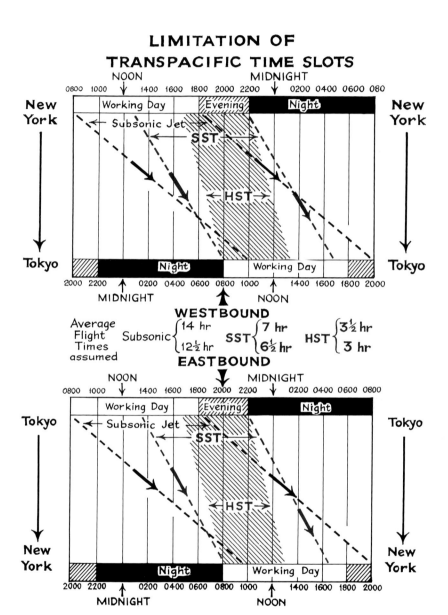

Average Flight Times assumed

Subsonic { 14 hr / 12½ hr } SST { 7 hr / 6½ hr } HST { 3½ hr / 3 hr }

Few airlines have shown much enthusiasm for a new supersonic airliner to succeed the Concorde. One exception is Northwest Airlines, which has attracted some attention, ranging from enthusiasm to scepticism, for its much-publicized Orient Express idea. (Northwest Airlines)

carry more than a few very rich or very privileged people. It will be, in effect, a supreme executive tool, for supreme executives, but with a difference: the costs will be borne by the taxpayer—but did I not hear someone say "No More Taxes?"

As long ago as 1960, an *Aviation Week* headline announced "Hypersonic Airliner Proposed for 1980s." The Bell Aircraft Corporation was proposing a 30-passenger, 15,000 mph aircraft that would have been carried piggyback fashion on a "six-engine turbojet-ramjet boost vehicle" and would take off from mounted guide rails "as it lights off its 165,000 lb thrust rocket engine." What with hydrazine and nitrogen tetroxide propellants, and double wall-type heat shields, and one thing and another, but "no break-throughs in the state-of-the-art," the project would have cost $1 billion (about a quarter of the cost of the Concorde) and take 15 years. Or so they said.

The language used by the hypersonic protagonists then was much the same as it is now. Will they never learn?

THE DAVIES LAW
OF THE SUPERSONIC MARKET
(D.L.S.M.—Mach 5/25 versions)

Total North Pacific Passengers (one way)

Passengers per year	25,000,000	35,000,000
x 6% First Class[1]	1,500,000	2,100,000
x 50% on top city pairs[2]	750,000	1,050,000
x 200% upgrade from first and business class[3]	1,500,000	2,100,000 ... T_{NP}

HST Passengers (one way, per aircraft)

Round trips per day 2	3	
Seating capacity[4] 250	300	
Passengers per day 1,000	1,800	
x 70% load factor 700	1,260	
x 365 days in year 255,000	460,000 ... P_{NP}	

North Pacific HST Market

$$\frac{T_{NP}}{P_{NP}} = \frac{1,500,000}{255,000} = 6 \qquad \frac{2,100,000}{460,000} = 5 .. M_{NP}$$

World HST Market

Assume North Pacific to be one
quarter of total transocean (or
equivalent) market[5] ....6 x 4 = 24   5 x 4 = 20 .... M_W

Note: As with the Concorde and U.S. SST calculations (pages 115 and 124), there are several elements of compounded optimism, indicated by
1. This percentage is higher than the 5% in the previous assumptions, even though the tourist market is growing at a faster rate than the premium-fare markets.
2. Higher than previous assumptions as the premium fare traffic could be dispersed to multiple Pacific Rim destinations.
3. (Simply an over-optimistic assumption. Concorde experience does not support evn 150%, as in previous calculations.)
4. Recent studies by leading manufacturers assumed (McDonnell Douglas) 300, and (Boeing) 400.
5. Pacific market is growing at a sustained higher rate than the Atlantic.

The Suspended Monorail

I n all forms of transport, the closing decades of the 20th century have witnessed the leveling of progressive performance improvements so that on land, sea, and air, no increase in speed of any significance can be visualized in the foreseeable future. Railroads are restricted by the need to reconstruct or build completely new track if they are to improve on the 100–125 mph normal top speeds achieved on main lines. Road transport organizations cannot plan on speeds of more than about 80 mph, even in Germany, where there is no speed limit, and certainly not in the U.S.A. where 65 mph is standard for high speed highways. Water transport is obsolete, except for freight and local tourism. The airlines' only objective is to bring into service more economical, not faster, airliner types.

An impasse seems to have been reached. The traveling public must resign itself to accepting the fact that, by the year 2050 A.D. the journey time from New York to London will be no faster than it is today—and the privileged Concorde travelers of today will appear only as memories in the pages of history books. The Concorde itself will be long gone; and there will be no successor unless a befuddled government manages to dupe its taxpayers into footing the bill for some wildly expensive supersonic executive airplane to carry a few politicians and tycoons. The plateau of achievement in long-distance journey times has already been reached, and this applies to all forms of transport.

Equally, the journey time between major cities in the medium-haul ranges of, say, 400—2,500 miles, will not change either. The U.S. transcontinental trip will still take about five hours non-stop, or six to seven hours via the multiplicity of hubs—the operational innovation which enabled large airlines to increase load factors and market shares. The same applies in Europe where, however, many travelers have the advantage of choice: trains there are still fast and efficient and invariably take people into the centers of the cities, which is where a large proportion of them wish to go.

On short-haul air routes, the prospect for improvement is bleak. A cursory glance at the history of busy routes in the 200–400-mile range bracket reveals that, for example, city center journey times between New York and Washington, or San Francisco and Los Angeles (conceding the doubtful assumption that the latter *has* a city center) are no better today than they were

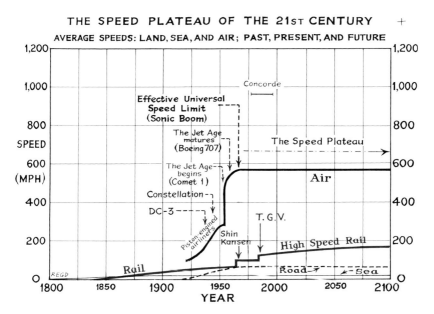

THE SPEED PLATEAU OF THE 21st CENTURY   +

AVERAGE SPEEDS: LAND, SEA, AND AIR; PAST, PRESENT, AND FUTURE

Almost like an Einsteinian constant, the conclusion seems inarguable that public transport, land, sea, or air, will never be faster than it is today. The Sound Barrier prevents airliners from flying faster, and airways congestion is even threatening to decrease average airport-to-airport speeds, as well as to increase times between city centers. High Speed Rail can be introduced albeit with high financial investment; while higher speeds on the roads can be achieved only at great risk to life and limb.

in 1930; and there is much evidence to suggest that it takes longer to go from Times Square to the White House today than it did 60 years ago. Only in Japan and in Europe have definite improvements been made, and these have been on specific routes only and not generally applied. The magnificent Shin Kansen high speed rail system of Japan opened a new era for railroading when the first route, on the Tokyo-Osaka Tokkaido Line, opened in 1964. Since then, all of Japan's major cities have been linked with the smooth-running, punctual, and frequent Bullet Trains, which maintain *average* speeds exceeding 100 mph. In Europe, the railroad companies of U.K. and France have many 100 mph lines radiating from London and Paris respectively, and in the latter case, the T.G.V.—Train à Grand Vitesse—travels between Paris and Lyon and from Paris to Nantes at 155 mph.

In 1994 the Channel Tunnel ('The Chunnel') fulfilled a 200-year-old dream of a link between England and France—and simultaneously threatened to wipe out most of the traffic on the air routes that connect London with Paris, Brussels, and Amsterdam. This may be no bad thing; for these 200-mile routes are uneconomic to operate and unbearably expensive to fly on.

Here, however, the story of reduction in travel time between big population centers during the next few decades takes a different course. The Japanese Shin Kansen program has come to a halt, because of the tremendously high cost of building the new, precision-laid track. The French T.G.V. was even more expensive; and while in Germany, Spain, and other countries of Europe, high speed lines are being built, these are as yet only on a few routes. Thus, for journeys of more than about 300 miles, and in spite of the inconvenience of going to and from congested airports, air travel will still continue to be the preferred transport mode; as only over the specially selected surface routes, as mentioned above, is the railroad or road alternative likely to be competitive. The problem is that, as the popularity of air travel increases, so does the congestion, and this is evident not only in the air traffic control delays (where a missed approach can add another 15–20 minutes and to be caught in the stack adds up to an hour or more) but more spectacularly on the ground. The modern obsession to use roads almost exclusively as a solution to public transport problems had led to the near certainty of a traffic jam at some point between airport and city center; and in the case of Los Angeles, which once had the finest urban transit system in the world, before the freeway mania took over, the certainty of stagnant four-abreast smog-creating phalanxes of cars is absolute.

The solutions that are the subject of experiment and proposal are pitifully inadequate. The term light rail has come into common usage. This is no more than a euphemism for street car, and is avoided as a description because this would thereby be an admission that the destruction of streetcars and tramways throughout the mid-twentieth century was a retrograde step. After the automobile-highway lobby fought off the threat successfully for about forty years, Los Angeles is finally to have an urban transit system—following closely on the lines of the old Red Cars that were destroyed in the 1950s. In Washington, D.C., firms are competing for the privilege of building some kind of rail system to Dulles International Airport. A suburban rail line used to go right by the airport location, but it was torn up.

The most extraordinary aspect of the entire history of the destruction of the streetcars is that they were the most efficient form of local transport ever devised. The electric power that drove them was cheap and pollution-free; and did not depend on foreign oil supplies to keep them going. Their main fault, apparently, was that they got in the way of the private cars. Certainly, at busy intersections, they were inflexible, and although electrically-driven

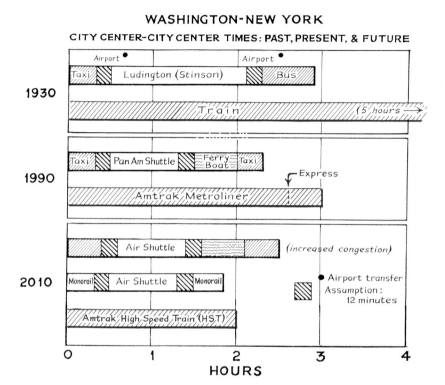

WASHINGTON-NEW YORK
CITY CENTER-CITY CENTER TIMES: PAST, PRESENT, & FUTURE

The journey time between downtown New York and downtown Washington was only about three hours back in 1930, when the connections to the airports were free of traffic gridlocks. Today, few travelers on the air shuttles make it in less time, and then only if the waiting time at the airport is at a minimum. The prospects of improvement in the future appear to depend on a revolutionary mode of ground transport to link the airports with the downtown areas.

buses were a partial solution, the politicians and the public alike turned to in- dividual cars and six-lane highways as the preferred method of going from one place to another.

The very availability of multi-lane highways is self-defeating. The more efficient they seem to be, the more traffic is attracted to them; and nowhere is this more evident than on highway links to airports. As an airport becomes more popular, the traffic to it becomes denser. Industry, commerce, and residential districts grow up, not as satellites of the city served by the airport; but as satellites of the airport itself. And the main highways become parking lots of record proportions during the rush hours—ask any regular user of the Long Island Expressway. People who complained bitterly at two-minute hold-ups on streetcars now tolerate half-hour delays on congested freeways, and spend an extraordinary amount of their free time in their cars, equivalent to years off their lives.

From the point of view of air transport—and this book, after all, is on that subject—this surface traffic congestion is critical and has to be solved if the journey times between city centers are to be maintained at their present levels, much less improved. The biggest danger is that the gridlocks will increase to unprecedented levels so that city center journey times will actually increase. To take one example: on the route from New York to Washington, D.C., simple arithmetic shows that to save ten minutes on the city center journey time, the alternatives are to speed up the flight, which is clearly impossible, or to speed up the taxi/limousine service by 9 mph, not impossible but clearly difficult. To save more than ten minutes involves the certainty of speeding tickets.

What, then, can be done? If airplanes cannot fly faster, the solution must be on the ground, and only an exclusive form of tracked vehicle system will do, as high speeds exceeding 65 mph on roads are unacceptable because of the inherent danger of loss of control for a variety of reasons. Orthodox rail will be prohibitively expensive, because of the problem of finding a tracked right-of-way, or a right-of-way suitable for a track, at least one that will permit high speeds and be flexible enough to penetrate the suburban congestion to reach the inner core of the city.

By process of elimination, therefore, an advanced form of elevated monorail—rather than a 19th century 'light rail'—seems to be the logical solution to a 21st century challenge to improve public transport. Elevation—reminiscent of the Chicago 'El' of bygone days—takes the tracked system off the city streets, where necessary. As will be demonstrated below, there are good reasons for selecting a suspended monorail system, simply because any other form of monorail offers little if any improvement over a standard two-rail tracked vehicle system.

Now the skeptics will argue that this idea is a supreme example of a fallacious fantasy—or a fantastic fallacy. Monorails, they will claim—with historical evidence to prove the assertion—have been proposed since the early 19th century. And this is true. Equally true is the conclusion that almost every

These two pictures demonstrate the advantages of one of the most successful urban transport systems ever devised. The Schwebebahn (Swinging Railway) at Wüppertal, Germany, has amply proved the versatile flexibility of the suspended monorail. The top picture shows it avoiding congestion at a street intersection; the lower view shows it making use of a convenient right-of-way over a river. (Wüppertaler Stadtwerke, A.G.)

THE ELEVATED MONORAIL
COMPARISON OF DIFFERENT SYSTEMS
(Assuming elevated independence and acceptable speed on all systems)

System	Example	Right of Way Easement	Horizontal Flexibility (Sharp Corners)	Vertical Flexibility (Moderate Gradients)	All-Weather Reliability (Track Protection)	Wide-Body Potential
SUPPORTED (Orthodox Rail)	BART (San Francisco Bay Area)	X	X	X	X	X
SUPPORTED (Single Beam)	ALWEG (Seattle,Tokyo, Disneyland)	✓	X	X	X	X
ASYMMETRIC SUSPENSION (Cantilever)	Schwebeban (Wüppertal)	✓	✓⋅	X	X	X
SYMMETRIC SUSPENSION (Box Rail)	SAFEGE (Chiba, Japan)	✓	✓	✓	✓	✓

X ... impossible or severe problem.   ✓⋅... with difficulty.   ✓... by design.

One reason why the idea of a monorail has never achieved wide success is be-cause the various systems offer few advantages over orthodox rail, except the rel-ative freedom of choice of route offered by the elevated track. Nevertheless, the longevity of the Wüppertal Schwebebahn has been remarkable, suggesting that a modern development of it would be worthy of careful study.

one of them failed. But not every one. In the approximately 100 years after the very first primitive line was built at the London docks in 1824 to carry goods at 5 mph for half a mile, more than a dozen so-called monorail projects of various kinds were launched. Some were never put into operation; some were not commercially operated. Those that were were regarded more as curiosities than practical forms of transport, the longest lived being the Listowel and Ballybunion Railway which operated in County Kerry, Ireland, for 36 years after its opening in 1888.

Significantly, two of the monorail lines did not fail, and both were of the asymmetrically suspended traction type. In 1929, the Bennie Railplane, designed by George Bennie, operated experimentally near Glasgow, Scotland, for a few months. Propeller driven by diesel-electric engines, sus-pended from an overhead track but with a guide rail below, it would not look out of place today in a promotional brochure. But even more impressive has been the continued success of the German Schwebebahn (Swinging Railway) which has operated continuously since 1901 in the narrow valley of the River Wüpper, connecting the cities of Elberfeld, Barmen, and Vohwinkel.

Why the designers, engineers, and project leaders concerned with solving the problems of efficient and rapid public urban transport do not make an annual pilgrimage to Wüppertal (the name for the amalgamated cities of Elberfeld and Barmen) is a mystery. After half a century of reliable operation, the Schwebebahn was, to the satisfaction of the local citizenry, modernized in 1951, and has been operating ever since. It strides swiftly and quietly along and above city streets, highways, canals, and assorted open spaces, without interruption; for it is isolated from gridlocks and other forms of congestion that plague the city streets of every major city in the world today.

Almost in defiance of following a proven winner, the monorails that have actually been built and operated, with limited success, during the past 30 years have been the lines of the Alweg system. Named after its designer, Axel Lennart Wenner-Gren, the cars are supported by a single rail and straddle it symmetrically. Subsidiary guide rails each side of a central beam stabilize the vehicle. The electric motive power is also contained in the overhanging portions of the cars. The Alweg system has been operated successfully at the World's Fair in Seattle, at Disneyland and Disneyworld, and in several cities in Japan, notably to connect Tokyo's Haneda Airport with the downtown area.

The Alweg lines demonstrate one main advantage of the monorail. The lines can be built relatively inexpensively—cheaper than, for example, a six-lane elevated freeway—to clear all obstacles such as street intersections, railroads, rivers, or canals. Running on rubber-tired wheels, it is also quiet, and is thus environmentally attractive. And it does not use up precious gasoline.

But there are limitations to the Alweg system that do not handicap the asymmetrical designs, of which the Schwebebahn is the outstanding example of success. Because it straddles the line, the Alweg car cannot negotiate sharp curves, at least not as sharp as those within the design capability of the Wüppertal line, because the car cannot bend with the track, and the trucks or bogies are not flexible in the lateral direction.

This leads to the conclusion that, accepting the fact that an elevated monorail offers distinct advantages over any surface-bound form of transport, the preferred traction methods should be of the asymmetrically suspended type. Can any improvement be made of the Wüppertal system? If so, than a closer look seems to be warranted, bearing in mind the uninterrupted onrush or ever greater airport-to-city transport congestion problems that are arising as we approach the 21st century.

Only one new idea appears to have had real merit. This was the French SAFEGE system that was first demonstrated at Chateauneuf-sur-Loire, near

The modern mono-rail systems shown here are (top) the German ALWEG at Disneyland, Ana-heim, California; and (bottom) the French SAFEGE, at the experimental track constructed in the 1960s at Cha-teauneuf-sur-Loire. (ALWEG and Rail-planes, Ltd.)

Orléans, France, in 1960. It differed from the Schwebebahn of Wüppertal in an ingenious way. L.F. Chadenson, a French bridge designer, had realized that the new wheels fitted to the trucks of the Paris Metro system—Line 11 was the first to be so fitted, in the late 1940s—had great merits of strength and adhesion, plus the advantage of low noise level. The wheels had pneumatic tires, with protective steel flanges, had no equal for adhesion in dry weather, and were capable of maintaining sufficient friction between rail and wheel to permit the trains to ascend much steeper gradients than hitherto. But in wet weather, the adhesion quality disappeared. Chadenson and the SAFEGE company came up with an answer: turn the truck (bogie) upside down and put a roof over it, to form a box-shaped channel for the truck to ride in, and suspend the car from the trucks.

The SAFEGE system was in some ways unique. Cars or trains were symmetrically suspended, and were therefore more inherently stable than those of the asymmetric system pioneered by the Schwebebahn and subsequently modified by other experimenters. The experimental line of box-railed track at Chateauneuf-sur-Loire appeared to prove everything claimed by the Societé Lyonnaise engineering combine which owned the SAFEGE patient. Speeds of 60 kph were achieved constantly without slackening of speed or passenger discomfort on a line less than a mile long and which included a section of 400-metre curvature. Its resistance to weather was proved on one occasion during a bad winter when, with all trains and roads icebound, the SAFEGE train made its daily run, even though the visiting dignitaries who were supposed to attend were stuck in Paris.

The SAFEGE system therefore shared with Alweg and the Schwebebahn the advantage of great flexibility because of the elevation of the track. It had the additional advantage over Alweg in that the trucks allowed it to negotiate tighter corners, especially useful in crowded cities. With Alweg, the rail beam bisects the lower side of the vehicle longitudinally, a defect that could only be overcome by complex articulation. And SAFEGE has the further

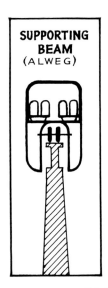
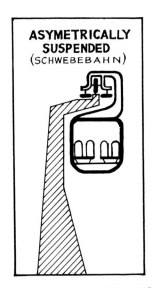
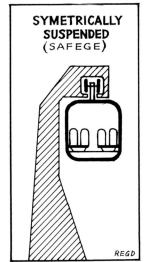

MAIN TYPES OF MONORAIL

This diagram illustrates the engineering and design characteristics that affect the operation of different monorail systems. The ALWEG system is handicapped by its inability to negotiate sharp curves. The Schwebebahn's rail is constantly exposed to the elements. The box-rail system, originally proposed by the French SAFEGE company, seems to offer the ideal solution.

WINDOW OF OPPORTUNITY

THE WIDE-BODIED MONORAIL

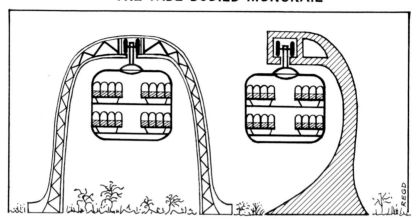

For all forms of land transport, vehicles are severely restricted in the maximum size permissible by the track upon which they travel. Railroad cars cannot be bigger because of loading gauges that have controlled the size of tunnel cross-sections and bridge clearances. On the roads, an item measuring ten feet is considered to be a wide load, requiring special exemption from the regulations. Because of the acute problems of congestion in many of the world's large cities, the time may be near when a revolutionary solution may have to be found, to increase carrying capacity.

additional advantage over both of its rivals in that the track itself is always kept dry, being on the lower side of a box-shaped cross-section.

The SAFEGE principle was examined very closely, not only in France but elsewhere. The British aerospace and engineering consortium, Hawker Siddeley, made many feasibility studies, as did the construction firm Taylor Woodrow in that country. The American Machine and Foundry Company took a license and studied the possibility of building an experimental line at the New York World's Fair; and several cities in other parts of the world, including Tokyo, also showed interest. But the idea never reached the stage of a serious and committed marketing plan, backed by sufficient capital to construct a demonstration line where it would be commercially visible. Had the Chateauneuf-sur-Loire line been transferred lock, stock, and box-rail to the center of Paris, or London, or Washington, D.C., or along the ocean boulevards of Rio de Janeiro, the story might have been different.

The SAFEGE system was promoted most energetically during the 1960s and a line was built in Chiba, Japan, in 1986. Perhaps it is a little ahead of its time. For in one particular aspect it had something to offer that no land-based transport system can match. Railroads are restricted to the rail gauge—the standard track width is 4 feet $8\frac{1}{2}$ inches although in a few countries it is a few inches larger. The loading gauge, i.e. the maximum width and height measurements permitted for overhead construction and tunnel clearance, is equally restrictive, so that railroad passenger cars (coaches) can, at best, offer only six abreast seating. The same applies to road passenger vehicles, buses, trolley cars, or street cars. Few countries permit vehicle widths of more than $8\frac{1}{2}$ feet. Both road and rail have resorted to double-decking to increase capacity that can be carried over the same track; but these have not been universally applied, partly because loading and unloading of passengers to and from the upper deck is time-consuming and cancels out much of the advantage of the extra capacity.

The asymmetrically-suspended monorail system offers, theoretically, the possibility of a wider passenger car, but the method of suspension opens up serious questions concerning balance and stability at high speeds. **Only the symmetrically-suspended monorail, i.e. the SAFEGE system, or one closely like it, can offer the unmatched advantage of wide-bodied passenger car capacity, and thus immeasurably improve the chances of relieving urban congestion by opening up new vistas of a revolutionary mode of transport.**

Is it beyond the wit of the U.S. manufacturing industry (or, for that matter, the German, British, French, Japanese, or Russian?) to meet the challenge? Is the United States, particularly, the country that has put a man on the moon, launched a fleet of giant nuclear-powered aircraft carriers, put into orbit hundreds of satellites, explored the Solar System, and mass-produced giant wide-bodied airliners, incapable of conceiving a straightforward successor for the 21st century that will be an improvement on the technology of the 19th?

What, the reader may ask, has this got to do with air transport? It has everything to do with air transport, for there is no other way to improve city center journey times. Airliners cannot go faster, and nor can trains or buses, each for different, track-related reasons. Only the suspended monorail, free from the bondage of a surface transport system that was laid down in the era of the stage coach, can offer relief.

The suspended monorail may not be a form of heavier-than-air airplane construction. But, as I once mused while gliding along the Chateauneuf-sur-Loire experimental SAFEGE track at 65 kph (40 mph), it is the nearest thing to flying without actually getting off the ground.

Bibliography

Chapter 1   The *Il'ya Muromets* (1913–1922)

There have been many sporadic references in books and periodicals in the past, and some historians have recognized the historical importance of this great Russian pioneering aircraft type. All the information has been difficult to obtain from primary sources. For additional data, however, the reader need go no further than:

Igor Sikorsky: The Russian Years, by Carl Bobrow and Von Hardesty: Smithsonian Institution Press, Washington, D.C., 1987

Chapter 2   The Lawson Airline (1919)

Lawson - Aircraft Industry Builder, published by Humanity Publishing Company, Detroit, 1939

A Two Thousand Mile Trip in the First Airliner by Alfred Lawson: Humanity Benefactor Foundation

The Airliner and Its Inventor - Alfred W. Lawson by Robert F. Brooks: Paper delivered to the American Institute of Aeronautics and Astronautics, Anaheim, California, 20 October 1969

Chapter 3   The Armstrong Seadrome (1923–1943)

"Commercial Ocean Transit by Airplane" by E.R. Armstrong: *Aviation*, 4 June 1923

"Airways of the Atlantic" by Stella Wolfe Murray: *Airways*, September 1926

"Seadromes and Ocean Flying" by E.R. Armstrong: *Aviation*, 28 Nov. 1927

"Legal Aspects of the Seadrome" by Earl Hanson: *Airway Age*: Vol 11, No. 12, 1926

America-Europe, via North Atlantic Airways, published by The Armstrong Seadrome Development Corporation, Wilmington, Delaware, 1927

"Armtrong Seadrome Project Progresses" by Earl Hanson: *Airway Age*, March 1930

Seadrome Ocean Airways, published by the Founders Syndicate, Armstrong
   Seadrome Airways, Wilmington, Delaware, 1930

Economics of Seadrome-System Ocean Airways (S.A.E. Paper presented by
   E.R. Armstrong at the Annual Meeting of the S.A.E., Detroit, 19-23
   January 1931)

When Will These Stepping Stones of Steel Span the Oceans? (Pamphlet published by Pennsylvania-Central Airlines, July 1943)

"The Armstrong Transoceanic Seadromes" by Dan Barber: *Airpost Journal*,
   January 1985

Chapter 4   The Dornier Do X (1929–1933)

*Erprobungs und Vorführungs flüge mit dem Dornier-Flugschiff Do X -
   D 1929*: Dornier Metallbauten, GmbH, Friedrichshafen, 1929

*Mit dem ersten Flugschiff der Welt Dornier Do X - D 1929 über drei Konti-
   nente*: Schweizer Aero-Revue A.G., Zurich-Oerlikon, 1930 and 1931
   (two volumes)

Aviation, 21 December 1929 and 4 January 1930

U.S. Air Services, February 1930

S.A.E. Journal, May 1330

Aero Digest, October 1930

Aeroplane, 12 November and 19 November 1930

Curtiss-Wright Review, October 1931

Vacuum Oil Company (Commemorative Booklet) 1931

L-Aéronautique, February 1931 and November 1932

Chapter 5   Legalized Murder (1934)

Final Report of War Department Special Committee on Army Air Corps: U.S.
   Government Printing Office, 18 July 1934

U.S. Postmaster General's Report, 25 January 1935

Airways by Henry Ladd Smith: Alfred A. Knopf, New York, 1942

The Air Mail Emergency, 1934 by Norman E. Borden: Bond Wheelwright Co.,
   1968

"Early Airlines - Accident List, 1926–1941" by Kenn C. Rust: *Journal of the
   American Aviation Historical Society*, Fall 1987

Chapter 6   The Big Flying Boats (1931-1948)

The Modern Airliner by Peter W. Brooks: Putnam, London, 1962

The Technical Development of Modern Aviation by Ronald Miller and David Sawers: Routledge and Kegan Paul, London, 1968

"The Intercontinental Airliner and the Essence of Airplane Performance, 1929–1939" by Richard K. Smith: *Technology and Culture*, July 1983

A History of The World's Airlines by R.E.G. Davies: Oxford University Press London, 1964

Airlines of the United States Since 1914 by R.E.G. Davies: Putnam, London, 1972 and Smithsonian Institution Press, Washington, D.C., 1982

Pan Am: An Airline and Its Aircraft by R.E.G. Davies: Orion Books, New York, 1987; and Paladwr Press, McLean, Va., 1992

Chapter 7   The Commercial Airships (1919-1937)

The books written about the rigid airships, predominantly the Zeppelins, would fill an entire library. The ones listed here are representative of those that approach the subject from an analytical, rather than a blindly emotional viewpoint. The last book in the list is strongly recommended.

Giants in the Sky by Douglas H. Robinson: University of Washington Press, Seattle, 1973

European Transport Aircraft by John Stroud: Putnam, London 1966

Historic Airships by Peter W. Brooks: Hugh Evelyn, London 1973

Lufthansa: An Airline and Its Aircraft by R.E.G. Davies: Orion Books, New York, 1991; and Paladwr Press, McLean, Va., 1992

Zeppelin: Rigid Airships by Peter W. Brooks: Conway Maritime Press (Putnam), London, 1992

Chapter 8   The Mayo Composite Aircraft (1938)

Mayo Composite Aircraft Company Ltd—Notes for Press, 14–17 February 1938

Flight, 6 December 1934, 7 and 14 November 1935, 17 February 1938, 3 March 1938, and 28 July 1938

Aeroplane, 6 October 1937

Chapter 9   The Romance of Early Air Travel (1919-1940)

During the formative years of commercial aviation, countless books were written about the joys of flying, not only for academic readers, but also for the popular book market. While the former tended to dwell on the theoretical advantages of air travel, and sometimes exaggerated them, the latter, somewhat paradoxically, often presented a more balanced account of what the air passenger really had to endure. The first two in the list that follows are examples of such books and are recommended for those readers who enjoy browsing in second-hand bookshops.

The Airway to See Europe by Eleanor Elsner: Albert E. Marriott, London, 1930

The World's Airways by Robert Finch: University of London Press, 1938

British Airways by C. St John Sprigg: Thomas Nelson, London, 1938

The Only Way to Fly by Robert J. Serling: Doubleday, New York, 1976

Croissants at Croydon (The Memoirs of Jack Bamford): London Borough of Sutton Libraries, in association with Les Anciens d'Air France, Sutton, Surrey, England, 1986

Chapter 10   The First Comet (1952–1954)

Report on Comet Accident Investigation: Royal Aircraft Establishment, Farnborough, England, September 1954

D.H. - An Outline of de Havilland History by C. Martin Sharpe: Faber & Faber, London, 1960

Enterprise, August 1949 (Staff journal of the de Havilland company)

"The Magnificent False Start" from *A History of the World's Airlines* by R.E. G. Davies: Oxford University Press, London, 1964

1949–1989 and the Next 40 Years of Jet Transport by J.M. Ramsden: Paper delivered at the Sir Geoffrey de Havilland Memorial Lecture, Hatfield, England, 15 March 1989

Chapter 11   The Concorde (1976–   )

The volume of written material on the Concorde, ranging from perceptive analysis to meaningless drivel, would comprise an encyclopaedia. The items selected below are some of the more penetrating that have appeared in the world's press, and which have filled the world's bookshelves; and none of them post-date the year in which the Concorde entered commercial service, and whose record then had to speak, with increasing embarrassment, for itself. Considerable credit is due to Andrew Wilson, Roger Eglin, and Mary Goldring, whose perceptive observations and analyses were isolated gleams of common sense amid a plethora of flag-waving self-deception during the 1970s.

"Lightweight Claims that Damn Concorde": Letter to the editor, by R.E.G. Davies, in *The Observer*, London, 21 May 1972

"Can Concorde Make a Profit?" by Peter G. Masefield, *Flight International*, London, 10 August 1972

"Tne Great Concorde Scandal" by Andrew Wilson: *The Observer*, London, 4 Februry 1973

"Why Concorde Must Die" by Andrew Wilson: *The Observer*, London, 2 February 1974

"Three Times Dearer by Concorde" by Mary Goldring: *The Economist*, London, 9 June 1974

"I'm Concorde, Fly Me": *The Economist*, 12 July 1975

"Concorde and the Environment": *Flight International*, London, 27 November 1975

"Concorde Legal Question Raised": *Aviation Week & Space Technology*, New York, 12 January 1976

"The Concorde Consipiracy" by John Barry, Peter Gillman, and Roger Eglin: *The Observer*, London, 8 February 1976

"Concorde Deserves a Chance" by Robert Hotz: *Aviation Week & Space Technology*, New York, 19 January 1976

"The Concorde Scandal" by Jeremy Bugler, *New Statesman*, London; April 1976

"Concorde Service Record" by John Belson and Jack Gee: *Flight International*, London, 31 July 1976

"Concorde Economics Keyed to Utilization" by Rosalind K. Ellingsworth: *Aviation Week & Space Technology*, 23 August 1976

"Concorde Claims Found to be Inaccurate": *The Times*, London, 2 December 1976

"Concorde's £17 million setback for British Airways": *The Times*, London, 28 July 1976

Concorde, The Inside Story by Geoffrey Knight: Weidenfeld and Nicholson, London, 1976

Chapter 12   The U.S. SST (1958–1971)

Like the Concorde, the United States supersonic airliner was the subject of intense competition and much controversy over a period of many years, embracing the entire decade of the 1960s. Hundreds of articles, papers, and learned reports were written and published, mostly in support of the project.

Outstanding among the antagonists was William Shurcliff, whose advocacy for level-headedness may have been the main contribution to the vital decision-making that led to the cancellation of the U.S. SST. The entire chronicle of one of the most important episodes in aircraft development history is narrated with meticulous precision in:

Clipped Wings by Mel Horwitch: M.I.T. Press, Cambridge, Mass., 1982

Chapter 13   Competition by Deregulation

The process of Airline Deregulation has been on public record and reported in the press and the media before and since the 1978 Act. This chapter summarizes the author's views rather than setting down the facts, which are simply a matter of historical record. These are synthesized in the Essay on Deregulation, which appears in the revised reprinting of the author's own book:

Airlines of the United States since 1914 by R.E.G. Davies: Smithsonian Institution Press, Washington, D.C., 1982 (Revised Reprinting)

Chapter 14   Short Take-Off and Landing (STOL) (and Commercial Helicopters) (1960s–1980s)

STOL Transport 188: Brochure prepared by McDonnell Douglas Corporation, December 1968

"London City Airport": *Highlift* (Boeing Canada magazine) Vol. 9, No. 3, Fall/Winter, 1988

"Aircraft Without Airports—The Tilt Rotor Concept and VTOL Aviation" by Dr. Hans Mark: *Aerospace* (Royal Aeronautical Society), London, March 1987

"Canada Has a Word for It—STOL" by Tom Weissman: *Esso Air World*, Vol. 23, No. 5, 1971

Chapter 15   The Specialized Commercial Air Freighter   (1946–1966)

Air Freight—15 Years of Development (Special Report) by Ray Lyne: de Havilland Aircraft Company, Hatfield, England, 16 May 1961

The Future of Air Freight and the Market for the Freighter Aircraft (Special Report) by Ray Lyne: de Havilland Aircraft Company, Hatfield, England, 4 August 1961

The Hungry Tiger by Frank Cameron: McGraw-Hill, New York, 1964

"Design Concepts for Future Air Freighters" by H.W. Withington: *Exxon Air World*, Vol. 30, No. 3, 1978

"Trunk, All-Cargo Line Showdown Looms": *Aviation Week*, 13 March 1961

"New Prey for the Flying Tiger": *Dun's Review*, March 1970

"Tigers is off to Fast Start in Deregulated Cargo Arena" by James P. Woolsey: *Air Transport World*, February 1983

"Recession and Deregulation Posing a Stiff Test for Flying Tigers" by Henry Lefer, *Air Transport World*, February 1983

Chapter 16   The DC-3 Replacement (1960s–1970s)

This essay is based on many research studies made at the de Havilland Aircraft Company (later Hawker-Siddeley Aviation) during the 1960s, when the search for the so-called DC-3 Replacement was at its height. The analyses consistently supported the conclusions summarized in this book. In the most promising category, the feederliner, de Havilland produced project studies for a 26-seat twin jet, the D.H.126, which later developed into the H.S.136, with an additional ten seats and a little more range. This aircraft, properly marketed, might have been a world-beater; but it never went beyond the project stage. Other attempts by many other manufacturers, all of whom produced voluminous literature, and went into production with feeder aircraft; have never succeeded completely in replacing the DC-3.

Chapter 17   The Orient Express

Today, the fanatical preoccupation with dreams of commercial supersonic flight continues, in a frightening repetition of the specious, but completely unsupportable advocacy of a previous generation of engineers, designers, and journalists; but not, to their credit, by economists. As before (see Chapter 12) the volume of words is heavily weighted in one direction.

"Hypersonic Airliner Proposed for 1980s": *Aviation Week*, 4 April 1960

To Asia and Back, The Future of the Hypersonic Transport in Commercial Aviation: paper delivered before the First High-Speed Commercial Flight Symposium, 22 October 1986, Columbus, Ohio, by John F. Horn, President and CX.E.O., Northwest Airlines

"How Different a Modern SST Would Be" by Cornelius Driver: *Aerospace America*, November 1986

"Into the 21st Century—Supersonically" by James P. Loomis: *New York Times*, 10 July 1988

"High Speed Transport Study Focuses on Lower Mach Range" by James Ott: *Aviation Week & Space Technology*, 29 February 1988

"The Final Frontier" by David Martindale: *Frequent Flyer*, March 1987

"Boeing Sees Bigger, Better SST Airliner for Service by 2015" by Barry Reinsberg: *Boeing News*, 30 June 1989

"Designing a Plane for the Leap to Space (and Back)" by Carl H. Lavin, *New York Times*, 3 October 1989

"The HOTOL Man" by Tom Huntington: *Air & Space*, December 1988

"HOTOL" by Peter J. Conchie, *Aerospace*, October 1989

Chapter 18   The Suspended Monorail

The Railplane System of Transport: Hitchins, Jervis & Partners, London, 23 July 1935

Das Beste von der Schwebebahn in 50 Jahren: Wuppertaler Stadtwerke, 1953

"Histoire des Monorails" by Andre Begue: *La Vie du Rail*, Paris, 9 Feb. 1958

Le Metro Aérien Suspendu: Société Lyonnaise des Eaux et de l'Eclairage (SAFEGE), Paris, 1960

The World Market for a Rapid Urban Transport System by R.E.G. Davies: de Havilland Aircraft Company, Hatfield, England, September 1961

Opportunities for Monorails in the U.S.A. by R.E.G. Davies: de Havilland Aircraft Company, Hatfield, England, November 1962

Monorails by H.H.C. Barton: Institution of Locomotive Engineers, London, 6 February 1962

The ALWEG Monorail: Alweg Rapid Transit Systems, Seattle, 1962

"Alweg Monorail at Century 21 World's Fair": *Modern Transport*, London, 7 April 1962

"The Monorail and the City-Centre-to-Airport Transport Problem" by R.E.G. Davies: *Flight International*, 19 April 1962

"The Use of Monorail Transport to Ease Transport Problems" by L.W. Passmore: *The Railway Gazzette*, 22 February 1963

"The Silent Revolution": *Bibendum* (Michelin Tyre Co., Ltd.), December 1963

"Prospects for Monorails Today" by R.E.G. Davies: *The Surveyor and Municipal Engineer*, 18 January, 1 February, 15 February, 29 February, 1964

Index

All entries are contained in a single index. References to items other than in the main text are dealt with by suffixes, as follows: E = Exhibit or Chart; M = Map; P = Photograph; T = Table. The more important subjects and page references, including main chapter topics, are shown in bold-face type.